god Helpe me shaver
He is good mam dont
bodd Touch
Hes good for us No for you

Fuck us
greenys   god bless me
              freind

Fuck evert
bodd

Also by Douglas Schoen

*Declaring Independence: The Beginning of the
End of the Two-Party System*

*The Power of the Vote: Electing Presidents, Overthrowing Dictators,
and Promoting Democracy Around the World*

*On the Campaign Trail: The Long Road of Presidential
Politics, 1860–2004*

Pat: A Biography of Daniel Patrick Moynihan

Enoch Powell and the Powellites

Also by Michael Rowan

*Como Salir de Chávez y de la Pobreza
(Getting Over Chávez and Poverty)*

Hugo Chávez
and the
War Against
America

THE THREAT CLOSER TO HOME

Douglas Schoen and
Michael Rowan

Free Press

New York   London   Toronto   Sydney

FREE PRESS
A Division of Simon & Schuster, Inc.
1230 Avenue of the Americas
New York, NY 10020

First Free Press hardcover edition January 2009

FREE PRESS and colophon are trademarks of Simon & Schuster, Inc.

For information about special discounts for bulk purchases,
please contact Simon & Schuster Special Sales at
1-800-456-6798 or business@simonandschuster.com

Designed by Ruth Lee-Mui

Excerpt from Thor Halvorssen, "Venezuela's Charades," February 7, 2008,
editorial section (page not listed)—courtesy of the *Washington Times*.

Manufactured in the United States of America

10   9   8   7   6   5   4   3   2   1

Library of Congress Cataloging-in-Publication Data

Schoen, Douglas E., 1953–
    The threat closer to home : Hugo Chávez and the war against America /
by Douglas Schoen and Michael Rowan.
        p.   cm.
    Includes bibliographical references.
    1. Chávez Frías, Hugo.   2. Venezuela—Politics and government—1999–
I. Rowan, Michael, 1942–   II. Title.
    F2329.22.C54S36   2009
    987.06'42092—dc22   2008038956

ISBN-13: 978-1-4165-9477-2
ISBN-10:   1-4165-9477-9

This book is dedicated to
Joshua Evan Schoen and to
Maria de la Rosa Rowan.

"America is very naive about the threat Chávez poses. Today Chávez is at least as dangerous as bin Laden; he's preparing his attack; he's even implementing the attack, but too many of America's leaders are still ignoring him. This could be a tragedy bigger than 9/11."

—Otto Reich, ambassador to Venezuela, 1986–1989; assistant secretary of state for western hemisphere affairs, 2001–2002

Contents

Preface

It's important for us to set out initially why we came to write this book—why we have spent the amount of time and effort that we have over the last few years writing about Hugo Chávez and working to change politics in Venezuela.

While admiring Chávez's intentions to eradicate poverty and corruption in his country, we have sadly come to believe that Chávez arguably presents a greater threat to America than Osama bin Laden does on a day-to-day basis, and this is our opportunity to set out the reasons why we believe this to be the case.

Both of us have had long years of experience in Venezuelan politics, and have seen firsthand the impact that Hugo Chávez has had on Venezuelan society as well as on the world at large. Hopefully, in this book we will set out the reasons why Chávez had the impact we attempt to document systematically here.

Michael Rowan was not involved in the 1998 presidential campaign in which Chávez was elected, and in many published articles he praised Chávez's stated *intentions* to reverse the poverty, inequality, and corruption that plague oil-rich Venezuela to this day. What became obvious over time—and this book documents it—was that Chávez was not interested in solving problems for Venezuela but in creating problems for America and doing all he could to use those problems for his own selfish purposes.

In 2004, Schoen and Rowan worked for the nonprofit organization

Súmate (Spanish for "Join Up"), which collected 3.5 million signatures for the recall of President Chávez, a referendum that Schoen's exit poll showed Chávez had in fact lost, despite his claims that he had won by close to 20 percent. We believe he rigged that referendum and in so doing, fatally damaged Venezuela's democracy.

Two years later, in 2006, Schoen and Rowan again collaborated in supporting the election of Governor Manuel Rosales, the unified opposition candidate running against Chávez. We believe that at the very least, Rosales probably came close to winning that election, but Chávez manipulated the vote count to show a landslide. Those efforts we believe foreshadowed his abortive attempt a year later to change the constitution to allow him to serve as president for life through another rigged referendum. Fortunately for the world, and certainly for the Venezuelan people, he was not allowed to cheat for what we think would have been the third consecutive time.

At the end of the 2006 campaign for president, faced with harassment, e-mail and phone threats, phone tapping, and computer crashes caused by Chávez's supporters, Rowan moved his family to the safety of the United States, where he currently resides.

While it is tragic that Chávez has not kept his 1998 campaign promises about fighting poverty and corruption in Venezuela, what has alarmed us since we began working together in 2004 is what Chávez is doing outside of Venezuela. This book documents Chávez's connections to Iran's nuclear program, his training and support of Hezbollah and Hamas, his provision of money and oil for Colombia's FARC guerrillas (who are little more than narcoterrorists), as well as his invitations to Russia to send warships to the Caribbean for joint military exercises with Venezuela. It also documents his purchase of billions of dollars in sophisticated weapons that he does not need, as well as the threatening of his neighbors in Colombia and Peru. Moreover, he has stood by, at the very least, as 280 tons of cocaine per year were delivered from Venezuela mostly to the United States, in addition to allowing terrorists to launder money through his country, all the while facilitating the transformation of Venezuela's society into one very much like Cuba's.

This book also reveals much for the first time about Chávez's publicity machine in the United States—the most lavish and effective of any foreign power—which will almost certainly be used to attack our work as "a CIA-financed plot to destroy Chávez and his revolution," which is the way Chávez deals with his critics.

We have written the book with our own resources, with no other purpose beyond telling the truth about a serious problem that we believe Americans and the world have overlooked. We have also provided as much documentation as we could to demonstrate how all this has unfolded.

It is our fervent hope that the United States will forge a long-term Latin American policy that addresses endemic poverty and inequality, and a short-term Venezuelan policy that reduces or eliminates America's dependence on Chávez's oil. As the reader will find, that is our central focus, and one we hope readers will think about as a new administration takes shape in Washington.

Michael Rowan
Douglas E. Schoen

THE THREAT CLOSER TO HOME

Introduction

Anti-U.S. networks are here to stay. Chávez is throwing his one-pipeline-state petrodollars around to cultivate bonds beyond comrades in Cuba, Nicaragua and Bolivia. Ties with Iran, Russia, China, Argentina, Ecuador and Caribbean states are intensifying. . . . Chávez wants to parlay his petrorevenue and pseudorevolution into a global anti-American role.

—Roger Cohen, *The New York Times,* December 3, 2007

Standing at the podium of the United Nations in September 2006, he seemed like any world leader we're accustomed to seeing at the General Assembly. Jet-black, short-cropped hair, dark complexion; a dark suit, crisp white shirt and red tie; he clasped his hands together in prayer gazing upward, the presidential teleprompters at either side. When he spoke, he sounded intelligent, informed, confident, imposing. He opened with a reference to one of Noam Chomsky's books. And shortly after some modest applause, he began referring to President Bush as "the devil" and the West's spokesman for imperialism. "Yesterday the devil was here right in this spot," he said, crossing himself as if anointed by the deity. "This table from where I speak still smells from sulfur," he added. "It would take a psychiatrist to analyze the U.S. president's speech from yesterday." When not bashing the leader of the free world, Chávez excoriated the UN it-self. "I believe that almost no one in this room would stand up to defend the system of the United Nations. Let's admit with honesty, the UN sys-tem that emerged after World War II has collapsed, shattered; it doesn't work."

Who is this man? one wonders. What is his agenda? How seriously should the rest of the world take his rhetoric? Does he back his words with actions? And when he does, how does it affect other nations? How should the United States respond? These are critical questions. This Latin Ameri-can potentate, unknown to the majority of the American public, is a far greater threat to our national security than the cleric with the long gray beard, the easily recognized religious zealot, Osama bin Laden. The cold reality is this: Hugo Chávez, the president of Venezuela, is a much more dangerous individual than the famously elusive leader of al-Qaeda. He has made the United States his sworn enemy, and the sad truth is that few peo-ple are really listening. More important, is our government listening?

Some see him as a clown, but his histrionics mask the danger he poses. Our economy is in shambles in large part because he has successfully driven up the price of oil to record levels. He's propped up Iran's economy over the last few years and so is supporting state-sponsored terrorism. He is also most likely advocating on behalf of Hamas and Hezbollah, and even tolerating Hezbollah's presence in his country. Further, recent revela-tions about the FARC—the Colombian guerrillas—show he has spent hundreds of millions of dollars to support terrorist activity in the southern hemisphere, perhaps even supporting the development of a dirty bomb. In the meantime, he's buying off American leaders across the political spectrum.

In sum, Hugo Chávez is one genuinely scary individual who suddenly has a much larger platform on today's geopolitical stage than anyone pre-dicted. "I'm still a subversive," Chávez has admitted. "I think the entire world should be subverted."[1]

"America is very naïve about the threat Chávez poses," says Otto Reich, a former Ronald Reagan ambassador to Venezuela and assistant secretary of state for the western hemisphere in the Bush administration. "Today, Chávez is at least as dangerous as bin Laden; he's preparing his attack; he's even implementing the attack, but too many of America's leaders are still ignoring him. This could be a tragedy bigger than 9/11."[2]

When our vulnerability was tested at the beginning of this century by an enemy without a country, we tightened security at our borders, scrutinized foreigners, and generally speaking, closed ranks. We grudgingly gave up some of our freedoms after the Office of Homeland Security was created. We reasoned that it was now a different world.

But it's not just our infrastructure that's vulnerable. It's not just our culture and American democracy. It's the very core of what makes us the envy of the free world: our economy.

Industry, imagination, and a willingness to strive are traits that we treasure. We are only 4 percent of the world's people but we provide more than 25 percent of the world's economic output—an enviable position of strength and prestige. But our very power and presence in an interdependent and interconnected world makes us a target for the rage and resentment of an attack from a few strategically placed people among the other 96 percent—the 6.4 billion non-Americans who populate the rest of the world.

Our trade deficit—$3.8 trillion since 2000—is enormous, unprecedented, and perilous, and makes the dollar vulnerable to an attack that's already begun. When the euro was first floated just a few short years ago, it traded at 90 cents. At the time of this writing, it has hit $1.55, weakening our buying power in the European Union. The dollar has declined against other major currencies as well.

Our shaky economy is being propped up by foreign investment at a perilous time for U.S. security. The United States is still the leader of the free world, but our foothold is weak. Our military forces are spread thin: we are conducting controversial, unpopular wars in Iraq and Afghanistan and are involved in humanitarian and security missions in 70 of the world's 192 nations. Some 200,000 U.S. troops are currently deployed to the Iraqi and Afghani theaters, and many troops are required to do multiple tours of duty. Our generals complain that our air fleet is dangerously outdated, with crucial planes, such as F-15s, frequently grounded; the other services say there is a pressing need for modernizations. Yet, whatever our shortcomings, our very reach and visibility continue to inspire envy and hatred, and make us increasingly vulnerable to attacks.

A generation has gone by since the Cold War thawed and two superpowers ruled the earth. We now live in a symbiotic society, where each country is beholden to another in some way or another—natural resources, food and health support, disaster relief, trade agreements, and so on. This symbiosis, happy or not, depending on the circumstances, leaves us open to criticism on the worldwide political stage. We cannot afford all the altruism we'd like to pursue, nor can we be everything to everyone.

Every day our position as economic and military colossus erodes slightly. Why? We import more than half the oil we need to operate our economy, which makes us vulnerable to volatile oil-producing regimes that are unfriendly to our way of life. Oil recently traded at $125 to $147 a barrel, causing significant pain for businesses and consumers, and fueling inflation in a number of sectors, especially food sales. A similar spike in oil prices—or a decision by the Organization of the Petroleum Exporting Countries (OPEC) and China to dump the dollar in favor of some other reserve currency—would inflict grievous harm on the U.S. economy and severely endanger its standing as the world's sole superpower. And as the fourth largest supplier of oil to the United States, Venezuela has made us one of her thirstiest customers, providing us with $29 billions' worth in 2007 alone.

Chávez has the means and motivation to harm the United States in a way that no other country—and perhaps no other terrorist organization—could. He prepared for this role at the feet of one of the world's most cunning and effective dictators, Fidel Castro. One cannot discount how much Castro's aura has shaped Chávez's thoughts and actions. We've already seen the halo effect on Chávez that allowed Fidel Castro to rule Cuba for half a century—mainly with Soviet support. The Nobel laureate economist Joseph Stiglitz has noted admiringly: "Venezuelan President Hugo Chávez seems to have succeeded in bringing education and health services to the barrios of Caracas, which previously had seen little of the benefits of that country's rich endowment of oil."[3]

A number of Venezuelans, however, believe that Stiglitz has been seriously misinformed. When Chávez was elected to the presidency in December 1998, polls showed that 80 percent of Venezuelans believed he would lead his nation out of endemic poverty. Three years later, fewer than 40 percent believed it and 800,000 Venezuelans took to the streets in a massive protest against Chávez's authoritarianism. He was briefly overthrown by his own military, which refused his order to shoot civilian protesters. Chávez claims this was the doing of white oligarchs in a conspiracy planned and implemented by the United States, the CIA, and President George W. Bush.

To those Americans who think they understand him, Hugo Chávez may seem like a blowhard, all bluster and little substance, a Castro pretender and acolyte known mostly for his baiting of President Bush. He has labeled Bush a genocidal maniac, a warmonger, a drunkard, a coward, and the world's number one terrorist. While Bush's favorability ratings hovered at a mere 30 percent in U.S. polls in the fall of 2008, by any decent critical standard, Chávez's calumnies are still over-the-top. Even Fidel had better manners when taking American leadership to task. Yet it's easy for Bush's adversaries and denigrators to find common ground in this Venezuelan autocrat.

When Chávez pontificates about Bush as Satan or decries capitalism as the world's worst horror ("Jesus Christ was the first Socialist and Judas the first Capitalist," he told Rome officials in 2005),[4] few Americans take him seriously and fewer still see in Chávez a real danger to this country.

This is a serious underestimation.

With Hugo Chávez commanding the Venezuelan pipeline, America is facing an unprecedented and unrecognized threat. When asked about the looming scythe over our heads, State Department officials merely shrug, though the U.S. military's threat assessment rule is to analyze an adversary's capabilities first and intentions second. There are many who harbor bad intentions toward the United States, but only a few who possess the capability to do anything about it. Chávez is one of these few because:

- His de facto dictatorship gives him absolute control over Venezuela's military, oil production, and treasury.
- He harbors oil reserves second only to those of Saudi Arabia; Venezuela's annual windfall profits exceed the net worth of Bill Gates.
- He has a strategic military and oil alliance with a major American foe and terrorism sponsor, the Islamic Republic of Iran.
- He has more soldiers on active and reserve duty and more modern weaponry—mostly from Russia and China—than any other nation in Latin America.
- Fulfilling Castro's dream, he has funded a Communist insurgency against the United States, effectively annexing Bolivia, Nicaragua, Dominica, and

    Ecuador as surrogate states, and is developing cells in dozens of countries
    to create new fronts in this struggle.

- He is allied with the narcotics-financed guerrillas against the government
  of Colombia, which the United States supports in its war against drug
  trafficking.
- He has numerous associations with terrorists, money launderers,
  kidnappers, and drug traffickers.
- He has more hard assets (the CITGO oil company) and soft assets
  (Hollywood stars, politicians, lobbyists, and media connections) than any
  other foreign power.

These are formidable and perhaps unique capabilities on the world scene.
But does Chávez intend to use these weapons against us? We believe he
means it when he says, "We have made it very clear. Our enemy is the
American empire,"[5] and "If the U.S. Empire succeeds in consolidating its
dominance, then humankind has no future, therefore, we have to save humankind and put an end to the U.S. Empire."[6]

    Chávez longs for the era when there will be no liberal international or-
der to constrain his dream of a worldwide "socialist" revolution: no United
Nations, no World Bank, no International Monetary Fund, no Organization for Economic Cooperation and Development, no World Trade Organization, no international law, no economic necessity for modernization
and globalization. And perhaps more important, he longs for the day when
the United States no longer polices the world's playing field. Chávez has
spent more than $100 billion trying to minimize the impact of each inter-
national institution on Latin America. He is clearly opposed to international cooperation that does not endorse the Cuba-Venezuela government
philosophy.

    "Look, I think the first thing to acknowledge when one goes to war,"
Chávez told the TV interviewer Carlos Croes in 2005, "is that one has to
begin hating the . . ." [Croes interrupts] "To hate him?" [Chávez contin-
ues] "To hate him! I mean, you cannot go to war loving the person. We
have to start getting ready to see the gringos as enemies, and that's the first
preparation for combat."[7]

    In fact, worldwide polls show that the United States is currently the
most despised nation on earth. Yale's Amy Chua believes it's because
"America today has become the world's market-dominant minority . . .

Americans have attained heights of wealth and economic power wildly disproportionate to our tiny numbers."[8] Chávez exploits this. He is deeply shamed by the history of slavery and subjugation of the Indo-Afro (dark-skinned) people and believes that confiscation of property, revenge, warfare, violence, and hatred are all justified as payback. We are dealing with a vindictive, vengeful man on the verge of megalomania, and we have not yet fully comprehended his potential to spread his wrath throughout much of the free world.

IN THE following pages, we'll examine five critical fronts of Chávez's initiative against what he calls "the evil empire." These are his oil; his alliance with Iran; the FARC's guerrilla war in Colombia; promoting anti-American states; and building friendly or so-called soft assets in the United States.

The "Oil Weapon"

By driving up the price of oil, Chávez is seeking to undermine the American economy—a goal he has declared publicly many times. He knows that higher oil will jack up inflation, exacerbating America's present economic downturn. The use of what Chávez calls the "oil weapon" is a conscious strategic initiative on his part that already has resulted in higher gas prices, economic dislocation, and oil market uncertainty.

His goal is to aggrandize himself at America's expense. As the *New York Times* columnist Roger Cohen has noted, "Chávez wants to parlay his petrorevenue and pseudorevolution into a global anti-American role. . . . High oil prices will tend to accentuate the long-term erosion of American dominance."

Chávez's first act as president was to seize absolute control over Venezuela's national oil company, Petróleos de Venezuela, S.A., PDVSA (pronounced "pay-day-VEY-sa"), which he had criticized as "a state within a state" during his presidential campaign. From 2001 to 2004, the Chávez takeover of Venezuela's oil sector (and the money and power that followed) involved a series of massive protests, a coup d'état that was reversed, a national strike that petered out, and a recall referendum against the president, all of which Chávez miraculously survived.

From early on, Chávez had helped to drive up the price of oil: from $8 a barrel when he assumed power in 1999 to $40 in 2004 and $147 in 2008. Over this period, Chávez shorted the oil market by 3 million barrels a day. Had this shortage been made available in 2008, it could have pushed prices down to the $50-a-barrel range—or about $2.25 for a gallon of gas in the United States. Americans think ExxonMobil is earning obscene profits, but its CEO's penchant for increasing the company's earnings is mild compared with Venezuela's. Of all the members of OPEC (the oil cartel was a Venezuelan idea), Chávez has lobbied most aggressively for the highest prices since its founding.

It's no surprise that oil is Chávez's weapon of choice. Today, Chávez estimates that Venezuela has reserves of 307 billion barrels of oil, second only to Saudi Arabia. And that's approximately ten times the amount of reserves held by the United States.

Venezuela's Alliance with Iran

Venezuela's ties to the radical Islamist regime in Iran have indirectly (and possibly directly) resulted in state-sponsored terrorism against the United States, its allies, and its interests. By directly supporting Iran with commercial projects and oil revenue, Chávez has provided much-needed resources to prop up the ailing Iranian economy. This, in turn, freed up Iranian money for terrorists whose goal is to undermine American interests in Iraq, Afghanistan, and indeed around the world.

Most Venezuelans were surprised when Chávez courted Iran shortly after taking office in 1999, but the record shows that Chávez had long intended to ally with Iran to harm the United States. When he was only a fledgling captain in Venezuela's military in 1982—three years after Ayatollah Khomeini's revolution deposed the Shah of Iran—Chávez swore allegiance to a military conspiracy to take power in Venezuela and to use oil, OPEC, and allied Middle East nations as weapons against U.S. dominance.

As president, Chávez made four official visits to Iranian president Sayyed Mohammed Khatami, who returned the interest with several trips to Venezuela. But he found his real soul mate in Iran's radical new president, Mahmoud Ahmadinejad, who was elected in 2005. In 2006, on an official visit, Chávez immediately pledged to join Iran against the "evil empire" of "the imperial U.S.," while Ahmadinejad praised Chávez as "a worker of God and servant of the people [who] works perpetually against the dominant system [the U.S.]."[9] Ahmadinejad visited Ecuador and Nicaragua, both allies of Venezuela and Chávez, in 2007.

The alliance has blossomed into a mutual defense pact against their common enemy, the United States. It also entails $20 billion of oil and military contracts and more than 180 trade agreements.[10] These contracts have created a joint bank, an oil industry technical program, and a joint fund. Additionally, they have created a jointly owned petrochemical complex in Iran, 51 percent owned by Iran and 49 percent owned by Venezuela. The two countries have constructed a second petrochemical complex in Venezuela, at a total combined cost of $1.4 billion.[11] Reports have documented the presence of Iranian-sponsored Hezbollah terrorists in Venezuela, and the strategic placement of Iranian missiles on Venezuela's border. The missiles are reportedly aimed against the democratically elected government of Colombia—the prime mover in the war against cocaine financed by the United States.

Guerrilla Warfare in Colombia

Chávez has tried to put pressure on the United States by supporting the Communist guerrilla insurgency in neighboring Colombia. Even as the United States has spent nearly $6 billion over the last decade in an effort to stabilize Colombia, curtail its cocaine traffic, and eliminate the insurgency (which is funded largely by drugs), Chávez has adopted the Colombian guerrillas known by the Spanish acronym "FARC" (Revolutionary Armed Forces of Colombia) as his revolutionary comrades-in-arms. Although he denies being involved with them, Colombia has provided documents to the Organization of American States that it says detail Chávez's support of guerrillas with deals involving arms, money, and cocaine. Chávez claims that Colombia fabricated the documents, but the preponderance of evidence shows—and most responsible Latin American authorities believe—that the alliance is a fact.[12]

The FARC is the largest of the Communist guerrilla insurgencies that have plagued Latin America for almost half a century, but in recent years its power and influence have waned. With U.S. aid, the Colombian government has managed in the last decade to reassert control over most of the guerrilla territory. It has disarmed the majority of the right-wing paramilitaries that once patrolled and terrorized the Colombian hillsides. Prosecutors have cracked down on the country's once ubiquitous cocaine cartels, and the FARC has dwindled to about 9,000 guerrillas hidden in the dense jungles along the 1,370-mile border with Venezuela.

Still, the FARC has not disappeared entirely. It may be reduced in number but it enjoys an estimated $300 million of annual income from cocaine smuggling (80 percent of the world's cocaine is processed in Colombia), kidnapping, and extortion. It engages in murder, recruiting of children for warfare, human rights violations, terrorism, and "crimes against humanity," according to Colombia's President Álvaro Uribe. According to reports from among its 2,400 former members, the FARC resembles a mafia crime gang more than a Communist guerrilla army, but Chávez disagrees, calling the FARC, "insurgent forces that have a political project." They "are not terrorists, they are true armies . . . they must be recognized," Chávez said.[13]

In September 2008, Chávez expelled the U.S. ambassador. In response, the next day the United States accused three high government officials of drug trafficking and providing arms to FARC members, whom it labels as terrorists. For the fourth consecutive year, the U.S. government indicated that Venezuela had not done enough to aid antidrug efforts.

Promoting Anti-American States

Chávez has built an alliance of anti-American states in Latin America and in the Caribbean, called the Bolivarian Alternative for the Americas or ALBA—which includes Cuba, Bolivia, Nicaragua, and Ecuador—in order to augment his power in the western hemisphere and curtail America's. He has propped up Fidel Castro's failing dictatorship with billions in oil subsidies annually since taking power. By its own admission, the alliance is frustrated with the "failure of the neoliberal politics imposed on our countries," and the birth of the alliance places Latin American and Caribbean people "on the road to their second and true independence." The declaration of the alliance laid out the founding principles in "firm rejection of the goals of the FTAA [Free Trade Agreement of the Americas]," and in agreement that the "cardinal principle that should guide [the alliance] is the great solidarity among the people of Latin America and the Caribbean as upheld by Bolívar, Martí, etc."[14]

Chávez met Fidel Castro for the first time in 1994. Chávez had just been released from prison, where he'd been incarcerated after his coup d'état attempt against the democratically elected president of Venezuela on February 4, 1992. From that point on, Castro became Chávez's mentor, strategist, and daily political consultant. Chávez's goals in life are to complete Simón Bolívar's dream to unite Latin America and Castro's dream to communize it.

Castro developed Chávez's strategy in the 1998 campaign for the Venezuelan presidency, and upon Chávez's victory, Castro developed the rewriting of the constitution and inspired the creation of a one-party state and the nationalization of the means of production. Castro also encouraged the militarization of society and the persecution of dissenters and of advocates of democracy. However similar they are, Venezuela is a large mainland country with porous borders and a history of democracy and freedom, whereas Cuba is an island ruled by a slew of dictators. Where Castro is an intellectual who showed he could manage agriculture, health, education, military, and security systems even as Cuba was failing miserably, Chávez is a quixotic if charismatic bloviator who has shown he can't even manage a nation rich in oil reserves.

Chávez, however, is still betting on a post-Castro Cuba, in short, by forging or continuing deals with Fidel's brother and successor, Raúl. They have an oil-for-services deal in which Venezuela ships 92,000 barrels a day to Cuba in exchange for the services of thousands of Cuban doctors in Venezuela's slums and other technical assistance. Venezuelan banks are financing fifty-eight Cuban manufacturing programs and more than a dozen agricultural development programs.

"Since the beginning, both Fidel Castro and Hugo Chávez have been determined to move the relationship between their countries beyond the oil-for-doctors swap and toward something that is much broader and has the potential for sweeping regional impact," says Dan Erikson, a Caribbean expert at the Inter-American Dialogue policy group in Washington, D.C. "Raúl Castro is strongly interested in moving beyond an alliance built on personalities by creating sustainable, institutional arrangements, and this has helped to cement the Cuban-Venezuelan relationship." [15]

Chávez is not only sympatico with Cuba but with Russia as well. In July 2008, Chávez made his sixth trip there, to cement relations with Vladimir Putin's handpicked successor, Dmitri Medvedev. Clearly, the two countries see themselves as allies and a countervailing force against the policies of the West.

The two nations agreed to coordinate their actions on the pricing and distribution of oil and gas, which will likely not bode well for their customers looking for free market value. Chávez had a serious interest in making such a deal. At the time of this writing, he was on the verge of buying $1 billion in arms from the Russians. They were expected to include as many as 20 S-300 Thor antiaircraft missile systems and three diesel-powered submarines. Venezuela is currently Russia's largest arms customer, having received in the past some 100,000 Kalashnikov assault rifles plus assorted fighter jets and helicopters, at a cost of almost $5 billion so far, totaling twelve contracts for weapons purchases between 2005 and 2007. The Russians have promised to jointly explore gas resources in Venezuela and to share nuclear power technology with Chávez as they previously did with Iran.[16] China and Venezuela also agreed to build two oil refineries, one in each country, as a means of reducing Venezuela's dependence on the U. S. market, which still accounts for 60 percent of Venezuelan exports.

Thanks to Putin, and now Medvedev, an oil-for-arms relationship with one of the world's superpowers will ensure that Venezuela is protected from any unexpected insurgencies. In August 2008, as Russia was about to invade Georgia, Chávez appeared in Moscow and offered Venezuelan airfields for refueling Russian bombers armed with nuclear weapons, which recalled the Soviet Union's attempt to build nuclear missile bases in Cuba in 1962. The Russians asked Chávez to withdraw the public invitation so they did not have to respond, and thereby avoided embarrassment on the world political stage.

But in September 2008, the Russians showed no such reticence. In short order, a pair of Russian TU-160 low-range bombers able to carry nuclear weapons landed in Venezuela. Russia also sent a number of ships from their North Sea fleet along with the unequaled nuclear cruiser, *Peter the Great,* to take part in exercises with the Venezuelan navy later in November of that year. And at the end of a two-day visit by Chávez to Russia that month, the Russian government also confirmed that they were offering a $1 billion loan so that Venezuela could purchase additional arms. A neutral analyst has indicated that the arms purchases were a deliberate attempt by both governments to "import cold-war tensions to the region."[17] Further, the *Wall Street Journal* called the deployment of Russian ships and planes to the west "unprecedented since the Cold War" and representing a potential increase in tensions between the United States and Russia, especially in the aftermath of the summer 2008 war in Georgia.[18]

Summarizing the emerging ties between Russia and Venezuela, Arthur Herman recently wrote, "These [military] exercises are a stark challenge to U.S. interests in South America and the Carribean . . . [and] mark a major step in Chávez's bid to become the leading power in the southern Western Hemisphere. They also put the seal on Russia's aggressive re-emergence on the international scene both in Eastern Europe and Asia, and now in the Western Hemisphere."[19]

Developing "Soft" Assets in the United States

Since he was elected, Chávez's public relations machinery has spent close to a billion dollars in the United States to convince Americans that he alone is telling the true story. The appealing narrative spun by Hugo Chávez features a poor, dark-skinned former paratrooper who defied the odds to defeat a predominantly white regime and now fights the prevailing bureaucracies to end poverty, war, and racism. If pressed, Chávez probably would liken himself to Nelson Mandela, though perhaps with a bit more testosterone.

With America's foreign policy on shaky footing, its image abroad at its nadir, and a lame duck leader in the White House, it wasn't hard to find sympathizers within our borders. They included former President Jimmy Carter, the Reverend Jesse Jackson, liberal Democrats such as Senator Chris Dodd (Conn.), Representative Dennis Kucinich (Ohio), and Representative William Delahunt (Mass.). Many of these politicians believe that Chávez is the victim of racism and fear that gripped the United States after the attack of 9/11. Chávez applies his Bush-bashing as a weapon of mass distraction from his ever-growing assault against America. While many might view this rhetoric as adversary politics-as-usual, U.S. Representative Charles Rangel (D-NY) had a rational response. When he heard that Chávez called Bush "Satan," he responded, "If there's any criticism of President Bush, it should be restricted to Americans, whether they voted for him or not."[20]

First among the many Americans who have delivered ringing encomiums to Chávez's revolution were African American studies professor Cornel West, the union activist Dolores Huerta, and the leftist organizer Tom Hayden, who along with Jesse Jackson wrote a letter to President Bush on the eve of Venezuela's 2006 presidential election in which they contended that "Since 1999, the citizens of Venezuela have repeatedly voted for a government that—unlike others in the past—would share their country's oil wealth with millions of poor Venezuelans," a claim that even Chávez's former economic experts disputed.[21]

Second, a string of Hollywood luminaries have been drawn to Chávez's version of his story. Some plan to put it on the big screen. Ed Asner, Danny Glover, Sean Penn, Kevin Spacey, Naomi Campbell, and a host of others have endorsed Chávez. Loaded with cash and aware of the power of the entertainment industry and the media, Chávez has funded his own film industry in Caracas, where Danny Glover picked up $20 million for a Chávez-inspired film noting parallels between how the French were expunged from Haiti and how Chávez is ridding Venezuela of America's influence.

Third, there are a number of influential Americans who have been attracted by Chávez's money. These include the 1996 Republican vice-presidential candidate Jack Kemp, who has reaped large fees trying to sell Chávez's oil to the U.S. government;[22] Tom Boggs, one of the most powerful lobbyists in Washington, D.C.; Giuliani Partners, the lobbying arm of the former New York mayor and presidential hopeful (principal lobbyists for Chávez's CITGO oil company in Texas); former Massachusetts governor Mitt Romney's Bain Associates, which prospered by handling Chávez's oil and bond interests; and Joseph P. Kennedy II of Massachusetts, who advertises Chávez's oil discounts to low-income Americans, a program that reaches more than a million American families (Kennedy and Chávez cast this program as nonpolitical philanthropy).

The official American response to the threat posed by the Chávez regime has been to ramp up diplomacy in the region. In March 2007, President Bush launched what one White House operative called "a diplomatic counter-attack"[23] to Chávez, visiting five Latin American nations relatively safe from criticism, or so they thought—Brazil, Uruguay, Colombia, Guatemala, and Mexico.

In Brazil, Bush was met by demonstrations and an editorial headlined "Uncle Scrooge's Paltry Package" in a conservative newspaper. *O Estado de São Paulo* wrote that the aid Bush was offering to Latin America amounted to "the equivalent of five days' cost of the war in Iraq, and a drop of water compared to the ocean of petrodollars in which Chávez is navigating at full speed."[24] Chávez had also upstaged Bush by firing up a raucous "anti-imperialist" rally in Buenos Aires, where he called Bush a "political cadaver" selling "American hypocrisy and greed. [Bush] thinks he is Columbus discovering poverty after seven years in power."[25]

As we reveal Chávez's inner workings, you will learn what many Venezuelans and other Latin Americans already have discovered: he is a charismatic, formidable leader; he understands the use of well-placed propaganda; he knows how to adeptly cultivate and manipulate allies; he rules with absolute authority. And when you deconstruct the man in some detail, you come to realize that he is a looming threat to the liberties we in America—and other countries in the free world—cling to with such fervor.

1

The Origin
of the Threat

Who is Hugo Chávez? Why does he hate and seek to destroy the United States? And why do so many otherwise astute observers of foreign affairs discount and even dismiss the danger he poses to our interests?

From a distance, Chávez can appear to be little more than a bumptious fool—a buffoon the likes of which Third World countries often present to the world. And to be sure, Chávez shares many traits in common with more ordinary backwater big men who pose no threat to America. Chávez used mostly familiar means to gain power, and much of his rhetoric resonates with people born into South America's troubled mix of extreme poverty, inequality, and racial injustice.

Indeed, many of Chávez's criticisms of his country are true. Although

Venezuela has long been one of the region's richer countries, since the coming of the Spanish in 1522 it has operated as a virtual caste system, with European whites at the top, controlling the government and most of the resources, and browned-skinned Indo-Africans on the bottom. It is a toxic arrangement that has helped to produce many a revolutionary over the centuries, including the great Simón Bolívar—legendary liberator of the lands that today comprise Venezuela, Bolivia, Colombia, Panama, Peru, and Ecuador.

Chávez came of age amid this mix of grinding rural poverty, racial isolation, and political and economic turmoil. He naturally sympathizes with those who suffer as he suffered, and he shares their resentments against their oligarchic oppressors in Caracas. It's easy to dismiss Chávez's rantings as the visceral responses of the poor, brown-skinned youth he once was.

But there is more—much more—to the story than this. Chávez is no simple tribune of the poor. He is a true radical, who imbibed deeply the Marxist and revolutionary ideologies that convulsed Latin America during his formative years in the 1960s and 1970s. And he joins his people's resentment to a wider hatred of the great republic to the north, which Chávez accuses of arrogance, theft, bullying, and a determination to humiliate him and his people.

Chávez's longtime psychiatrist Edmundo Chirinos (also a leftist writer, former university rector, and presidential candidate) believes that Chávez's anti-American feelings form the very core of his personality: "Chávez feels a genuine scorn for oligarchic people, not only in the sense of possessing money but of affectation, through gestures, language . . . and so in that respect, he exhibits an evident bipolarity, of an affinity for the humble and a rejection of the all-powerful."[1]

By the time he graduated from the Venezuelan Academy of Military Sciences in 1975, Chávez had channeled that rage into an ideologically coherent plan to subvert the government of Venezuela and launch a regional and even wider assault on his hated enemy. Some of this thinking was simply a product of his environment. Other elements stem from formative experiences in his life. But perhaps the most important was the influence of key people he met, learned from, and came to admire over the course of his long rise to power.

From his birth in 1954 to his coup d'état attempt in 1992, Chávez's mental state, formative thoughts, and early behavior were entirely consistent with what was to follow. He would take over Venezuela by whatever means and use its oil wealth to launch a revolution against the superpower, the evil empire, the United States.

Chávez's formative years offer clues to what would come later—provided one studies them with an open mind, and is willing to look past his buffoonish exterior. History teaches us that the grandiose plans of buffoons sometimes succeed, and their grandiose plans occasionally come to fruition.

Childhood

The man who fancies himself the twenty-first century's Bolívar was born on July 28, 1954, in the tiny village of Sabaneta. Located in the state of Barinas, it borders Colombia, where the Andes Mountains slope down to the vast savanna. The region has long been famous as a breeding ground for cattle, lawlessness, and rebellion. As in most of the Americas, from the British West Indies to Louisiana, slaves did nearly all of the work until the mid-nineteenth century.

Sabaneta itself is nothing but a few strips of dirt lined with shacks and stores and one little cinema. It was typical of the towns inhabited by Venezuela's poor, brown-skinned, uneducated masses. From an early age, Chávez soaked up the grievances of Venezuela's rural poor and nurtured the resentment that is a by-product of surviving the daily battle against poverty.

Chávez's schoolteacher parents—Hugo de los Reyes Chávez and Elena Frías de Chávez—could not afford to raise all of their six children at home, so the two oldest boys, Adán and Hugo, were sent to live with their grandmother, Rosa Inés. Several distinguished Chávez-watchers, including Álvaro Vargas Llosa, have theorized that his being locked in closets at home and then sent away by his parents to grow up elsewhere constituted a seminal rejection that gave rise to what Vargas Llosa calls Chávez's "messianic inferiority complex"—his overarching yearning to be loved and his irrepressible need to act out.

"Mamá Rosa," as young Hugo affectionately called his grandmother, was the real mother figure in young Hugo's life. It was she whom he talked to, cared for, wrote to, identified with, and remembers. His first letter after entering the military academy was written to her: "I have always felt proud to have been raised by you and to be able to call you *Mamá*."[2]

Mamá Rosa fired Hugo's and Adán's imaginations with tales of daring deeds of the rebels Ezequiel Zamora and Maisanta (whom Chávez would later falsely claim was his great-grandfather), imprinting them with dreams of valor, glory, and power that inspire him to this day.

And she—or at least her example—reinforced the frankly racialist thinking that was far from uncommon in poor areas. Asked by his biographers in 2004 to describe his grandmother and mother, Chávez used racial terms: "My grandmother was a mix of black and indigenous," he says. "My mother was fair skinned and really pretty." Chávez may admire or loathe people based upon their skin color perhaps in part because his alienation from his mother was also personal. According to his early lover of nine years, Herma Marksman, as a youngster in Sabaneta, Chávez would cross the street so he didn't have to say hello to his mother and would avoid eye contact with her. Hugo often said he didn't love his mother.[3]

Like a virus that never goes away, poverty affected every aspect of young Hugo's life, from his meager breakfast to street baseball and other humiliations. On his first day in school, the boy was sent home because he lacked proper shoes. Mamá Rosa had no money for anything that would pass for shoes and Hugo's parents had nothing left over after supporting their own household as well as Mamá Rosa's. Hopeless, she sat down on the earthen floor of her tiny palm-thatched hut and cried. It was an incident that little Hugo would never forget—and that indeed still figures into many of his stories.[4]

In an interview with Lally Weymouth of *Newsweek,* Chávez recalled childhood memories of his poverty: "I was in close contact with poverty, it's true. I cried a lot. . . . I had to go with my father in the wee hours of the morning to help him fish to be able to eat. I sold sweets that my grandmother baked in the public square to have money to buy shoes and notebooks."[5] Chávez goes on to remember Jorge, a child with whom he played ball every day. "Then one day, he didn't come to school. We asked why. They told us his mother had died in childbirth. This happened a lot, because there were no doctors for anyone." Since Jorge's father had also died, "he was forced to go to work and become a child-laborer. He had little brothers and sisters, and they had to be fed."

Then he pauses, remembering his own little brother.

"Yes, I saw the pain of poverty. My little brother was called Enso, he was a very beautiful child but he became ill. I remember him lying in a hammock. He was always smiling. But he died. There were no doctors, nothing. We buried him in a bag. He was one of those children who are swallowed by poverty."[6]

Yet, in spite of all the hardship, childhood was for Chávez "a very happy period. I would give anything to go back to one day in my childhood. I was indeed a poor child, a peasant, but I was very happy with my grandmother. She filled me with love and solidarity."

Adolescence:
The Young Communist Rebel

Chávez is remembered as a studious but unruly child. A teacher, Elgilda Crespo, remembers the boy throwing a notebook at her and not handing it to her as she had asked. "Hugo, pick it up, you don't throw things," she instructed, whereupon he picked up the notebook and threw it at her again. It took him a long time to calm down.[7]

In high school in nearby Barinas, Chávez early fell under the influence of accomplished peers whose young lives were already in the service of worldwide Communist revolution. Two of Hugo's school friends were the sons of José Esteban Ruiz Guevara, a historian, poet, writer—and zealous Communist. Ruiz more than anyone shaped Hugo's basic ideas about capitalism, communism, and revolution.

Ruiz was a leader of the Communist Party in Barinas, an avocation that had once landed him in jail. His commitment to the party and its ideas ran deep. He was part of a Communist network—backed by Castro—planning an insurrection in Venezuela against the elected government of Rómulo Betancourt, the so-called father of Venezuelan democracy. Adán Chávez and later Hugo joined this network of Communist subversives as teenagers.

Ruiz even named his own two boys Vladimir (for Lenin) and Federico (for Engels). These brothers became young Hugo's fast friends. They called him Goofy, from the Disney cartoon, and often invited him to study in their father's huge library, the only one of its kind in the small town.[8] It was filled with the works of revolutionaries such as Marx and Mao, and also with books by political philosophers such as Machiavelli and Rousseau. "You better get Marxism into your brains, and good," the elder Ruiz told him.[9]

Federico and Vladimir Ruiz, however, downplay their father's influence on young Hugo. Both state that, while Ruiz might have talked of communism from time to time, he and Hugo never had elaborate conversations, and they deny that he indoctrinated the boys with leftist literature.[10] But Ruiz's wife, Carmen, remembers differently. "Don't you get tired of talking about communism?" she once asked Chávez in the family library. "Good God, I have had it up to here with communism! I don't want to hear another word about it."[11]

Another favorite topic of Ruiz's lectures was the heroics of Simón Bolívar and Ezequiel Zamora, a soldier and leader during Venezuela's mid-nineteenth-century Federal War. Zamora in particular was famous for his hostile view of the Venezuelan oligarchy and for the land reform program he developed to benefit the peasants.[12] Other Ruiz heroes were Fidel Castro and his Argentine revolutionary sidekick Che Guevara.

Thus it was Ruiz who first linked for Chávez the Venezuelan nationalism of Bolívar and Zamora with the communism of Castro and Che. Chávez himself would later define his Bolivarian Revolution in precisely these terms.

Ruiz was not the only influence on the young Hugo. As he listened to Ruiz's sermons, events all around him seemed to confirm their essence. Latin America and the Caribbean were on fire with Communist insurgencies, providing stories of heroism that enthralled the young Chávez. Collective memories of the Cuban revolution, and the subsequent American failures to overturn it, were fresh.

Hugo was not old enough to appreciate events in Cuba as they unfolded. As a ten-year-old in 1964, he witnessed the Brazilian military—aided by the CIA—overthrow the elected, left-leaning president João Goulart because of his ties with labor organizations.[13] And as a teenager he thrilled to tales of Che Guevara's derring-do in his attempts to foster revolution in Bolivia. But he was still naive. When he heard the news that Che had been cornered and killed in 1967, the thirteen-year-old Hugo wondered why Castro didn't send helicopters to save him.[14]

Later in Chávez's life, the "dirty wars" in Argentina—state-sanctioned assassinations and "disappearances" carried out against left-wing politicians and trade leaders—and the American support for the anti-Communist Nicaraguan Contras further deepened his hatred of the United States and his resentment of U.S. meddling in Latin America.

The Cadet

A military career might seem an unlikely path for a young man on fire with revolutionary zeal. But the Venezuelan Academy of Military Sciences was one of few options for a poor boy determined to further himself. Unlike the military in Chile and Argentina, there was no discrimination in the Venezuelan military; anyone could reach military rank and many senior officers came from poor families.

Of the six Chávez boys, Adán was the only one who made it into university and managed to graduate. But Hugo's school grades were too low to qualify. He applied to the military academy at seventeen, over the objection of Mamá Rosa, who lit candles in church against it: "I am praying to the saints to get this idea out of your head," she told him. "You, Huguito, are a rebel. One day you could get yourself in trouble." [15]

Despite his poor grades—and his failures in science, which should have dashed his hopes for entry—Chávez was accepted into the academy for his athletic prowess. The academy reviewer, sympathetic to the boy and searching for a way around his record, asked him, "Do you play a sport?" That he did. "Baseball saved me," Chávez recalls. [16] He entered the academy in 1971 as a baseball player.

The Venezuelan Academy of Military Sciences is Venezuela's oldest military school and offers a four-year training program for officer cadets. Chávez entered amid a transformation. The curriculum had recently been restructured to provide a more humanities-based education, more akin to what civilian universities were teaching. The cadets were encouraged to go on to graduate schools rather than the U.S.-run School of the Americas in Panama, where they'd gone in the past.

These reforms created a divide between the old and the new military. Before Chávez became a cadet, Venezuela's military had a long tradition of joint education, training, and exercises with the United States—as do many Latin American nations to this day. The old Venezuelan military elite not only learned U.S. military tactics; they built close ties with their American counterparts. Chávez's class was one of the first for which such training was not mandatory, and for which the maintenance of close ties to the United States was not emphasized.

As he explained in 2004: "After my generation entered the FAN [Spanish acronym for Venezuela's military], U.S. influence went into a progressive decline. The nationalist sentiments that arose among the Venezuelan military grew in us. For example, when we went to the anti-guerilla camps there were no longer any gringo advisors. Fewer and fewer officers went to study in U.S. military academies.

"I didn't go [to the U.S.] but . . . many of those who did take those courses not only were not poisoned by U.S. teaching but on the contrary, it reinforced their nationalist feelings. The ideological process that was underway in the barracks distanced itself from imperialism. We were studying Bolívar and the logical consequence of this was an absolute rejection of imperial ideology." [17] The class before his was, Chávez has said, "the last gasp of fascism and of anti-communism," while his 1975 graduating class was, he claims, "the first to discover Bolívar." [18]

Chávez was as poor a cadet as he had been a student. He acknowledges being continuously disruptive in academic classes. "I argued with my superiors, I never remained silent," he says. [19] His particular grievance was the army's suppression of the Communist guerrillas in Venezuela, whom he almost quit the academy to join. "I even founded the Army for the Liberation of the Venezuelan People," a cadet activist group, but he could find only a few sympathizers among the corps, so it withered. [20]

In 1974, Chávez visited Lima, Peru, with other Venezuelan military cadets to celebrate ceremonies commemorating the 150th anniversary of the battle of Ayacucho, the last battle against Spanish rule on the continent. There, Chávez met the left-leaning Nationalist general Juan Velasco Alvarado, who had seized power in 1968 and then confiscated large farms, enterprises, and banks. "Plan Inca," which Chávez had read about enthusiastically in the military academy library, would serve as a model for him when he became president in 1999.

He recalls, "They took us to the government house and Velasco was there at a reception for officers and cadets where he spoke a few words and sent two books to us, *The Peruvian National Revolution* and the *Manifesto of the Revolutionary Government of the Armed Forces of Peru*. After listening to

Velasco, I drunk in the books and even learned almost all of some speeches by heart. I kept those books until 4 February 1992" (the date of his coup d'état attempt).[21]

These visits, and those books, were not the sole influences on Chávez during his years at the academy. He also came under the sway of Jacinto Pérez Arcay, an officer in the military and a teacher at the academy. Arcay would later serve Chávez as a brigadier general, one of the top military aides advising him during the 1992 coup. Chávez felt his debt to Arcay keenly: after coming to power in 1999, he would thank the general by giving him an office in Miraflores, the presidential palace.[22]

Arcay claims that preventing the Americans from stealing Venezuela's resources has always been Chávez's primary motivation. "Hugo knew early on that that was the biggest threat to the country, that he was destined to lead the greatest battle against the United States, which for centuries had coveted our nation.[23] . . . The main battle is not against the country's oligarchy," the general says, "the great battle is against the empire."[24] And as Chávez sees it, he is not bringing that battle to the United States but fighting a defensive battle for Venezuela's liberation: America "will never give up the idea of winning over, of turning people against a revolution which has openly said that the empire is its main enemy."[25]

Chávez graduated in 1975, the last in the class of sixty-seven students—an outcome he blamed on his teachers. Years later, he reflected on his journey. "The Hugo Chávez who started at the academy was a boy from the countryside. Four years later a second lieutenant who had set out along a revolutionary path graduated."

Chávez was now a secret guerrilla, with a fierce anxiety to act heroically on his beliefs. In his personal diary on October 25, 1977, he wrote: "This war is going to take years . . . I have to do it. Even if it costs me my life. It doesn't matter. This is what I was born to do. How long can I last like this? I feel impotent. Unproductive. I have to get ready. To act."[26]

Guerrilla in Uniform

On graduation day 1975, Hugo Chávez officially became a lieutenant in Venezuela's military. He received his sword from the hand of President Carlos Andrés Pérez[27]—the man he would try to overthrow seventeen years later. He was already dreaming of power, writing ambitiously to his girlfriend, "I wish I could one day have the responsibility of the whole fatherland, Great Bolívar's Fatherland." [28]

Thereafter, Chávez began living the life of a Communist double agent. "During the day I'm a career military officer who does his job," he told his lover, Herma Marksman, "but at night I work on achieving the transformations this country needs." [29] His nights were filled with secret meetings of Communist subversives and co-conspirators, often in disguises, planning the armed overthrow of the government.

In this clandestine life, Chávez became a master of daily deception. "He is marvelous at deceiving people," his psychiatrist Dr. Edmundo Chirinos notes.[30] Chávez's co-conspirator in the 1992 coup, Francisco Arias Cárdenas, who accused Chávez of killing civilians in April 2002, remembers that "When we were in the army, Chávez took a course in psychological warfare in El Salvador. He became a big proponent of reverse psychology, baiting opponents into underestimating your strength." [31] After opposing Chávez in 2000, Arias Cárdenas reversed field to become his ambassador to the UN.

Apart from his brother Adán, Chávez told his family nothing about his subversive activities. Mamá Rosa would die in 1982, having no idea what was really going on in the life of the little rebel she had weaned on stories of General Zamora.

Rebellion was stirring all over the Latin American countryside, driven by unprecedented economic turmoil. The crash of the Bretton Woods system of exchange rates fixed to the gold standard by "First World" nations created a tidal wave of economic depressions throughout much of the Third World, and especially in Latin America. The region's poverty was worsening, and would double in a decade, from 120 million poor people in 1980 to 240 million in 1990.

Fresh out of military school, Chávez was sent to put down a Maoist uprising in his hometown. "It is there I began to see," he says now. "The peasants were subject to huge repression. [The army would] burn their houses down, accuse them without respecting the rule of law. I saw how peasants were tortured by my own side. I saw it happen." [32]

In 1977, his unit was transferred to the eastern state of Anzoátegui, where sects of ultraleft guerrillas were fighting. In the spring of 1978, he transferred to Maracay in central Venezuela—and there he began meeting with revolutionaries and making speeches. In 1979, he was transferred to Caracas to teach at his former military academy.[33] It was the perfect perch from which to build a network of officers sympathetic to his revolutionary cause.

Chávez also expanded the circle of his ideological mentors. By far the most important of these was Douglas Bravo, an unreconstructed Communist who disobeyed Moscow's orders after *détente* to give up the armed struggle against the United States. Bravo was the leader of the Party of the Venezuelan Revolution (PVR) and the Armed Forces of National Liberation. Chávez actively recruited his military friends to the PVR, couching it in the rhetoric of "Bolivarism" to make it more palatable to their sensibilities.

Bravo articulated a four-part armed struggle strategy that Chávez would later implement as president. The key insight Bravo added to the prevailing Marxist theorizing of the time was a strategy to employ Venezuela's oil as a weapon against the hated United States.

His strategy was simple to understand, if not necessarily easy to execute: First, use Venezuela's oil as a weapon against U.S. capitalism and imperialism by convincing OPEC to limit production and raise prices. Second, ally with Islamic oil nations in a bloc against Israel and the United States. Third, stir up nationalism and militarism in Venezuela by using Bolívar as a symbol and thereby crushing the oligarchy. Finally, build on these successes to initiate a triumphant revolution in Latin America and the world.[34]

In short, Bravo added both oil and Iran to Chávez's intended revolution.

Chávez found Bravo's strategy exciting. It meshed with the ideas culled from his conversations with Mr. Ruiz in Barinas, and with his lifelong readings of revolutionary tracts. And, satisfyingly, it pitted him squarely against the current government—which at that time was drawing closer to the hated United States.

In particular, Venezuela was the one OPEC member to reject the 1973 Arab oil embargo and to continue and even increase its shipments to the United States. This not only infuriated the country's OPEC partners in the Persian Gulf; it helped to further radicalize Douglas Bravo, Hugo Chávez, and other Venezuelan revolutionaries who sought to deny oil deliveries to the "capitalist and imperialist" United States.

Where Chávez the guerrilla differed with the sometimes democratic-minded Bravo was over the way to take power. Bravo was an experienced coup plotter. He had played a role in the 1958 popular uprising that overthrew the Pérez Jimenez dictatorship and culminated in a democratic election. Bravo aspired to repeat this success.

Chávez, however, rejected both a mass movement and an election in favor of a surprise attack by a military force that would then rule by diktat, as in Cuba. "We wanted the civil society to participate in the revolutionary movement," Bravo recalled in 2006. "But this was exactly what Chávez didn't want. He wanted civil society to applaud him but not to participate."[35] To Chávez, it was his way or the highway, and Bravo was eventually dismissed from Chávez's inner circle.

The Oath

In December 1982, a few months before the Venezuelan economic crash known as "Black Friday," Chávez was chosen to make a dinner speech at an air force base in Maracay honoring the death of Simón Bolívar. His superiors asked him to provide a written copy of what he planned to say, as military procedures required. "Major, Sir, I have no written speech," he told the chief of staff of the parachute regiment. "I am going to say a few words."[36] In reality, Chávez rarely had only a few words.

Instead of the expected nationalistic speech honoring the hero, Chávez condemned the current administration, intermixing his denunciations with stem-winding exhortations recalling not just Bolívar but also Zamora and Maisanta, the rebel leader Chávez falsely claims as his great-grandfather. Finally, Chávez also called for revolt.

After the dinner, Chávez and three officer friends walked privately to the nearby sacred tree "Saman de Guerre," where Bolívar is said to have napped before the fateful battle of Carabobo, and formed a new radical organization called the Bolivarian Revolutionary Army-200.[37] There, the four military conspirators repeated Bolívar's oath:

"I swear by the God of my fathers, I swear by them, I swear by my honor and I swear by my homeland that I shall give no respite to my arm nor rest to my soul until we have broken the chains that the powerful have placed upon us."[38]

It would be Chávez's life's work to keep that oath. And ten years after making it, he had his first real chance to fulfill it.

2

Por Ahora—
"For Now"

Like many a dictator before him, Chávez had to endure failure before finally tasting success. Indeed, his very failure to seize power on the first attempt—his botched 1992 coup attempt—laid the foundation for his successful second try. And the ridiculous quality of the first paradoxically helped as well: it caused seasoned observers to dismiss Chávez as a joke, and downplay any threat he posed. Sadly, this response endures to this day, despite his success at seizing and consolidating power.

Yet the true lesson of 1992 is precisely the opposite. That failed putsch illuminates Chávez's methods and motivations, offers a window into both his strategy and his tactics, and shows how he honed his mastery of asymmetric, deceptive warfare. If anything defines the life and times of Hugo Chávez, it is deceiving his enemies. By his own account, he was a double agent "living a double life" for two decades.[1] Perhaps among all recent world leaders, only the career KGB agent Vladimir Putin compares in talent for, and experience in, calculated deception on a grand scale.

The 1992 coup is also important because it marked the first time that the private Chávez revealed himself fully to the public eye. Those who knew the man personally could have little doubt of his antidemocratic, antigovernment, anti-American, pro-rebel, pro-Castro, pro-Communist, pro-revolution fervor. But to the Venezuelan public—and to the world at large—all this was as unknown as the man himself. In 1992, Chávez burst onto the scene by launching a coup d'état attempt against the democratically elected government of Venezuela. Unlike his hero in Cuba, who concealed his true intent until he had power firmly in hand, there would be no ambiguity about what Chávez stood for in the years that preceded his finally taking power in 1998.

Chávez's masterstroke was his insistence on being allowed to make a live televised statement to all Venezuelans in surrendering his coup attempt—and the lie he told to make it happen was arguably the most consequential lie of his career. Promising to call on his troops to stop fighting, Chávez instead rallied his supporters to fight another day. All was over, he said, *"por ahora* (for now)." But his chance would come again.

The 1992 coup attempt failed to install Chávez in power. But his actions—and especially the speech that ended it—succeeded in transforming Chávez into a popular hero and a national figure. Absent the '92 failure, there could have been no '98 success.

The Path to Insurrection

As a young officer with radical proclivities, Chávez had to carefully walk inside the line of acceptable soldierly behavior. The Venezuelan military had a long legal and political tradition of detachment from politics. Indeed, from 1958 to 1998, Venezuelan soldiers were constitutionally barred from voting.[2] (Chávez would reverse this upon his election in 1998; the military gained the vote in 1999, and by 2006 Chávez was publicly instructing soldiers that it was their patriotic duty to work for his revolutionary political party or resign from the service. He also posted military officers as heads of hundreds of civilian institutions.)

The pre-Chávez military culture frowned on political activities, especially in the barracks. If a military officer was found associating with the Communists (the mutual enemy of both the military and the major political parties throughout the Cold War period), that would spell the end of his career—and maybe worse. Cold War proxy fights were being waged throughout Latin America, and the Venezuelan government was a loyal U.S. ally. Many Venezuelan officers—and almost all the generals—had served on a tour or two studying at U.S. military academies. These men identified with the United States. Very few had any experience in the Soviet Union or Cuba.

Chávez spent the years between the 1982 saman tree oath and the 1992 coup profitably, carefully recruiting fellow conspirators, plotting strategy, and waiting for the opportune moment to fulfill his lifelong dream. As a child, he had learned sympathy for Venezuela's rebels and guerrillas. As a high school student, he learned to admire the Communists. And as a lieutenant, captain, major, and lieutenant colonel, he attempted to unite both leanings into a conspiracy to take power by force.[3]

Chávez quickly gained a reputation among his fellow soldiers as a supporter of the rebels they were supposed to be fighting. To those who listened, he was also known to support Castro in Cuba, Che in Bolivia, and Allende in Chile; and he was against the United States in every case. Some of this was bluster, some a by-product of Chávez's irrepressible hatreds and revolutionary enthusiasms. But it was also propaganda devised to attract fellow travelers to his cause.

In 1983, on Simón Bolívar's two hundredth birthday, Chávez founded a movement within the Venezuelan military called the Revolutionary Bolivarian Movement-200 (*Movimiento Bolivariano Revolucionario*-200, or MBR-200). Chávez himself described the purpose of the organization in a 1994 speech in Havana:

"We had the audacity to found a movement within the ranks of the Army of Venezuela. We were tired of the corruption, and we swore to dedicate our lives to the creation of a revolutionary movement and to the revolutionary struggle in Venezuela, straight away, within Latin America. We started doing this the year of the bicentenary of the birth of Bolívar." MBR-200 would form the nucleus of the *Chavista* movement, and its adherents would help Chávez mount the '92 coup.

Chávez's recruiting efforts were helped by the structure of the Venezuelan military. The armed forces were top-heavy with generals: several times the number of senior officers served in the Venezuelan army as served in comparably sized military forces of other countries—and by design. The multiplicity of generals—all of whom enjoyed high pay and numerous perks—made the corps a conservative force.

The central government, in any case, counted on their loyalty to a system that generously provided for them. Diosdado Cabello, a lieutenant who would become one of Chávez's co-conspirators, once recalled that "the then governor of Bolívar State, Andrés Velásquez, had warned President Carlos Andrés Pérez about a possible coup d'état. The President asked who was behind it. 'Some majors,' the governor answered. 'Oh, they'll get over it when they get to be generals,' Pérez said." [4]

This arrangement had its drawbacks, however. For the younger officers—the lieutenants, captains, majors, and lieutenant colonels—pay grades and perks were only a pitiful fraction of what the generals enjoyed. Even with the top-heavy command structure, their chances of making general were slim, and the wait for such an appointment could take a lifetime. Chávez and his fellows were eager to take things into their own hands.

But to mount a coup meant taking command of troops. Castro may have taken over Cuba in 1959 with a few hundred guerrillas; many more would be necessary to overpower a large, spread-out country like Venezuela.

From 1981 to 1984, a determined Chávez began secretly converting his students at the military academy into co-conspirators; ironically, his day job was to teach Venezuelan military history with an emphasis on promoting military professionalism and noninvolvement in politics. By 1984, Hugo Chávez and his fellow officer Francisco Arias Cárdenas were the clear leaders of a loose cabal of young officers.

Chávez also turned to old friends, such as his uncle Narcisco Chávez Suárez; his lover Herma Marksman; the Communist intellectual and rebel leader Douglas Bravo; and an air force officer, William Izarra;[5] to form a tightly knit cabal. He reduced the inner circle, and tried to limit access to a circle of trusted allies.

Chávez's recruitment efforts were not always successful. Interestingly, Raúl Isaías Baduel, one of the four saman tree oath-takers of 1982, refused Chávez's entreaties to participate. He felt that Chávez was not being truthful in calling it a revolution when it was a military coup pure and simple: "I call it a coup d'état with no ifs, ands, or buts," he told a startled Chávez. He continued to argue that Chávez had not prepared a clear political project and had no idea how to run the country. Chávez went ahead without Baduel, who noted, "In the eyes of the military hierarchy I was a coup supporter and in the eyes of my comrades, a defector."[6]

Bravo and Izarra were older than Chávez and had begun plotting against their country long before Hugo got involved. They also had an extensive network of lesser conspirators, and conducted their activities using code names (Chávez's own was "Che María"), disguises, dead drops, third-party cutouts, and safe houses familiar to readers of Tom Clancy novels. Always, Chávez was fearful of detection, distrustful of conversations, wary of being tracked, and felt "isolated and watched."[7]

Despite their caution, Chávez had his share of close shaves. The closest came in 1986, when a lieutenant Chávez had tried to recruit informed on him to military security. But unluckily for the military, a sympathizer alerted Chávez that he was under suspicion just in time for the conspirators to burn boxes of evidence. According to his collaborator and lover at the time, Herma Marksman, Chávez was able to talk his way out of trouble (that time and several times afterward) because the security investigators were incompetent or didn't follow up on evidence of conspiracy. "I can't believe they didn't discover what he was doing," Marksman recalls.[8]

The plotting and secrecy went on for days, weeks, months, years; it went on for more than a decade. The delays so frustrated Chávez that he feared the coup would never happen.[9] Izarra originally wanted to launch it in 1982. That plan was delayed to 1986, then 1989. The reason was simple: the conspirators still did not have sufficient adherents to pull it off, because they had not yet been assigned to important enough commands to build a suitable following. Until they had a large and loyal number of troops, all the talk about coups was just talk.

Chávez's rise through the ranks was slow. Distrusted by his superiors, he was given small commands or assigned to nonoperational duties such as teaching. Even there, he got into trouble. In July 1984, the director of the military academy received repeated complaints from the parents of his students that the academy had become "the center of a conspiracy." Chávez was reassigned to a motorized squadron in remote Elorza, Apure, close to the Colombian border. The transfer made it more difficult for him to stay in touch with potential recuits and central command.[10] But the transfer didn't stop him; it only made his road trips longer.

Promoted to major in 1986, Chávez was given command of another civilian-military unit on the border. In 1990, he was promoted to lieutenant colonel and given a civilian affairs garrison, though his brother officers serving at these ranks typically commanded larger, far more heavily armed units.

But in 1991, Chávez's fortunes finally and dramatically changed. As the fortunes of his nemesis President Carlos Andrés Pérez waned, Chávez's prospects rose.

Pérez had been a popular president of Venezuela during the oil boom years of 1974 to 1979, when the country was flush with petrodollars. After a decade out of office, he was reelected in 1988 with nearly 53 percent of the vote. His second term, which began in 1989, would not be nearly so happy as his first.

Economic conditions in Venezuela were poor, and deteriorating. The oil boom of the 1970s gave way to the oil glut of the 1980s, a reality that the Venezuelan economy was ill prepared to handle. In response, President Pérez sought to reform his country's oil economy in concert with an International Monetary Fund loan program requiring the reduction of the domestic oil subsidy (a gallon of gasoline in Venezuela costs only 12 cents even today). The resulting price hikes of energy products and services triggered massive popular uprisings. Bus fares doubled overnight, as gasoline prices increased by 100 percent, all without notice or explanation from government. In February 1989, people thronged the streets and were quickly joined by university students, as well as labor, business, and political interests. As the cities descended into looting and chaos, Pérez instructed the military to use whatever force was necessary to restore order in the streets.

Chávez himself was at home with the chicken pox and thus did not have to take part in military actions against rioting citizens in the streets. But in a blow to his conspiracy, one of the four 1982 saman tree oath-takers, Felipe Acosta, was killed that day. And hundreds—perhaps thousands—of looters, vandals, innocent civilians, and military were also killed. It was a turning point for the conspirators and the people of Venezuela. Pérez had become an ogre. Two years later—right before Chávez made his fateful attempt—62 percent of Venezuelans told pollsters that they favored a coup against Pérez.

Chávez may have safely avoided having to show his loyalties during the riots, but suspicions against him mounted, first within the military and then among government officials. On December 6, 1989, Hugo Chávez and other MBR-200 members were taken into custody—"Some fifteen of us, all majors, got arrested that day," he recalls[11]—and charged with conspiring to assassinate President Pérez.

Instead of being interrogated in a jail cell, however, Chávez was invited to dine with General Fernando Ochoa Antich, the defense minister. Little did Chávez know at the time that Ochoa sympathized with his disaffected officers. But over the course of the dinner, he learned. According to his own account, Chávez not only talked his way out of going to prison, but even converted the general to his revolutionary cause.

Chávez recalls, "Ochoa said good-bye to me and told me, 'you can count on me.' "[12] Thereafter, an investigative panel reviewed Chávez's case but made no charges against him. General Ochoa arranged to have Chávez transferred to his first real command, a parachute brigade of some six hundred troops in the Maracay military base a few hours' drive southwest of Caracas. Seven months later, Chávez would launch his coup.

The Fateful Day

In mid-1991, Chávez was nearly ready. Civilians—including Douglas Bravo—were purged from the group in favor of a purely military operation.[13] The plotters scanned the calendar for a date when President Pérez could easily be assassinated, and when their own logistical difficulties could be overcome. They settled on February 3, 1992, the night that Pérez was returning from the World Economic Forum in Davos, Switzerland, where he had been all week. The plan was to capture the president after he landed at the airport.

The first gunshots rang out around the Maracay base, fifty miles from Caracas. Despite the fact that senior generals had been alerted to the imminent coup hours before it began, government forces at first seemed unable to resist the rebels.

In the early hours of February 4, Chávez's comrade Commander Francisco Arias Cárdenas had taken control of Maracaibo, Venezuela's second largest city and the oil production heart of the country. He also had the governor of Zulia state in custody.

Commanders Jesús Urdaneta and Jesús Ortiz were fighting successfully in the Maracay and Valencia industrial areas. Commander Acosta had seized control of the military airport at La Carlota and arrested the head of Venezuela's air force.[14] Maracay and Valencia fell to the rebels in the dark hours that followed. The only power base remaining in government hands was Caracas, where Chávez himself commanded the *putschistas*.

He began by loading 460 paratroopers under his command into twenty buses, ostensibly for a night exercise to Cojedes. But he immediately diverted the buses to Caracas, telling the drivers there was an emergency in the capital—a lie that Chávez would make come true. "Of those men, only a very small group of officers knew what we were going to do that night, the troops didn't know a thing," Chávez acknowledges.[15]

His destination was the Military History Museum at La Planicie, a mile from Miraflores, that he intended to use as a central headquarters. Upon arrival, Chávez and his men were met with machine-gun fire from the garrison. But they quickly gained control over the museum after convincing the military garrison inside that there was a riot in Caracas, which he was ordered to squelch.

That would prove to be the high point of the night for the conspirators. From then on, everything went wrong.

In a change of protocol, President Pérez was met at the Simón Bolívar airport by Chávez's secret patron, Defense Minister Fernando Ochoa Antich, who reported that rumors of a coup attempt had been flying about since 3:00 p.m. The minister's presence made capturing the president at the airport impossible; Ochoa may have seemed sympathetic but apparently his sympathy only carried so far.

Pérez instructed Ochoa to launch an investigation in the morning. Then the president was driven to La Casona, his residence in eastern Caracas. Chávez's men had another chance to capture the president as his car traveled through a tunnel under the mountain highway heading toward Caracas, but they botched it.[16]

By then, things were going from bad to worse for the conspiracy. Military radios stopped working; no one knew what was happening elsewhere—

including the conspirators. The battery for Chávez's personal cell phone died, making coordination impossible.

Meanwhile, Pérez was updated on the situation around midnight, and decided to drive from his residence to the presidential palace of Miraflores. On the way, his car passed through lines of tanks commanded by officers loyal to Chávez, but the officers didn't recognize the president, and they let him pass. Once Chávez realized that Pérez had reached Miraflores, he ordered twelve tanks to surround the palace and break down the front door—an effort that was captured on TV for everyone to see. The whole country got up from bed to watch.

Surrounded, Pérez decided to escape to the Venevision TV studio and fight from there. But Chávez's tanks were blocking the rear exit. Pérez's top military aide stepped outside and asked the tank commander why he was there. "To protect the president," he said. "The president is protected, thank you," Pérez's military aide said. "Please move your tank so we can pass by." The officers, cowed by the authority of the president, let him go. Pérez, hidden in a limousine, escaped to Venevision, where he would squelch the coup.[17]

Chávez had now failed to capture Pérez four times in three hours: at the airport, in the tunnel from the airport, on the drive from his residence to Miraflores, and in Miraflores itself. Diosdado Cabello admits that Chávez's part in the coup was amateurish: "The plan involved stealing tanks, but none of us knew how to operate them," he recalls. "That's why the President called us 'the Caracas Kamikazes.' That's how we went out, to wing it."[18]

At 1:00 a.m., the TV was turned on in the museum, but instead of Chávez announcing the insurgents' victory, there was Pérez saying he had squelched the takeover. While Chávez's soldiers had taken over a TV station, they didn't know how to transfer his rebellion video announcement to the proper format for broadcast.[19] Chávez's announcement never made it onto the air. But Pérez's announcement informed the loyal military in the museum what Chávez was up to and they soon encircled him.[20]

Chávez now realized he was finished: "A caged tiger—I didn't know how to face it, what to do."[21] Yet he had one more brilliant stroke of genius up his sleeve. Seven hours later, in the act of surrender, Chávez created the sense of inevitability that Pérez was finished and that one day he himself would be president instead.

In the hope that lives could be saved—since hundreds had already been killed—Pérez's military began negotiating with Chávez to surrender. Chávez's protector Defense Minister Ochoa suggested a friend of Chávez's, General Santeliz, to negotiate terms.[22]

Surrounded, outnumbered, and beaten, Chávez agreed—to the astonishment of his comrades. But even as he did so, his co-conspirators held tight to their positions at the La Carlota airport, and garrisons at Maracaibo, Valencia, and Maracay. They were bargaining chips; Chávez wanted something in return.

President Pérez's effective use of television during the crisis impressed Chávez and gave him an idea. He conditioned his surrender on being allowed to broadcast a live statement to the people of Venezuela. Asked to write down his statement, Chávez refused, saying, "I'm not going to write anything. I'm going to call for surrender. I give you my word of honor. I shall go out on air with dignity."[23]

The military, led by Defense Minister Ochoa, argued for allowing Chávez to go on TV, ostensibly to persuade his collaborators to surrender as he had. Astonishingly Pérez agreed.[24] As calls or telegrams poured in to Pérez from supporters as diverse as President George H. W. Bush and President Fidel Castro, Chávez went on the air wearing his paratrooper uniform and red beret:

First of all I want to say good morning to the people of Venezuela. This Bolivarian message is for the brave soldiers who are presently at the Paratrooper's Regiment in Aragua and the Armored Brigade in Valencia. *Compañeros,* unfortunately, *for now,* the objectives we established in the capital were not achieved. That means that we, here in Caracas, did not succeed in taking control. You did an excellent job out there, but it is now time to avoid more bloodshed, it is now time to reflect. *New situations will present themselves.* The country must find the definite path toward a better destiny. Listen to what I say. Listen to Commander Chávez, who sends out this message so that you will please reflect and lay down your weapons, because now, truly, it is impossible for us to meet the objectives we established on the national level. *Compañeros:* listen to this message of solidarity. I thank you for your loyalty, your bravery, your generosity, and as I stand before the nation and

all of you, *I assume the responsibility for this Bolivarian military movement.* Thank
you very much. [Emphases added].[25]

The colossal newspaper headline POR AHORA, the next day turned Hugo
Chávez into the folk hero he had always wanted to be. In a 1999 article, one
of Latin America's most famous writers, Gabriel García Márquez, wrote
that "what seemed to be a surrender was actually the first speech in his
campaign for the presidency." [26] The poet and politician Tarek William Saab
went further: "It's more than that—those were the words that *made* him
president." [27]

With those words, Chávez became the repository of hope for the poorest, most indignant element of a society that had long dreamed of sweeping the corrupt white elites out of power and ending crony capitalism and
government malfeasance. For the 62 percent of Venezuelans who had told
pollsters they favored a coup, Hugo Chávez was now a saviour in waiting.
His biographers found among his San Carlos prison papers a prayer brought
to him in jail by an anonymous Venezuelan:

Our Chávez's Prayer

Our Chávez who art in prison
Hallowed be thy coup.
Come and avenge us, your people,
Thy will be done
In Venezuela
As it is in your army.
Give us today our lost faith,
And forgive not the traitors
As we forgive not
Those who arrested you.
Lead us not into corruption
But deliver us from Carlos Andrés Pérez.

Chávez in Jail

Imprisoned, but not charged or convicted of a crime (even though hundreds had died or were severely injured in the coup attempt), Chávez read

Marx and Sun Tzu, burnishing his revolutionary credentials with a manifesto calling for rebellion against the oligarchs, corruption, and poverty. Imprisonment, a common enough breeding ground for revolutionaries, was the critical stage in the development of the Chávez saviour myth.

Chávez's popularity put him into contention with the top politicians in the country.[28] Prison guards turned the other way as hundreds of Venezuelans pretending to be relatives or friends of Chávez lined up every day outside the jail at Yare to visit him. This included Luis Miquilena, who would become his mentor; José Vicente Rangel, who would become his vice president; and Tarek William Saab, who would become the head of his National Assembly's foreign relations committee.

In prison at Yare, Chávez continued to plot. In a July 12, 1992, letter to co-conspirator Luis Reyes Reyes, Chávez wrote in code that "You must work very closely with (6) and (7) [co-conspirators still on the loose] at a convergence of X [code for military uprising] and Y [a general strike]."[29] In November, a second coup attempt by Chávez supporters was easily put down.[30]

The following summer of 1993, President Carlos Andrés Pérez was impeached for making a $2 million contribution to Nicaraguan presidential candidate Violetta Chamorro. (Ironically, Chávez would contribute a thousand times that amount to foreign countries a decade later without a peep from his rubber-stamp National Assembly or Supreme Court.)

The 1993 presidential elections were held, but—in a harbinger of his later disdain for suffrage and the rule of law—Chávez still wasn't prepared to recognize the legitimacy of democracy. Instead of endorsing a candidate from prison, he called on the public to abstain from voting. It didn't, and in December 1993, Venezuelans elected a new president, Rafael Caldera, the archenemy of Pérez, who had led the fight for Pérez's impeachment and praised Chávez's coup attempts on the floor of the Venezuelan Senate.

In the spring of 1994, President Caldera summarily dismissed the case against Lieutenant Colonel Hugo Chávez, as opposed to pardoning him for treason and the killings committed during his coup attempt; this opened the path for a Chávez presidential campaign. Under the 1961 Constitution in effect at the time, convicted felons were not allowed to run for high office in Venezuela. By dismissing the charges against Chávez, Caldera wiped his record clean. He did so only to put the last nail in the political coffin of Carlos Andrés Pérez, not knowing what he had given birth to.

It was a risky gambit. A sworn enemy of the Venezuelan government—one who had promised not to rest until he saw the established order toppled—was now a free man. Only four years later, a stunned and diminished Caldera would pass the sash of the presidency to none other than Hugo Rafael Chávez Frías.

3

The Democratic Dictator

Second only to the assertion that Chávez is harmless is the protestation that he was democratically elected. Why this should excuse the very real harm—harm that subsequent chapters will detail at length—that Chávez is attempting to inflict on America is never explained.

That aside, the premise of the claim is itself fundamentally flawed. It is true that Chávez won election to the presidency fairly and honestly in 1998, when he was not in control of the election machinery. But after he took power in 1999, the 2000 elections were marred by severe—and sadly underreported—irregularities. The Carter Center, which monitored the second election, reported that "the significant politicization of the elections and organizational deficiencies contributed to a lack of confidence in the process and the nonpresidential results, thus leading us to characterize the July 2000 elections as flawed."[1] These irregularities, however, pale in comparison to the massive fraud that Chávez orchestrated four years later to defeat a 2004 recall referendum—a process that coauthor Schoen witnessed firsthand, and this time with Jimmy Carter's imprimatur.

Of course, Chávez has governed like anything but a democrat. He has moved at every turn to consolidate power into the hands of his own office, remake the other branches of government into rubber stamps responsible solely to him, strip away his rivals' influence in and out of government, limit freedom of the press, and transform his office into a personal fief with unlimited powers for the length of his life.

Chávez openly admires the world's leftist and anti-American dictators— above all Fidel Castro—and seeks to emulate their success. To the extent that Chávez believes in democracy at all, he holds to the cynical maxim of all tyrants who use the electoral process to gain power: "one man, one vote, once." Chávez's attempt to outdo Castro has culminated—so far—in a referendum he forced onto the ballot in December 2007 that would have granted him near-absolute power and the possibility of election for life. For once, he was defeated at the polls so soundly that even his vast expertise in electoral manipulation could not save him. Angry at what he perceives to be the ingratitude of the Venezuelan people, Chávez nonetheless remains undaunted, repeating his famous phrase *"por ahora."* The power grab had failed, but only "for now." Another attempt is surely coming.

Since he was a small boy, Hugo Chávez had dreamed of triumphing in a glorious military conquest and becoming a utopian saviour like Simón Bolívar for Gran Colombia, Juan Velasco Alvarado for Peru, or Fidel Castro for Cuba.[2] Like him, they were all military men. But unlike them, Chávez was hamstrung by the checks and balances of a constitutional democracy. He despaired of his prospects of taking power by the sword.

Chávez's solution to this dilemma was to launch a democratic coup, to use the electoral process for undemocratic ends. He declared his 2000 election to be a revolution, giving him a mandate to change everything in Venezuela—the constitution, the time zone, the currency, the national shield, the national holiday, the military salute (which became "Fatherland, socialism or death"),[3] even the country's very name—for all time.

Or so Chávez hopes.

The Path to Power

Chávez emerged from jail in 1994 a hero to Venezuela's poor. He had also, while imprisoned, assiduously courted the international left, who helped him build an impressive political war chest—including, it was recently revealed, $150,000 from the FARC guerrillas of Colombia.[4]

He moved into the small apartment of Luis Miquilena, a longtime Communist. Miquilena saw in Chávez a potential revolutionary leader and got to know him by visiting the young firebrand in prison.

While they shared the overarching goal of remaking Venezuelan society, they differed on tactics. Chávez's dream of triumphing in a glorious military conquest like another Bolívar or Castro—and his desire for sole control—was mitigated by Miquilena's more cautious, overly political approach.

In April 1994, Chávez announced the Fifth Republic Movement (MVR in Spanish) to "restore the nation's lost honor" by eliminating poverty and corruption with oil money.[5] This political party would form the backbone of his support in his quest for the presidency in 1998.

Chávez also looked abroad for help—and he found it. The FARC—the narcoterrorist group operating in the Colombian interior—helped finance the rise of his political party. And to Hugo's delight, Castro received him lovingly in Havana in December 1994. Castro saw Chávez as a second chance for his world Communist revolution, and took the extraordinary step of meeting the rebel paratrooper from Venezuela at the airport,[6] as though he were a head of state.

Back home, he continued his populist campaign championing Venezuela's poor and decrying the upper classes and the government. To this traditional mix, Chávez added something new: overt anti-Americanism. In a 1996 demonstration calling for the ouster of President Caldera—the same man who had pardoned Chávez only two years earlier—Chávez supporters burned an American flag and denounced "the imperialism of the *yanqui* aggressor."[7] It was the first time the Venezuelan people had heard anti-Americanism injected into mainstream political discourse by a political figure with real promise, and it came to many as a shock.[8]

In 1997, Chávez formally established the MVR as a political party and registered as its presidential candidate.[9] A young journalist for the *Caracas*

Daily Journal, Richard Brand, tried to interview Chávez as a throng of security men in Chávez's characteristic military red berets pushed them both toward Chávez's Land Cruiser. "As somebody who tried to overthrow the government by force," Brand asked Chávez as he ducked into his vehicle, "do you think you can get elected president?" With Brand still squeezed between Chávez's bodyguards and the vehicle, the electric window rolled up and Chávez stared ahead as his vehicle rolled over Brand's foot, breaking his toe. It was a chilling augur of Chávez's future treatment of the independent media.[10]

The leading issues in the 1998 election campaign were, as ever in Venezuelan politics, poverty and corruption, though this time the poor and disenfranchised seemed angrier than ever—and receptive to a populist with an iron fist, a benevolent king. Or maybe a queen: The early front-runner at 60 percent in the polls was the former Miss Universe, Irene Saez, who promised to save Venezuela from pandemic corruption and poverty. Chávez, by contrast, was running fourth with less than 10 percent of the vote. Few believed he could go anywhere.[11] But as usual, the traditional political elites grossly underestimated him.

During the campaign, Chávez delivered a blend of anger, rage, nationalism, and vengeance that was crude, humorous—and effective. He savaged PDVSA, the national oil company, as a "state within a state" controlled by Venezuelan oligarchs, thieves, and U.S. oil companies. He promised to fire its corrupt managers and give oil money to the poor.

The populist appeals worked. Chávez climbed in the polls, alarming—among others—John Maisto, the U.S. ambassador to Venezuela. At one point, Maisto called Chávez a "terrorist" because of the coup attempt and denied him a visa to visit the United States. In reply, Chávez mocked Maisto by taking his Visa credit card from his wallet and waving it about, saying, "I already have a Visa!"[12] He also boasted of the incident in a visit to the University of Havana. "We are honored as rebel soldiers by the fact that we are not allowed to enter North American territory," Chávez said to Castro and his ministers. Polls showed that Chávez got a 5 to 10 percent bump from the incident.[13]

Chávez ignored the other candidates for president and they—to their peril—largely ignored him, at least at the beginning. His fellow candidates refused to criticize Chávez's connections to Communist revolutionaries and refrained from rebuking his open anti-Americanism. Only the private media dared raise such issues, and Chávez in turn denounced all such commentary as a U.S.-backed smear campaign of lies and defamation.[14]

On December 6, 1998, the Venezuelan electorate awarded Chávez with 56 percent of the votes.[15] He had achieved the perch from which he could wage his asymmetric war against his hated enemy: the United States.

But before taking office, Chávez paid his respects to his hero and campaign strategist Fidel Castro by jetting to Havana. It must have been a happy reunion. Here was a man with not just the will to pursue Communist revolution and humble America, but the oil resources and the rage to make it happen.

President Chávez

Hugo Chávez entered office with approval ratings in excess of 80 percent. He wasted no time in leveraging that popularity into more power for himself.

In rapid succession, Chávez proposed to convene a new Constituent Assembly to draft a new constitution. The people enthusiastically agreed, and elected 131 delegates, who set to work in August 1999. Before getting down to the business of drafting the new constitution, however, the assembly first selected a small "judicial emergency committee" meant to remove judges who were ostensibly suspected of corruption but, in truth, were merely believed to be skeptical of Chávez's plans. Nearly two hundred judges were fired without recourse to appeal.

The Constituent Assembly then declared a "legislative emergency" and used that as an excuse to forbid the national legislature from passing laws or even holding meetings while the assembly did its work. It did so quickly, submitting the new constitution for popular ratification only four months later. It was easily approved.

Called—inevitably—the Bolivarian Constitution, the new document formally changed the name of the country to the Bolivarian Republic of Venezuela. The substantive changes were far more ominous. The new framework abolished the old bicameral legislature in favor of a single house whose members were to be selected on the basis of a proportional representation scheme designed to favor Chávez's party. Chávez naturally billed the move as replacing "a corrupt representative democracy with a superior 'direct democracy' and substituting 'twenty-first-century social-ism' for 'savage capitalism.' "[16]

In addition, the term of president was extended from five to six years, and the clock on term limits was reset. Hence Chávez could run again in 2000 and 2006, extending his time in office until at least 2013. Unlike every other Venezuelan president since 1958, Chávez would not simply serve his five years and depart.

Chávez would easily win reelection in the first ballot under the new con-stitution, in 2000, taking 56 percent of the vote and carrying into office with him a clear MVR party majority in the now-single-house National Assembly.[17]

Corruption—a problem endemic in Venezuela for decades—continued to bedevil the country. As co-author Rowan wrote in 1999, "Corruption in Venezuela is systemic. . . . The bloated bureaucracy, the demonic delays, the variability of rules, the destruction of precedent, the hopelessness of rational appeal, the infinitely exaggerated transaction steps, the nuclear mushrooming of paperwork, and yet the astonishing lack of records or ac-countability, are all typical of hierarchical distribution systems designed to make theft convenient. That's the idea."[18]

Corruption made a good campaign issue for Chávez, but when the time came to do something about it, he balked. Chávez initially appointed Jesús Urdaneta—one of the four saman tree oath-takers—as anticorrup-tion czar. But Urdaneta was too energetic and effective for the president; within five months, he had identified forty cases of corruption inside Chávez's own administration. Chávez refused to back his czar, who was eventually pushed out of office by the very people he was investigating. Chávez did nothing to save him.[19]

Rather than fight corruption as he had promised in his campaign speeches, Chávez became an expert practitioner. In 1999, he started a give-away project called "Plan Bolívar 2000." Implemented by Chávez loyalists organized in neighborhood groups called Bolivarian Circles, the project was modeled after the Communist bloc committees in Castro's Cuba. The plan was basically a social welfare program that mirrored the populist ethic. Social services included such items as improving schools, public works, and "popular markets" where the military distributed food at dis-counted prices. Plan Bolívar continued to harness support from Chávez's core constituency—the poor. In eighteen months, Bolívar 2000 had become so corrupt that it had to be disbanded.[20]

But such examples of retreat were the exception. The rule has been continued and widespread corruption. Chávez's "revolution" merely emulated the corrupt system of his predecessors, as the omnipresence of Rolex watches, Humvees, and cases of twenty-five-year-old Scotch whiskey among the Bolivarian elite immediately attested.[21] Accusations of nepotism became rampant: Chávez's father and five brothers were elected or appointed to high-level government posts and have allegedly enriched themselves with impunity.[22] Only a few years into Chávez's presidency, a former president of Venezuela's Central Bank opined that $3 billion in oil funds were simply missing and wondered aloud what the final tally would be if Chávez stayed in power and the oil barrel price increased—both of which have since come to pass.[23]

Independent studies estimate that the amounts taken from Venezuelan poverty and development funds by middlemen, brokers, and subcontractors—all of whom charge an "administrative" cost for passing on the funds—range as high as 80 percent to 90 percent. By contrast, the U.S. government, the World Bank, nongovernmental organizations, and international charities limit their administrative costs to 20 percent of project funds; the Nobel Peace Prize–winning Doctors Without Borders, for example, spends only 16 percent on administration.

With rampant favoritism in government procurement and payments, kickbacks in contracting, and criminal activities by government officials, police, and the military, public scandal was inevitable. When called to account, Chávez invariably charged that the stories were fabricated by the United States in order to discredit his revolution. The song sheet sometimes changes slightly: Chávez also likes to complain that he is the victim of racial discrimination by rich white South American oligarchs, but his rhetoric always returns to the claim that the evil empire to the north is secretly turning the dials.[24]

When the International Monetary Fund and the World Bank insisted on anticorruption programs accompanying their loans to any government, including Venezuela's, Chávez broke all ties to them and claimed they were corrupt puppets in the U.S. war against his legitimate government. When Transparency International showed that Venezuela under Chávez was creeping to the top of the list of the world's most corrupt countries, Chávez accused the organization of being a propaganda arm of the CIA.[25] When a British journalist for *The Economist,* Phil Gunson, reported undisputed corruption in the government, Chávez went on his *Aló Presidente* (*"Hello, President"*) TV program to castigate Gunson as an American CIA agent paid to do a hatchet job on Chávez personally.

From the beginning of his reign, Chávez sought and received extraordinary executive powers. In November 2001, using the powers of edict granted him by his new rubber-stamp legislature, Chávez issued forty-seven edicts that restricted private property and human rights while expanding the president's powers over economic and political life.

He would eventually confiscate or expropriate 3.4 million acres of farming and grazing lands from legitimate owners and producers for redistribution to his political supporters—"the deserving poor," as he likes to call them, who generally precipitated the land transfer by invasion, violence, and sometimes kidnapping.[26] Chávez boosted the popularity of these actions by selectively prosecuting rich foreigners, such as the British absentee land baron Lord Vecsey. His lands were expropriated with cameras rolling and the military siding with the poor, hungry invaders. The economist Dr. Carlos Machado Addison later lamented, "We are witnessing a mechanism to perpetuate poverty in the countryside."[27]

Thousands of private farms and ranches were taken over in this way, but the tens of thousands of revolutionary peasants who took over the land knew little about large-scale food production. Consequently, agricultural investment and productivity declined sharply. In the first four years of Chávez's administration, Venezuela's cattle population fell from 14 million to 10 million.

Chávez worsened the food crisis by tightening price controls, rendering it impossible for the remaining private farms and ranches to make a profit, and then prosecuting them for hoarding product or not producing anything.[28] When that measure inevitably failed, Chávez created a chain of Mercal mission stores that sold government-subsidized, mostly imported consumer goods to poor people, falsely promoting it as an endogenous solution. Mercal had captured about 40 percent of the national food market by 2006—which put the government in the unenviable market position of losing a little bit on each transaction and hoping to make up losses in volume. An attempt at an "endogenous" solution to get poor urban barrio residents to build chicken coops or grow vegetable gardens on the tin roofs of their shacks also failed, and by 2008 the shortages of basic foodstuffs even at the Mercal stores—and malnutrition among infants and children—stood at epidemic proportions.[29]

"The country is turning into Africa, with everyone trying to benefit from the oil bonanza," the banker and columnist Oscar García Mendoza observed in 2006. "Production is falling and government spending is rising. It's a celebration of irresponsibility and ignorance without limits."[30]

Chávez adopted similar measures toward private manufacturing. Five years into his rule, more than half the manufacturing enterprises in Venezuela had disappeared; unemployment spiked to 18 percent while more than half of the Venezuelan labor force toiled for pennies in the black market. Imports of foreign manufactures went through the roof as Venezuelan consumers, to Chávez's consternation, spent what little money they had on goods from the evil empire.[31] Few domestically produced goods remained.

To replace bankrupt private enterprises, Chávez organized thousands of peasant cooperatives with government capital and managed them with his political and military appointees. These rapidly and predictably blew through billions of dollars while producing fewer manufactured goods. By April 2006, *The Economist* ranked Venezuela seventy-eighth of eighty-two countries—fourth from the worst—measured for free enterprise investment.[32]

Chávez's antidote to manufacturing failure was to do more of the same—but on a grander scale. After the presidential election of 2006, he nationalized every American-linked company in the country, starting with Venezuela's oldest private enterprise, Electricidad de Caracas (EDC), owned by the U.S. energy company AES. The country's telephone utility, CANTV—owned primarily by the U.S. telephone giant Verizon—soon followed. Investments by American oil companies in the high-producing Orinoco region were also seized, along with the country's cement and steel firms, a major bank owned by Santander, and hundreds of retail gasoline stations owned by private enterprise.

These property confiscations, expropriations, and acquisitions cost the government of Venezuela untold billions of dollars as the efficiency and effectiveness of the economy continued—and continues—to decline.

Chávez also worked to undermine nongovernmental institutions that could potentially serve as a check on his power—in particular, the private media. The news media treated Chávez very well in his 1998 campaign, but the honeymoon ended when Chávez began to commandeer, according to his own Ministry of Information, approximately forty hours per week of TV time on all stations, co-opting entertainment programming and news and revenue-producing advertising—all during a time in which reports of corruption and incompetence in his first years of government became routine.[33] Chávez called these marathon broadcasts "participatory democracy." His goal was to rule directly, with no checks on his power and no intermediaries in his communications. On live TV, Chávez routinely announced the hiring and firing of ministers and PDVSA executives (often without telling them first), launched major programs, and even prepared for war with Colombia.[34] So far, he has spent some 20,000 hours on television since 1999.[35]

In 2004, Chávez pushed a law through his rubber-stamp National Assembly that sharply restricts media content.[36] Called the "Gag Law" by its many critics, it allows the government to imprison or fine journalists, publishers, and station owners for disrespectful speech or obscene materials—as defined by the government.[37] Those who tried to remain undaunted witnessed spectacular high-profile prosecutions—notably the trial of Francisco Uzon, a retired military general sentenced to five and a half years in prison for disputing the government's account of a fire in a military prison (to the general, the evidence suggested a flamethrower, not the matches alleged by the government). Programs and personalities offensive to Chávez tended to disappear from the air.

Having lost the goodwill of the nation's private media, Chávez used Venezuela's oil revenues to buy media properties and establish new ones loyal to him.[38] He eventually funded five new government TV stations, including Telesur—a Latin American "news" station modeled after Al Jazeera and intended to suffocate CNN en Español[39]—and a score of "community" TV stations broadcasting pro-Chávez propaganda and boasting of Venezuela's "miraculous improvements."

Where Chávez couldn't buy the media outright, he bought up the advertising and soon became the major advertiser in the country, effectively controlling TV, radio, and print media sympathetic to his ad dollars if not his message.

Chávez has justified every encroachment on democracy—whether centralizing power in the presidency, extending presidential terms, downgrading independent institutions such as the legislature and judiciary, eliminating effective checks and balances on executive power, controlling the electoral system, taking private property, criminalizing criticism of his authority, or trampling upon the freedoms of speech, press, assembly, and dissent—as a further perfection of it.[40]

The results were predictable. The domestic failures that flowed from Chávez's policies became immediately apparent to his top aides only months into office. Francisco Rodríguez, Chávez's chief economist from 2000 to 2004, later documented in *Foreign Affairs* magazine how Chávez's "pervasive chronic failures" spawned corruption, widened the gap between the rich and poor, increased infant mortality, inflated the currency, shrank the food supply, turned Venezuela into the murder center of the hemisphere, and did nothing to alleviate poverty or illiteracy despite tens of billions of dollars allotted to solve these problems.[41]

After only eighteen months in office, as Venezuela's economy deteriorated and its democracy was systematically curtailed, Chávez's favorability rating had tumbled from close to 90 percent at the start of 1999 to 50 percent upon his reelection in 2000. He had nearly tripled the amount of time he could remain in power, as compared to the previous constitution. But he paid the price of polarizing the country into two factions: one for and one against his self-declared, authoritarian revolution. Chávez had defined the people who were for him as loyal patriots fighting for a just revolution and the people who were against him as evil traitors to the nation and puppets of the United States.

It was a difficult tightrope to walk. And to succeed, Chávez needed an external threat to his Bolivarian Revolution. One enemy above all fit the bill.

The "American Coup"

In 2002, Chávez was removed from office for forty-eight hours. Chávez—and Venezuela's history textbooks—contend that the U.S. government inspired and arranged the coup attempt. What actually happened was very different.[42]

On April 11, 2002, 800,000 Venezuelans marched in a peaceful protest organized by Carlos Ortega, the leader of the CTV (Confederacíon de Trabajadores de Venezuela), Venezuela's largest labor union. They marched to support the PDVSA workers' demand that they be hired or fired based on job merit, not political loyalty to Chávez.

When the march neared Miraflores, gunshots from snipers on building tops and a bridge overpass felled more than a hundred people in the crowd, thirteen fatally (a disproportionate number of them wearing press credentials or holding TV cameras). The snipers disappeared into the woodwork, never to be found. Chávez supporters caught on video and identified were later judged by a Chávez-controlled court to have repeatedly fired into the unarmed and peaceful marchers in self-defense—against whom, the court didn't say.

As the shooting started, Chávez ordered TV news stations to black out the march and begin airing one of his videos of peaceful and empty streets or his own past speeches. Some privately controlled stations complied with the letter, but not the spirit, of the order by splitting the screen, showing Chávez's oration on one half and the bloody street clash on the other, for which Chávez would exact his revenge. He then ordered "Plan Ávila" into action.

The week before the march, Chávez had met in Miraflores with Defense Minister José Vicente Rangel, Vice President Diosdado Cabello, Attorney General Isaías Rodríguez, Supreme Tribunal of Justices president Franklin Arrieche, senior officials of the MVR party, and the senior military command of the Venezuelan armed forces. They all knew the march was coming, and in fact had worked strategically to provoke it. Chávez wanted to turn the march into an excuse to crush his opposition once and for all.

He stated that if the marchers crossed a thin line of police near Miraflores, he would consider that "an act of war" that justified a massive retaliation using deadly force: Plan Ávila. *VenEconomy Weekly* of Caracas later commented that had Plan Ávila been executed as Chávez envisioned, it "would have turned downtown Caracas into the Latin American equivalent of Tiananmen Square."[43]

Everyone in the room agreed except Justice Arrieche, who replied that marching was not an act of war but a civil matter that could be easily prevented by packing soldiers a dozen deep and using tear gas to disperse any civilians who crossed the line.

Furious at this reproach, Chávez dismissed Arrieche from the meeting with the admonition that he was ignorant about military strategy. (Months later, Arrieche agreed to testify in the U.S. Senate about these events, but then refused for undisclosed reasons.) He was removed from the court a year later and went silently into retirement.

But on the crucial day, the majority of Chávez's military not only refused to shoot peaceful marchers already fleeing from the scene but arrested Chávez for giving the order to do so. General Lucas Rincón, Chávez's handpicked minister of interior and enforcer, announced on television that "The high military command condemns the appalling incidents that occurred yesterday in the nation's capital. In light of these facts, the president of the republic has been asked to resign, and he has agreed to do so."[44] (When later restored to office, Chávez denied ever promising to resign; Rincón has never publicly spoken of the incident since.) Chávez and his family were prepared to be flown to Havana immediately.

On April 12, the military announced that Pedro Carmona, a business leader backed by former President Caldera and conservative Catholics, had been asked to run a transitional government, whereupon Carmona issued an unconstitutional edict abolishing the constitution, the National Assembly, and the changed name of the country. Carlos Ortega, though clearly no fan of Chávez, was appalled at the unconstitutional edict by Carmona. He split with Carmona on the spot—though he would later be prosecuted for treason by Chávez all the same. The Organization of American States, meeting in Costa Rica at the time, refused to recognize Carmona as president, because his edict broke the constitutional transition of power.

The unconstitutional seizure of power provoked more outrage than the Chávez policies that had inspired the initial protest. Riots and looting broke out everywhere and soon the whole country was on fire. Panicking, the military reversed itself and restored Chávez, who in turn appointed General Lucas Rincón—the man who had announced the resignation that Chávez swore he never gave—as his top military chief. This astonishing twist remains unexplained to this day.

Chávez was returned to Miraflores where, for about a week, he appeared to be a different man: shaken and humble, like someone who has gone through a near-death experience. He was apologetic, low key, and attentive. On April 14, two days after the coup, he publicly admitted mistakes in his handling of the march, and promised to consider the demands of the striking PDVSA workers. (True to form, a few weeks later he fired 18,000 of them.)

But it didn't take long for Chávez to regain his pluck. His first order of business was to turn this frightening near-death experience into a net benefit for himself. He would find a way to blame the coup on the United States.[45]

The evidence was nonexistent. At the time of the coup, U.S. naval forces had been conducting an exercise in the Caribbean, but such exercises were frequent and routine. American diplomats had spoken to Carmona during his forty-eight hours in Miraflores, but so had diplomats from dozens of countries. There was nothing tying the United States to General Rincón, who had accepted Chávez's "resignation"; to the military, who had refused to obey Chávez's order to shoot civilians; to the snipers, who had started the firefight; or to Carmona and his supporters. But Chávez managed to find what he needed.

In the early hours following the coup—after Rincón announced that Chávez had resigned but before Carmona's unconstitutional edicts of April 12—White House spokesman Ari Fleisher commented that "Chávez brought it [the coup] upon himself."[46] A few days later, when Chávez was restored to Miraflores, national security adviser Condoleezza Rice said, "We do hope that Chávez recognizes the whole world is watching and that he takes this opportunity to right his own ship, which has been moving, frankly, in the wrong direction for quite a long time."[47]

Chávez seized upon these innocuous statements as "proof" that the United States had financed and implemented a coup d'état against him and that Pedro Carmona, Carlos Ortega, the private TV stations, the Catholic Church, the opposition political parties, and even the 800,000 marchers were puppets duped by the U.S. government into taking part in an act of treason against the republic. Since 2002, Chávez has vocalized this claim so often that it appears he might even believe it. Responding to *Nightline*'s Ted Koppel in 2003, Chávez emphatically and repeatedly promised to "send the proof" that the United States was behind his coup; he never did so, and for a good reason—it doesn't exist.[48]

But Chávez knows that if any story is repeated often enough, some of it may stick, and to his credit as a propagandist, nary a news story about Chávez has gone by since 2002 that doesn't allege, suggest, or state as fact that the United States was behind the 2002 coup.

Savvy about American sound bites and media spins, Chávez spread his anti-American message everywhere and suppressed further inquiry into the facts behind his escalating allegations about the coup.[49] Chávez's assertion that his coup was a plot hatched by George W. Bush earned him support from the Congressional Black Caucus[50] and leading liberals Christopher Dodd, Dennis Kucinich, and William Delahunt, among others.[51]

With his "U.S. coup" story, Chávez had fabricated the hook he would use in a hundred trips around the world to explain his war against America. It also served him well at home, where he could now purge his enemies while looking like a democrat. "April 11 did us a great favor," a Chávez minister recalls, "because it forced a necessary purge that got rid of the traitors."[52]

The Recall That Wasn't

Hugo Chávez's hold on power had temporarily been solidified, but his popularity remained weak, and the ranks of disaffected Venezuelans continued to swell. A sixty-one-day national strike followed the 2002 coup attempt. When it came to an end, having failed to influence Chávez to moderate his policies, its leaders decided to return to the ballot box. They would attempt to recall their president.

Chávez wasted no time in stacking the deck against a recall. He filled the election commission (Consejo Nacional Electoral, or CNE) with a certain majority of members in his favor.[53] He launched a barrio mission that added 2 million new voters to the rolls, including many Colombian visitors and some FARC guerrillas.[54] He forbade an independent audit of the voter rolls even after thousands of new voters were found to have the same names and birth dates, or were supposedly 120 years old, or were known to be long dead.[55] And he altered the voting location for 2.6 million voters—mostly opposition voters identifiable from the recall petition signatures—forcing some to travel to a polling place hundreds of miles away.[56]

Chávez also replaced the country's election machines that had served Venezuela well for his own elections and for dozens of elections before he came to power. He gave no reason for this expensive, unnecessary move—but the reason was clear enough. The replacement machines were linked to a mainframe that performed a centralized electronic count that was easily corrupted to rig the vote, as tests in Illinois and Pennsylvania were later to reveal.[57]

Even the way these machines were purchased raised questions. Two young Venezuelans living in Florida were given $200,000 in start-up capital by the Venezuelan government to found a company named Smartmatic.[58] Before long, they had their first client: a $131 million no-bid contract from the Venezuelan government to build 29,500 new voting machines.[59]

In the lead-up to the recall referendum to be held on August 15, the election watch group Súmate ("Join Up")[60] which had collected the signature petitions for the recall, called for an independent audit of the e-voting machines to guarantee that they could not corrupt the vote count. The CNE refused. Súmate also protested the government's use of new electronic fingerprint machines—total cost, $165 million—at every voting station. Ostensibly there to prevent fraud, they could also be used to identify and intimidate those 3.5 million voters who had signed the recall petition. Again, the government refused to take any action. Indeed, the list of all those who signed the petition—including names and addresses—was later illegally put on the Internet by a Chávez legislator named Tascón. The infamous Tascón list was used as a black list to deny citizen services, jobs, and contracts in both the public and private sectors to the 3.5 million signatories,[61] a practice that continues to this day.

To prevent vote rigging on election day, Súmate worked with Penn, Schoen and Berland (PSB), a leading American polling firm—cofounded by Douglas Schoen—to conduct an extensive exit poll. Thousands of voters in representative samples were interviewed upon leaving the voting areas.

On Sunday, August 15, voter turnout surpassed all expectations. Across the country, Venezuelans lined up, some waiting more than twelve hours to cast a ballot. In PSB's experience, high turnout is almost always inspired by dissatisfaction with the incumbent. True to form, early exit poll data showed that Chávez was in serious trouble. This wasn't going to be a nail-biter; Chávez was losing big. At the end of the day, the exit poll showed an 18-point margin for the recall of Chávez, 59 percent to 41 percent.

As far as the CNE's rector Jorge Rodríguez, a Chávez loyalist, was concerned, those numbers were perfectly correct—only they were reversed. Despite the fact that the government had repeatedly claimed that the new machines would make available the results nearly instantaneously, the Venezuelan people had to wait seven hours to learn Chávez's fate. At 3:00 a.m. on the sixteenth, Rector Rodríguez (who would be rewarded by being named Chávez's vice president soon afterward) announced that Chávez had beaten the recall: 41 percent had voted in favor and 59 percent against.

Former President Jimmy Carter, whose Carter Center was monitoring the vote, confirmed the result.

No one had checked the machines' results against the paper ballots, still in possession of the government. All the voters had was the government's word that the CNE and Smartmatic had counted the votes honestly.

After a firestorm of criticism, Chávez and Carter acceded to a recount to be conducted internally (in effect, secretly) by the CNE's computers. Yet the day before that audit was to get under way, Carter said, "We have no reason to doubt the integrity of the electoral system or the accuracy of the referendum results." [62]

At the end of the week, the OAS announced its results. "The audit is completed," declared Secretary-General César Gaviria. "The results we have obtained with this check are totally compatible with the results of the electoral council." [63]

Two Boston-based academics, Dr. Ricardo Hausmann of Harvard University and Roberto Rigobon of MIT, later examined the computer results and found statistical anomalies so striking and so unlikely that they concluded fraud was the most logical explanation for the announced result. [64] Their conclusion was later corroborated by a multidisciplinary team, including a former rector of Simón Bolívar University, the former rector of the CNE, as well as two academics. [65] It appeared that results in certain voting tables had been changed through transmissions from the central computer so that neither Carter nor the OAS observers noticed.

When the questions raised by these academics were put to Jennifer McCoy of the Carter Center at the Inter-American Dialogue in Washington, D.C., while she defended the methods, practices, and conclusions of the Carter Center she also acknowledged she did not have any certainty as to how Venezuela voted on the recall." [66] Thereafter, President Carter went out of his way to criticize the PSB exit poll, [67] and to reaffirm his support of Chávez's legitimacy.

"Reelected"

In December 2006, Chávez won another six-year term as president. The CNE reported a landslide of 64 percent to 36 percent over Zulia state governor Manuel Rosales, a left-of-center unified opposition candidate. [68] Yet once again, PSB and Mexican exit polls showed a different result. [69]

And once again Chávez benefited from voter intimidation. A Penn, Schoen and Berland poll one month before the vote found that 42 percent of the voters believed that the CNE's fingerprint machines could tell the government how they had voted; and 47 percent believed that Chávez himself would be given the information.[70] The *Financial Times* reported that significant numbers of voters were fearful of opposing Chávez as well.[71]

Rosales campaigned hard, and managed to eat away at Chávez's support. His three key pledges—to distribute 20 percent of Venezuela's oil revenues in direct payments to the population; to stop Chávez's $100 billion foreign spending spree and spend the money at home; and to stop the crime wave that had turned Venezuela into the murder center of the hemisphere and perhaps the world[72]—were supported by more than 70 percent of the voters. Rosales was so popular in the slums—Chávez's longtime base of support—that his rallies there consistently drew far larger crowds.

Chávez had reason to be worried. So he resorted to an extraordinary measure: he publicly commanded Venezuela's 3 million civilian government employees, and its 1-million-strong military reserve, to vote for him or lose their jobs. He also used his control of the media to ensure a massive advantage in campaign coverage: for every twenty-two Chávez-oriented stories that made the press, Rosales received only one.[73]

On election night, exit polls showed that Rosales had lost by less than 5 percent. A subsequent academic study showed that 5,400 brand-new and unaudited Smartmatic e-voting machines were used for that election, and in several of the individual machines, Chávez had defeated Rosales by 98.5 percent to 1.5 percent, a margin Castro could only envy.[74]

Yet Rosales decided to concede early, disappointing many of his supporters who wanted to fight for the correct number rather than appearing to have lost by an apparently large number. Nevertheless, he proved that an opposition with a unified message and compelling messenger could compete with Chávez—despite the latter's enormous advantages and virtually unlimited funding. It was a harbinger of things to come.

President for Life?

By the middle of 2007, rampant crime, persistent poverty, and some of Chávez's more ill-considered decisions had driven his approval rating down to 37 percent. In particular, his heavy-handed decision not to re-license

RCTV—the oldest private channel in Venezuela, and one that spent most of its on-air hours broadcasting apolitical soap operas—caused outrage. Eighty percent of Venezuelans opposed the move, and *VenEconomy* editorialized, "President Hugo Chávez has finally discarded completely any façade and has shown his contempt for democracy, the rule of law and freedom of expression." [75]

Massive student protests—for free speech and against Chávez—followed. The protests made headlines worldwide and garnered sympathy throughout Latin America, from the Catholic Church, the Organization of American States, Europe, and the United States.[76] Chávez, true to form, called the protesting students "fascist children of the rich" and proclaimed himself once again the victim of an "imperialist aggression." [77]

In response, he decided to do what he does best: go on the attack. Claiming that his 2006 reelection "landslide" gave him a mandate to serve as president for as long as he could get elected, Chávez proposed a constitutional referendum allowing unlimited terms. He boasted of ruling until 2050. Other provisions included lengthening presidential terms from six to seven years, turning over control of the Central Bank to the president, limiting the size of landed estates, giving the president new powers over elected state governors, and allowing the president sweeping powers to declare states of emergency. Certain populist measures like shortening the official workweek and extending pension benefits to workers in the underground economy were thrown in as sweeteners. "Without the constitutional reform it will be impossible to continue constructing socialism," Chávez said, prompting students and slum residents alike to protest anew.[78]

"The real coup d'état is coming from Chávez, who wants to perpetuate himself in power," student leader Jon Goicoechea told the *New York Times*.[79] Chávez's former defense minister, the retired General Raúl Baduel—a saman tree oath-taker in 1982, and the man whose military unit had saved Chávez on April 12, 2002—agreed with Goicoechea that Chávez was performing a constitutional coup to become dictator de facto.[80] "Voters are being led like lambs to the slaughter," Baduel warned. Chávez called him a liar and a traitor.[81]

When the Catholic Church announced that the referendum was "morally unacceptable" because it gave the state absolute power over individual freedom, the Venezuelan cardinal was jostled in his car in front of the cathedral and Chávez opined that "The Cardinal and bishops are dolts, mental retards." [82] When the business group Fedecámeras opposed the referendum, Chávez threatened, "I'm going to take away every business you have." [83]

And when Chávez's former wife, Marisabel Rodríguez, said that Chávez wanted to be a dictator, Chávez bristled. In retaliation, he filed a custody suit for their daughter Rosinés in courts totally beholden to the president, but later abruptly dropped the suit. Marisabel's lawyers said she "would release the names and dates of those who engaged in promiscuous and illegal activities that she had witnessed in Miraflores." [84]

A June 2007 poll by Hinterlaces, an opinion research firm, showed only 19 percent support for the constitutional changes. [85] Never to be counted out, Chávez turned up the heat considerably, pouring billions of dollars onto the street and urging his government workers, soldiers, and party apparatchiks to turn out to vote, saying, "We're obliged to win this battle of world proportions. The final attack begins." [86]

Chávez was unmistakably worried. In the last two months leading up to the referendum, hoping to rally people to the flag, he threatened to go to war with the United States three times, once in defense of Iran, once in defense of Bolivia, and once in defense of Venezuela against Colombia.

He also made a Herculean effort to turn the election into a referendum on patriotism and on Bush. "Whoever votes against the referendum is against me; he who says he supports Chávez but votes 'no' is a traitor, a true traitor," he warned. [87] "Who votes 'yes' is for Chávez, who votes 'no' is for George W. Bush," he said, in a last-gasp effort to sway voters. [88]

On December 2, 2007, exit polls showed that Venezuelans rejected Chávez's referendum by 12 percent. [89] Results among military voters were leaked early onto the Internet (the military vote before the public and on separate machines) and showed Chávez losing 81 percent to 19 percent. [90] But when the CNE fell silent for hours after the polls closed, speculation rose that the vote was being changed by the election computers—exactly what experts believe happened in 2004 and 2006.

Former General Baduel went on TV when the polls closed to say that he had seen the actual vote totals and that Chávez must accept those totals or else—civil war being the implied "or else." [91] After hours of intrigue, Chávez backed down. At 1:00 a.m. on December 3, the CNE reported that with 87 percent of the vote counted, the 50.7 percent to 49.3 percent loss was "irreversible." It's unlikely that Chávez would have given up with 13 percent of the vote remaining to be counted unless he knew the margin of his loss to be much greater than he let on. Many believe that a face-saving deal had been cut between Chávez and Baduel.[92]

Chávez had lost and the opposition had won a "shitty" victory, as he called it.[93] Some 44 percent of the Venezuelan electorate did not vote—3 million of them Chávez voters from the 2006 presidential race. Chávez's margin of support had so badly contracted that rigging the Smartmatic machines was no longer possible.

On the other hand, Chávez had lost nothing—not a drop of oil, not a scintilla of power, not a bolivar (Venezuela's official currency) of money. Chastened but undaunted, he lamented loss with the words *"por ahora no pudimos* (for now, we couldn't)." As we have seen, the last time he used a similar phrase, it proved prophetic.

4

Oil Is His Most Potent Weapon

Only the very well off in America—the upper middle class and the wealthy—can wake up in the morning and not worry at all about the price of oil. For too many people, $4-a-gallon gas and $1,000-a-month heating bills are a frightening nightmare that has become an occasional reality that they have little or no control over. These two items alone are enough sticker shock for most of us to bear. Yet the price of oil—and yes, imported oil—affects the consumer price index, or inflation, in ways we don't often think about: plastic bags (made from oil), the cost of shipping goods and foodstuffs, the retail price of almost anything manufactured requiring machines and fuel to operate them. When the prices of fruits and vegetables go up, it's convenient to blame the farmer.

Instead, blame Hugo Chávez, who is indirectly more of the cause.

Imported oil also affects the purchasing power of the U.S. dollar, the availability of reasonable credit, the number of jobs created or lost each month, and how deep and long recessions last. Even current President Bush once famously acknowledged that we are "addicted to oil." The United States is the major global consumer of oil, mainly because we're a nation that cannot fathom a world without automobiles. While comprising only 4 percent of the world's population, we consume over one quarter of the world's oil, mostly for gasoline. This is the harsh reality. Our energy use is literally driven by cars, and this is not likely to change soon. Yet until alternative fuel sources are sufficiently developed, oil is a necessary dependency.

Much of what we end up paying for oil stems from Chávez's manipulation of the foreign import market. When he effectively seized control of the pipelines in Venezuela, he first began to exert outsized influence on the economies of Latin America, the Middle East, then on to those of Cuba, Bolivia, Ecuador, and Nicaragua. As the clock turned over to the new millennium, he was able to become one of the most important and powerful rulers in Latin America simply by the systematic easing and tightening of his nation's fuel spigots. Oil means money, and together they create power.

In short, oil quickly became Chávez's sword of Damocles. He knew we had an unquenchable thirst for it and by squeezing the world supply to the extent that he did, he could potentially bring the U.S. economy to its knees, or if not that, at least worsen the economic downturn in 2008, which may be the worst since the Great Depression.

Prior to the summer of 2008, Chávez personally shorted the oil market of 3 million barrels a day. Leading OPEC, he had every producing nation but Saudi Arabia following suit. This effectively removed a cushion of global supply that was keeping the oil price at manageable levels. He exploited U.S. vulnerability by reducing the global oil supply and by increasing the political risk premium paid for oil. Saudi energy minister Ali al-Naimi has said that oil price is partially determined by the geopolitical uncertainty over supply.[1]

Chávez understands scare tactics, as well as the political risk premium. He coupled the shortage with a massive media campaign to send a message that war, terror, or conflict was going to cut off the global oil supply. It had to be the most expensive media campaign ever. Typical headlines predicted that oil would go to $200 or $300 per barrel, and some speculators believed it. Chávez and Iran's Ahmadinejad even urged OPEC and the developing world to abandon the dollar as an international currency.

The President as Oil Baron

Hugo Chávez is implementing a sophisticated oil war against the United States. To understand this, you have to look back to 1999, when he asked the Venezuelan Congress for emergency executive powers and got them, whereupon he consolidated government power to his advantage. His big move was to take full control over the national oil company Petróleos de Venezuela, S.A. Chávez replaced PDVSA's directors and managers with military or political loyalists, many of whom knew little or nothing about the oil business.[2] This action rankled the company's professional and technical employees—some 50,000 of them—who enjoyed the only true meritocracy in the country.[3] (CITGO, Venezuela's wholly owned national gasoline company with 14,000 retail stations in the United States, later received similar treatment.)[4]

Chávez in effect demodernized and de-Americanized PDVSA, which had adopted organizational efficiency cultures similar to its predecessors, ExxonMobil and Shell, by claiming that they were ideologically incorrect.[5] Chávez compared this cleansing to Haiti's elimination of French culture under Toussaint L'Ouverture in the early 1800s.

The president's effort to dumb down the business was evident early on. In 1999, Chávez fired Science Applications International Corporation (known as SAIC), an enormous U.S.-based global information technology firm that had served as PDVSA's back office since 1995 (as it had for British Petroleum and other energy companies). SAIC had saved Venezuela $100 million a year while making PDVSA more productive and efficient. Chávez's case against SAIC was that it was an American company that had worked for the CIA (he actually noted that SAIC is CIA's spelled backward) and was "stealing PDVSA's secrets" for the American government.[6]

SAIC appealed to an international court and got a judgment against Chávez for precisely the opposite crime. The court decided that Chávez was stealing SAIC's knowledge without compensation.[7] Chávez ignored the judgment, refusing to pay "one penny."[8]

Stripped of SAIC technology and thousands of oil professionals who quit out of frustration, PDVSA steadily lost operational capacity from 1999 to 2001. Well maintenance suffered; production investment was slashed; oil productivity declined; environmental standards were ignored; and safety accidents proliferated.[9] After the 2002 strike that led to Chávez's brief removal from power, PDVSA sacked some 18,000 more of its knowledge workers. Its production fell to 2.4 million barrels per day, which is where it stood in 2008.[10]

After Venezuela's 2006 presidential election, Chávez seized "what might be the world's richest oil fields, a huge swath known as the Orinoco Belt that Big Oil has spent a decade and nearly $20 billion developing."[11] He told three American oil companies—ExxonMobil, ConocoPhillips, and Chevron—to turn over 60 percent of their heavy oil exploration and production property to the government or leave Venezuela. Only Chevron stayed in Venezuela as a minority partner in its own business.[12] In retaliation against Venezuela seizing its property, ExxonMobil briefly tied up $12 billion of Venezuela's global assets in a 2008 arbitration dispute in British courts. The asset freeze was later reversed on technical grounds.[13] Yet, at the end of the day, Chávez had virtually banished the American oil companies from Venezuelan lands.

In eight years, Chávez had trebled Venezuela's estimated reserves while halving what PDVSA was producing compared to its pre-Chávez plan, actions which gave him a lot more leverage over world oil supply and thus price.

The oil weapon was in place.

Venezuela's Rich Oil Fields

Venezuela has a lot of oil—Chávez claims over 300 billion barrels in reserve—and is second only to Saudi Arabia, the difference being that the Saudi oil is light, cheap, and easy to refine while 90 percent of Venezuela's is heavy, expensive, and difficult to refine, which means it requires a lot of technology and investment to process.[14] The U.S. Geological Survey describes the heavy-oil Orinoco Belt, a region southeast of Caracas, as "the largest single hydrocarbon accumulation in the world."[15]

But Venezuela is minimally developing its oil resources. While Saudi Arabia is producing 8 mbd (million barrels per day) and could go to 10 mbd if needed, Venezuela is producing only 2.4 mbd (1.3 mbd of that goes to the United States) and its production capacity is falling.[16] Historically, this is a huge decline for Venezuela, but it is intentional. Chávez has squeezed the world supply and increased the price of oil. If Venezuela was at 5.4 mbd in 2008,[17] as it had planned before Chávez took over, that 3 mbd supply cushion, added to the 85 mbd the world consumes daily, could cut the oil price in half.[18] But that's just the opposite of what Chávez wants to do.

Oil Has Ruined Venezuela

Even after the nationalization of Venezuela's oil more than thirty years ago and the intermittent spikes in the price of oil since then, Venezuela's standard of living has dropped precipitously. Its middle class has been decimated. Significant corruption and several scandals have scarred each successive government administration. More than half the population wound up in poverty, and voters simply gave up their hopes for a democracy.

How can such an oil-rich nation's government so ill serve its people?

Before Chávez, it actually meant well. The reforms President Carlos Andrés Pérez enacted in 1989 did increase productivity in Venezuela for the first time since the 1970s, but it was too little too late for the benefit of those reforms to trickle down to the population. Venezuelans had no idea what Pérez was trying to do when he rationalized the subsidized price of gasoline that year.[19] The result was the coup d'état attempt by Chávez and the populism that was to follow. Pérez was impeached and his nemesis Rafael Caldera elected in 1993. Caldera abandoned Pérez's government reforms, which damaged the economy even more.

Nevertheless, Luis Giusti, the president of PDVSA, pushed on with the oil reforms. He opened up Venezuela's heavy-oil industry in the Orinoco Belt to $20 billion of U.S. private oil company investment and participation in 1995, only to have it shut down by Chávez five years later. Under Chávez's oil policy, Venezuela is producing 3 mbd less than it would have if Giusti's oil opening had continued,[20] while institutionalized corruption actually escalated.[21]

Venezuela's abject failure at "sowing the oil" in its population in the 1976–98 period made the appearance of Chávez—or a populist just like him—politically inevitable.[22] That failure also opened the door for Chávez to realize his dream of becoming the revolutionary instrument of America's decline—taking revenge, as he sees it—which was perfectly suited to his anti-American rage.

Oil and Recessions

The concentration of oil in the Middle East has complicated the turmoil between Arabs and Israelis and the international effort to contain terrorism. The global coincidence between oil and conflict—from Iraq to Sudan to Venezuela—is an incontrovertible fact.[23] Since the collapse of the Soviet Union, oil has become a much more critical element in world politics. But it's taken nearly twenty years for this salient fact to become apparent.

Consider the recent history of the relationship between and among war, oil, and recession. The United States has had five recessions directly precipitated by international oil trade:

- 1973 after the Yom Kippur War and the Arab oil embargo, with oil at $45 a barrel;
- 1980 after the Iranian revolution by Islamic fundamentalists, with oil at $103;
- 1990 after the Persian Gulf war, with oil at $65;
- 2001 after the 9/11 terrorist attack, with oil at $45;
- 2008 after years of turmoil in oil states like Iraq, Iran, and Venezuela, with oil at a high of $147.

"Higher oil prices hurt the economy because they act like a tax increase," *The Economist* explains. "Firms that use oil face higher costs, which, if they cannot be passed on in higher prices, might mean that some production becomes unprofitable. Consumers paying more for their petrol and heating oil have less to spend on other things. If they look for higher wages to compensate for a drop in purchasing power that will only lead to job losses."[24] While oil may play a secondary instead of a primary role (to the home mortgage crisis) in the 2008 economic crash, as it did in previous downturns, there is no question among economists that oil is a huge contributor to the problem.[25]

U.S. oil imports increased from 35 percent of American oil consumption in 1973 to 60 percent in 2006, providing Venezuela alone with $37 billion in that year.[26] The world burned 85 mbd of oil in 2007, up from 75 mbd in 1999, and demand is increasing not just in America but also from 3 billion new customers in China and India alone.[27] Thus, American vulnerability to oil exporters and eventually someone like Chávez has grown exponentially.

Concerned about its vulnerability to oil imports and roller-coaster recessions, the United States instituted some energy conservation measures in the 1980s—smaller cars, more efficient engines, and home insulation are the big ones—which tempered demand and drove the oil price down to $30 or less until around the year 2000.

Yet in the robust bubble economy of the 1990s, SUVs and big engines sapped up those conservation benefits, and the oil market grew tight as energy demand expanded dramatically from rising demand in the developed world, augmented by new economic growth in China and India.

But supply and demand are not the only factors in setting the world oil price.

Why Oil Prices Are Rising

From 2000 to 2008, the oil price steadily rose from $10 per barrel to an all-time high of around $147 in 2008. In strict supply-and-demand terms, the oil price should have been less than half that, according to the Saudi Arabian oil minister Ali al-Naimi, but it multiplied because of what he calls the "political risk premium"[28] paid for geopolitical uncertainty. The conflicts in and around oil states make them a very risky market bet, and that is the major driver of oil prices today.

"The [oil] market is increasingly driven by geopolitical events," the president of OPEC, Mohammad bin Ahaen al-Hamli, has said, rather than by classical supply and demand economics.[29] The political risk premium paid for oil is psychologically driven by news from Iraq, Iran, Venezuela, Afghanistan, Syria, Nigeria, Sudan, Russia, and other places that mix oil production and conflict—some of it generated precisely to spike the oil risk premium. Chávez, for example, declared in March 2008—at the height of his crisis with Colombia—that "we are headed to $200 oil."[30] He exaggerated by $53, but he made his point.

Global Transfer of Wealth

Oil has caused a massive shift in the wealth of nations. All told, $12 trillion has been transferred from the oil consumers to the oil producers since 2002.[31] This is a very large figure—it is comparable to the 2006 GDP in the United States—and it has contributed greatly to our unprecedented trade deficit; a weakening of the dollar (which buys only half the euros it did five years ago); and the weakness of the U.S. financial system in surviving the housing mortgage crisis.

Two decades ago, private oil companies controlled half the world's oil reserves, but today they control only 13 percent. Oil has been nationalized as in Venezuela and is no longer available to what used to be called "big oil." While many Americans believe that big oil is behind the high prices at the gas pump, the fact is that the national oil companies controlled by Chávez of Venezuela, Ahmadinejad of Iran, and Putin of Russia are the real culprits.

"Part of the cost of absorbing past oil-price hikes has been higher consumer debt and a huge trade deficit, both of which make America's economy more vulnerable," *The Economist* noted in 2007.[32] And this massive transfer of wealth will increase over the short term because the share of oil reserves controlled by nationalized oil companies (not U.S. companies) is increasing, while the share controlled by private oil companies (some of which are U.S. companies) is decreasing.[33]

Oil, Corruption, and Dictatorship

Waste and corruption have fundamentally ruined many oil states through what economists call "the Dutch Disease," where oil outprofits other economic activity in the country to such a degree that the entrepreneurs spend all their time getting in on the profitable oil action rather than working at farming, manufacturing, or banking. This is why, forty years ago, Venezuela was a food-exporting country, while today it imports 60 percent of what it eats and its manufacturing base has been decimated. Recently, Chávez's controls over prices, wages, currency exchanges, profits, investment, and property have fed this destructive trend with new incentives for theft that made manufacturing and food shortages dramatically worse.[34] These he blamed on capitalism, hoarding, speculators—and the CIA.

"In many poor nations with oil," the *New York Times* reported in 2007, "the proceeds are being lost to corruption, depriving those countries of their best hope for development," of which Venezuela is a prime example: "Transparency International, an organization that tracks corruption, ranks countries from least to most corrupt, and in its 2007 index, Venezuela was ranked at 162 of 179 countries."[35]

Venezuela is by no means the only oil state cursed by institutionalized oil corruption. Of the top twelve nations exporting oil to the United States (the 2007 crude exports in thousands of barrels per day to the United States are noted in each case), nine of those nations are oil-cursed in this sense: Saudi Arabia (1,483), Venezuela (1,339), Nigeria (1,133), Iraq (484), Algeria (663), Angola (508), Kuwait (181), Ecuador (182), and Libya (117).[36]

Consequently, global markets reasonably see nondemocratic oil states as volatile, undependable, and unstable, and that drives up the price of oil—the political risk premium at work, if you will.[37] In that sense, the lack of democracy in OPEC countries relates directly to the rising price for oil.

To run our economic engine, we are depending on undependable countries heading in the opposite direction on the road to free market democracy. The *New York Times* columnist Thomas Friedman argues: "The higher the average global crude oil price rises, the more free speech, free press, free and fair elections, an independent judiciary, the rule of law and independent political parties are eroded."[38] This pattern of behavior, which Friedman calls "the First Law of Petropolitics," identifies the U.S. conflict between its interests and values as it looks for oil around the world.

Oil dependence on corrupt autocracies places the United States in a direct conflict between its interests and values, a vulnerability an oil-producing enemy like Chávez can easily exploit by describing his constitutional dictatorship as another kind of democracy. "North American imperialism [imposes] the division of powers, the alternation in power, and representation as the basis of democracy—Big Lies!" Chávez argues.[39]

The Chávez-Castro Condominium

When Chávez's plane first landed in Havana in 1994, Fidel Castro greeted him at the airport. What made Hugo Chávez important to Castro then was the same thing that makes him important to the United States now: oil. Castro's plan to weaken America—which he had to shelve when the

Soviet Union collapsed and Cuba lost its USSR oil and financial subsidy—was dusted off.[40]

The Chávez-Castro condominium[41] was a two-way street. Chávez soon began delivering from 50,000 to 90,000 barrels of oil per day to Castro, a subsidy eventually worth $3 billion to $4 billion per year, which far exceeded the sugar subsidy Castro once received from the Soviet Union until Gorbachev ended it around 1980.[42] Castro used the huge infusion of Chávez's cash to solidify his absolute control in Cuba and to crack down on political dissidents.[43]

In successive years, Cuba's allocation of Venezuelan oil would be increased to 100,000 barrels per day, and by 2008 it was estimated to total a market value of $24 billion.[44] On December 22, 2007, Chávez dedicated a $166 million refinery at Cienfuegos that gives Cuba the capability to refine Chávez's oil gifts plus offshore oil of its own. The U.S. Geological Survey reports that Cuba has 4.6 billion barrels of offshore oil available, some sites of which are only sixty-five miles from Florida's coast.

It's certainly conceivable that Chávez and Castro could conduct an oil-funded revolution right on America's doorstep.

Chávez's generosity to Cuba was a quid pro quo, of course. In turn, Cástro has sent over 20,000 doctors, sports trainers, and security personnel[45] to service Cuban health clinics in Venezuela's slums, to train Venezuelan athletes, and to form a security net around Chávez. Cuban security has penetrated deeply into Venezuela's military and security apparatus in order to prevent his assassination or a coup either internally or by the United States, which Chávez has predicted every year since 1999.[46]

As Chávez gained control of power, oil, and money in Venezuela, he demonstrated some skill at being able to ward off public disapproval of his performance, which Castro has miraculously achieved over the decades in Cuba.[47] In both cases, Castro and Chávez blame their lack of domestic economic performance on the United States, Castro because of the embargo dating back to the 1960s and Chávez because the United States is conspiring against him and his revolution.

Chávez's Influence within OPEC

Chávez's relationship with OPEC allowed him to ally his nation with Iraq, Iran, Libya, and Syria, and also to exploit Islam's rage against America's position on Israel, nuclear proliferation, and various Western values and traditions.

Arab and Venezuelan interests formed the Organization of the Petro-leum Exporting Countries in 1949 in an effort to formulate export policy and control the price of oil. A Venezuelan, Juan Pablo Pérez Alfonso, ap-proached and won the support of Iraq, Iran, Kuwait, and Saudi Arabia to create the cartel. While OPEC under Saudi control but not Venezuelan had an interest in harmonizing the price so it reflects both producer and con-sumer interests—avoiding recessions that reduce the demand for oil, among other things—it is still fundamentally a cartel for producers who live in the Islamic world. Altogether, the national oil companies of OPEC controlled three quarters of the world's oil reserves and provided 40 per-cent of the oil consumed in 2007.[48]

As member countries join, they are provided a quota for oil production so that OPEC can exert control over global export supply and thus maxi-mize the world oil price to the producers' advantage.

The cartel's power was displayed most dramatically when, in the after-math of the 1973 Yom Kippur War between Israel and its Arab neighbors, OPEC imposed an oil embargo on the United States and Western Europe, which triggered mile-long gasoline station lines in the United States, a global recession, and high inflation that lasted until the early 1980s. Be-cause of Venezuela's close ties to the United States at that time, Venezuela did not comply with the oil cutoff to the United States. Yet OPEC had demonstrated to the world its ability to humble our economy, a fact that Hugo Chávez, then a military cadet who sided with the Arab oil embargo against us, would never forget.[49]

Two more global recessions thereafter would be caused by Middle East-ern oil-state conflicts, including the Iranian Islamic revolution of 1979, which featured the U.S. hostage crisis; and the Iran-Iraq War, which re-sulted in a million casualties—and may have convinced an isolated Iran that it should produce a nuclear weapon.[50]

For a Latin among Middle Eastern potentates, Chávez has wielded a huge amount of influence. Once in office, he embarked on whirlwind trips to a dozen OPEC nations, chaired a lavish OPEC meeting in Caracas, got his leftist coup co-conspirator Alí Rodríguez appointed president of OPEC, and prompted OPEC to reduce supply and thus increase the world price at every turn.[51] Over world objections, Chávez became the only head of state to visit Saddam Hussein in Iraq in 2000, calling him "brother" and praising Saddam's regime as peaceful while criticizing the United States as warmongering.[52]

In short order, Chávez became the leading hawk for higher oil prices, strongly supported by OPEC members Iran, Syria, and Libya, which had also joined him in strategic alliances against U.S. policies on nuclear proliferation, terrorism, and Middle East conflicts.[53]

Chávez also proposed Russia, Oman, Angola, Bolivia, and Ecuador as OPEC members in order to stack organizational votes in his favor. (Ecuador was a former member.) Saudi Arabia remained the lone but powerful voice in OPEC loosely allied with the United States. But the Saudis couldn't stop Venezuela, Iran, and the anti-American price hawks from shorting global supply, frightening the markets, and driving the price of oil to whatever heights it could reach.

In November 2007, Chávez and Iran's President Mahmoud Ahmadinejad proposed at an OPEC meeting in Riyadh, Saudi Arabia, that OPEC should openly use its oil as a political weapon against the United States. They urged OPEC nations to abandon the "worthless" U.S. dollar as the exchange currency for OPEC's oil and as the reserve currency for OPEC nations and their oil sovereignty funds, in which several trillion dollars are kept in reserve.[54] Saudi Arabia was able to delay consideration of the Venezuelan-Iranian proposal only by insisting that a global run on the dollar and recession would be instigated merely by talking about it—the obvious intention of Chávez and Ahmadinejad.[55] It was obvious who was in control of world oil supply and the price—and it wasn't the Arabs.

The Paradox of Plenty—Why Venezuelan Oil Matters

Venezuelan oil once played a constructive role for the world economy and for Venezuelans, but not now. From 1920 to 1960, Venezuela was the world's biggest exporter of oil,[56] fueling for itself the best economic growth and lowest inflation in the world for that period, and also creating Latin America's first electoral democracy—in 1958. As *The Economist*'s Michael Reid has noted about that period, "Caracas became the most 'Americanized' capital in Latin America. . . . Venezuela's income per head was the highest in Latin America." [57] (Venezuela in 1998 was first among oil exporters to the United States, but by 2000 under Chávez it was only fourth and declining—Chávez's oil to America was starting to go to China, and by 2011 a great deal more will be going there.)

Many observers in the 1960s believed Venezuela was on track to be the first nation in Latin America to join the rich world; but it did not happen. Since the late 1970s, Venezuela has failed to spread oil benefits to its population, and since 1999 (when Chávez took command) Venezuela has been dramatically reducing its oil production and exports.

Much of the world's oil is possessed by unstable countries that are driving up its global price while turning against democracy and withholding oil's benefits to their populations—a potentially disastrous situation for their citizenry. According to a Rice University study of 2007, 77 percent of the world's 1,148 trillion barrels of proven reserves is in the hands of national oil companies and fourteen of the top twenty oil-producing companies are state-controlled, so the instability is going to increase. [58]

The infamous "oil curse" [59] fosters monopoly and theft that reduces or eliminates the chances for widespread development and democracy. The economist Terry Lynn Karl describes this "paradox of plenty" as the fundamental cause of internal instability in the oil-producing states she has studied. [60] The "curse," as Karl puts it, arises because, typically, a powerful cabal appropriates the oil wealth at every turn, leaving the vast majority to go poor and hungry. Corruption is thus institutionalized in oil states by combining monopoly, discretion, and secrecy inside an elite power cabal at the top of the political pyramid. [61]

In Venezuela, this cabal historically included the mostly white, rich, and educated minority that controlled the two main political parties through the Pacto de Punto Fijo, a 1958 power-sharing agreement that effectively excluded the country's brown-skinned and poor majority from enjoying the benefits of oil revenue. Before Chávez, every military dictator and president of the twentieth century came from Venezuela's white elite ruling caste, where two of the top claims to fame for the country were the highest per capita consumption of Scotch whiskey and small plane ownership in Latin America.

After Chávez, the monopoly, discretion, and secrecy stayed the same while the elite cabal came from his close military, family, and political appointees. President Hugo Chávez changed the names of the people but not the corrupt system he inherited from the oligarchs, so he wound up with the same corrupt result.

Without Chávez in power, Venezuela would have produced 5.4 mbd in 2008 and be on the path to increase this figure to 8 mbd by 2010. It could have helped ease the transition from carbon to less harmful fuels.

Whether Venezuelan poverty and inequality would have been eliminated under leadership other than Chávez in the last ten years, we don't know, but we do know it could hardly be worse for the poor than what has happened under Chávez.

5

Bad Neighbor

Chávez's predatory, undemocratic, and destabilizing actions are not limited to Venezuela. Far from it.

Chávez is not merely a domestic revolutionary. He is, or aspires to be, the leader of an international movement. His strategy is global. But one important aspect remains close to home.

Chávez is striving to remake Latin America in his own image, and for his own purposes—purposes that mirror Fidel Castro's half-aborted but never abandoned plans for hemispheric revolution hatched half a decade ago.

Yet Chávez is blessed with resources that Castro could only dream of. Thanks to record-high oil prices, he has money to spend—money that he liberally spreads around the region supporting candidates sympathetic to his leftist and anti-American aims, and opposing those he deems insufficiently committed to the cause, or worse, actually supportive of free markets and good relations with the United States.

Yet there is nothing "democratic" about these activities. As in the United States, most Latin American nations have laws that prohibit foreign interference—and especially foreign funds—from playing any role in their domestic elections. That has not stopped Chávez, of course. Stories routinely circulate about suitcases full of cash—usually American dollars, but sent from Caracas—showing up in Latin American capitals around election time and finding their way into the hands of left-wing politicians. Chávez, true to form, denies all involvement, but the evidence increasingly says otherwise.

With Chávez's assistance, left-wing leaders have been elected throughout the region. And the political climate has shifted markedly in the direction Chávez has sought to move it.

More sinister than Chávez's support for the politicians he likes is the treatment he metes out to those he dislikes. Here he crosses the threshold from mere illegality into destabilizing interference, saber rattling, and even real violence. Under Hugo Chávez, Venezuela has become the western hemisphere's second state sponsor of terrorism.

The supreme—and utterly inexcusable—example is Chávez's continued support for the FARC, the notorious narcoterrorist group operating out of the Colombian jungles. Part band of revolutionary ideologues, part drug traffickers, and part kidnapping ring, the FARC is Latin America's most dangerous entity. Yet Chávez embraces it without hesitation because it shares—at least in theory—his ideological goals, and because its common archenemy, the legitimate president of Colombia, favors the free market and is an unabashed ally of the United States. To Hugo Chávez, no sins are as unforgivable as these.

Per his pattern, Chávez has denied any involvement. But in March 2008, dramatic proof established beyond any doubt his ties to terrorism.

Americans may think that these Communist guerrillas fighting in Colombia's jungles have nothing to do with them, or that "we have no dog in the fight." But that is wishful thinking. The war in Colombia relates directly to worldwide terrorism, the cocaine trade, and gangs and urban crime in our own cities. And the guerrillas waging that war have for almost a decade received millions in funding from the Venezuela of Hugo Chávez—funding that is critical to their terrorist activities in the western hemisphere and to their trade in the potent drugs they have peddled to Americans and around the world.

Mentor

Hugo Chávez sees himself as leading the revolutionary charge that Fidel Castro always wanted to mount but was never able to spread beyond the shores of the island prison he created in the Caribbean. Yet four decades after taking power, Castro found a surrogate, a right arm who could carry on the work that he could not. Or rather, that surrogate found him.

Chávez has idolized Castro since his boyhood. But most boys never grow up to forge friendships, much less working relationships with their idol—and even less a working relationship in which the idolizer holds more cards than his idol. Chávez is an exception.

Chávez travels frequently to Havana, a practice that, as we have seen, began long before he even came to power. In the wake of the failed 1992 coup Castro saw something more than failure; he saw the young officer's potential.

Chávez returns the favor, in part by constantly gushing over his mentor. He speaks of the elder man as his "father" and "comrade" and "companion" and—in his more expansive moods—as the "father of all revolutionaries." Rare for the usually bombastic and dominant Hugo, he is always deferential toward Castro. Fidel fills the dominant role of teacher, mentor, and surrogate father, while Hugo acts the dutiful son and eager student.

But it is not an act—at least not entirely. Hugo can be prone to gushing: "You are the one with an exceptional mind, not me"; "We follow your example"; "Yes, Fidel. I have become, well, you have turned me into an emissary, a source"; "But you, Cuba and its example of dignity, of battle, courage and its infinite solidarity has always and will always be with us as an example"; "I do not have any qualms about calling you 'father' in front of the world. Onward to victory"; "In those days [1989] I saw you from afar and I wanted to get close to greet you, but I could not, but we were already involved in the revolutionary movement . . . now that I am listening and talking to you, what an honor." Yet his affection appears genuine.

Castro at least must think so. Since he became ill in 2006, very few people have seen him, and hardly any on a regular basis. Chávez is one of the few with virtually unlimited access to the Cuban dictator.

Castro offers Chávez political advice, and also more tangible benefits.

Most observers agree that Castro is a moderating influence on Chávez—if not in terms of overall goals, at least in terms of tactics and strategy. Chávez's enthusiasm for confrontation sometimes gets the better of him. For instance, early in 2008 Chávez nearly provoked a war with Colombia by massing troops at the border after Colombian forces had attacked a FARC camp in Ecuador (the opposite side of Colombia from Venezuela). Castro reportedly played an instrumental role in convincing Chávez to back down.[1]

As to the more tangible benefits, Chávez travels with a retinue of Cuban doctors; Venezuela's health care system is much less sophisticated than Cuba's. But that is just the tip of the iceberg. Cuban doctors work throughout Venezuela, particularly in the poorest areas, and thousands of Venezuelans travel to Cuba every year for medical treatment. Castro has also sent hundreds of Cuban teachers and—more important—intelligence agents to Venezuela. The spies both train Chávez's own intelligence service and conduct operations on behalf of the larger revolutionary project.

In return, Castro receives an all-important lifeline: some 90,000 barrels of oil per day, worth more than $3 billion per year at current prices. This is essential support, given Cuba's bleak poverty, and the only significant outside help Castro has received since the collapse of the Soviet Union and the end of Moscow's subsidies.

Buying Friends and Influencing Nations

Chávez sends Venezuela's oil to states other than Cuba. He routinely uses oil to bribe Latin American states into lining up against the United States, either by subsidizing oil in the surrogate state or by using oil to interfere in other countries' elections.

For instance, in 1999 Chávez created Petrocaribe, a company that provides discount oil with delayed payments to thirteen Caribbean nations. It was so successful at fulfilling its real purpose—buying influence and loyalty—that two years later Chávez created PetroSur, which does the same for twenty Central and South American nations, at an annual cost to Venezuela's treasury of an estimated $1 billion.[2]

Chávez does not just give oil; he also uses oil revenues to finance other largesse. To free Argentina and Ecuador from the U.S.-controlled International Monetary Fund (IMF), Chávez purchased $6 billion of Argentine debt and $300 million of Ecuadorian debt, and advanced $1 billion in capital for his pet Bank of the South to replace U.S.-controlled World Bank financing in Latin America.[3]

From 2005 to 2007 alone, Chávez gave away a total of $39 billion in oil and cash; $9.9 billion to Argentina, $7.5 billion to Cuba, $4.9 billion to Ecuador, and $4.9 billion to Nicaragua were the largest sums Chávez gave. Also on the dole: Uruguay, Brazil, many of the Caribbean nations, Vietnam, Syria, and Malaysia. Even rich countries have their hands out. Former London mayor Ken Livingstone (a longtime hard-left socialist formerly known as "Red Ken") inked a deal in 2007 to fuel London buses with Venezuelan oil and to subsidize the travel of low-income Londoners. Even Chávez's archenemy the United States benefits. CITGO—the American arm of Venezuela's national oil company—operates an oil subsidy program in twenty-three states.[4] As we will see in a later chapter, several prominent American politicians are only too happy to take Chávez's money even if it means assisting his anti-American crusade.

At a time when U.S. influence is waning—in part owing to Washington's preoccupation with Iraq and the Middle East—Chávez has filled the void. The United States provides less than $1 billion in foreign economic aid to the entire region, a figure that rises to only $1.6 billion when security aid to Colombia is taken into account. Chávez, meanwhile, spends nearly $9 billion in the region every year.[5] And his money is always welcome because it comes with no strings. The World Bank and IMF, by contrast, require concomitant reforms—for instance, efforts to fight corruption, drug trafficking, and money laundering—in return for grants and loans.

Consequently, over the course of a handful of years, virtually all the Latin American countries have wound up dependent on Venezuela's oil or money or both. These include not just resource-poor nations; in Latin America, only Mexico and Peru are fully independent of Chávez's money.

One consequence: at the Organization of American States (OAS), which serves as a mini–United Nations for Latin America, Venezuela has assumed the position of the "veto" vote that once belonged to the United States.[6] Not surprisingly, when Chávez is questioned at the OAS about buying $5 billion in arms, providing safe havens and money to Colombia's FARC guerrillas, or destroying democracy in Venezuela, the countries that stand up in his defense are Bolivia, Nicaragua, Ecuador, and Argentina, while virtually all other nations go mum. Since Chávez has been president of Venezuela, the OAS has not passed one substantive resolution supported by the United States when Chávez was on the opposite side.[7]

In all, since coming to power in 1999, Chávez has spent or committed an estimated $110 billion—some say twice the amount needed to eliminate poverty in Venezuela forever—in more than thirty countries to advance his anti-American agenda. Since 2005, Chávez's total foreign aid budget for Latin America has been more than $50 billion—much more than the amount of U.S. foreign aid for the region over the same period.[8] Many of these expenditures have been hidden from the Venezuelan public in secret, off-budget slush funds.[9] Details are hard to come by, but an investigation by the U.S. Congress found some $3 billion in offshore bank accounts, accessed by powerful people in Chávez's circles.[10]

The result is that Chávez is now, by any measure, the most powerful figure in Latin America. In a huge majority of the thirty-seven Latin American capitals, Chávez and Venezuela are the major foreign players in town, while the U.S. role continues to shrink. Chávez's transparent military alliance against the United States now includes Venezuela, Cuba, Bolivia, Nicaragua, and Dominica, with Ecuador close to joining. The Monroe Doctrine passed away without a funeral.[11]

Electioneering

Chávez is a powerful and effective campaigner at home, but some of his most impressive electoral victories have been scored abroad. Since taking office, he has insinuated himself into all the major presidential campaigns in Latin America—overtly by campaigning for those who support his anti-U.S. message, covertly by providing the cash to help friendly candidates win.

In the most celebrated case, a suitcase with $800,000 allegedly intended for Cristina Fernández de Kirchner, wife of a former president of Argentina and now that country's current president, was carted to Buenos Aires by alleged Chávez bagmen on a PDVSA plane in August 2007. Chávez denied any involvement. U.S. officials filed a criminal complaint in Miami, alleging that the men involved met in Florida to hush up details of the plot. Both the Venezuelan and the Argentine governments immediately complained that the Miami court case was fabricated by the U.S. government to embarrass their countries. The trial in that case is ongoing.

Rarely is evidence so direct ever found, however. While Chávez's money is difficult to trace, there is credible reporting that, since 2005, his cash has found its way into elections in Bolivia, Brazil, Costa Rica, Mexico, Peru, Ecuador, Nicaragua, and Argentina.[12] Chávez-backed candidates won in five of those elections: all except Costa Rica, Mexico, and Peru. Even there, his protégés lost by 1 percent, 1 percent, and 4 percent, respectively.

The amount of "walking around money" Chávez spends on elections (whatever the precise figure) pales in comparison to the more official help he eagerly commits to help favored candidates. This takes many forms: debt purchases, sweetheart deals, direct foreign aid, and various special projects. All of it has one purpose: to help Chávez's friends and punish his enemies—especially if those enemies happen to be friends of the United States.

Chávez's closest ally in the region (after Castro) is Evo Morales, the president of Bolivia, whom Chávez helped elect in 2005.[13] Morales—the first indigenous head of state since the Spanish conquest—ran a campaign against American-sponsored efforts to reduce coca leaf production. Bolivia, along with Peru, is the region's major producer of the leaf, which Colombian drug cartels process into cocaine (that Venezuelan smugglers then transport to the United States, with Chávez's tacit approval). Like his Andean ancestors, Morales chews the leaf, and he once convinced Chávez to try it on live television. Thereafter, Hugo became an energetic promoter of coca leaf agriculture for Latin America, and found another reason to attack the American government.

During Morales's first year in office, 2006, Chávez contributed a whopping $1 billion in aid to Bolivia (equivalent to 12 percent of the country's GDP). He also provided access to one of Venezuela's presidential jets, sent a forty-soldier personal security guard to accompany Morales at all times, subsidized the pay of Bolivia's military, and paid to send thousands of Cuban doctors to Bolivia's barrio health clinics. In return, Morales has opened up access to Bolivia's natural gas reserves to development by Chávez's PDVSA, nationalized the entire sector, and all but kicked out private sector multinational energy companies. He has even submitted Bolivia's application to join OPEC, in order to give Chávez another reliable ally—and vote—in that organization.

Chávez has assiduously sought to bring Bolivia into his new Latin American Bolivarian alliance. He has taken up Bolivian diplomatic causes as his own, notably Bolivia's century-old demand to reclaim the seacoast town of Arica—taken during a war in the nineteenth century—from Chile. He offered to sign a treaty pledging to help Bolivia resist a U.S. invasion and an assassination attempt on Morales, which Chávez—providing no evidence—insists the United States is planning.[14]

And he has brought Morales into the charmed circle of those granted audiences with Fidel. Morales, Chávez, and Castro have met openly a handful of times since 2006 to coordinate strategy,[15] denounce the United States for imperialism and colonialism, and to oppose the U.S.-backed Free Trade Area of the Americas in favor of Chávez's Bolivarian Alternative for the Americas (ALBA). Together, the three countries have even signed a mutual defense pact against any potential aggression by the United States.

Bolivia's opposition, led by former President Jorge "Tuto" Quiroga, has charged that Chávez has been interfering in the internal affairs of Bolivia since 2000. In April 2008, Quiroga appealed to the Roman Catholic Church, the governments of Brazil, Argentina, and the OAS to intervene.[16] Chávez, responding for himself and Morales, claims that Quiroga is a handpicked puppet of the United States.

After his political success in Bolivia, Chávez has aggressively supported every anti-American presidential candidate in the region. U.S. policymakers console themselves by claiming that Chávez's favorites have mostly been defeated by pro-American centrists. The truth is more complex. Chávez came close to winning every one of those contests, and lost only when he overplayed his hand. More troubling, U.S. influence and prestige in Latin America is at perhaps its lowest ebb ever; today, being considered America's ally is the political kiss of death.[17]

In Brazil, the socialist Lula da Silva was reelected easily, with a happy Chávez visiting him several times to announce joint oil deals or just appear with the candidate laughing it up on television. Chávez subsequently tried to leverage his close relationship with Lula to force the Brazilian Senate to approve Venezuela's membership in the trading bloc MERCOSUR, but the Senate has not yet given in.[18]

Similarly, in Ecuador, Chávez's candidate Rafael Correa was elected easily on an anti-American platform. President Correa promptly sold

$300 million of Ecuador's debt to Chávez, and went on to sign oil refinery deals that provide his country with hundreds of millions more in revenues. Correa has also expelled American oil companies from Ecuador, canceled the U.S. government's lease on a major drug interdiction airport center,[19] and sided with Chávez and against the United States on virtually every issue that comes up in the UN or OAS. Ecuador is rejoining OPEC at Chávez's suggestion.[20] Castro's doctors are also working in Ecuador's barrios—paid for by Chávez.[21]

In Nicaragua, Chávez traveled to visit his comrade-in-arms, former President—and longtime socialist and Castro ally—Daniel Ortega. Chávez donated millions of Venezuela's oil dollars to Sandinista (Ortega's political party) mayors throughout the country, and promised much more if the former president were to regain office. Upon Ortega's election, Chávez sent hundreds of millions of dollars to shore up Nicaragua's oil infrastructure and ports, as well as other, smaller outright gifts.[22] Ortega, long a foe of the United States, also eagerly joined Chávez's budding anti-American alliance.

In Argentina, Chávez provided an estimated $9 billion in bond purchases, aid, and subsidies to President Néstor Kirchner, and also purchased $5 billion of Argentina's old debt, allowing that troubled country to escape from the discipline of borrowing from the IMF. Beyond the notorious $800,000 suitcase, Chávez's aid to Kirchner allowed him to spend freely on the campaign of his wife to succeed him, and she was easily elected in 2007. Chávez has also shown himself willing to go the extra mile for his friends: one of the aims for his bus oil deal with London was to gain political support in the UK for returning the Falkland Islands to Argentina.[23]

Most of Chávez's failures are better described as near misses than outright repudiations. In Mexico, Chávez's candidate Andrés Manuel López Obrador unexpectedly lost by less than 1 percent to the pro-NAFTA, pro-American centrist Felipe Calderón. Calderón made headway against his opponent by effectively running against Chávez as well as his true opponent. Calderón's television ads alleged that Chávez had too much power in the region and accused the Venezuelan president of trying to buy the election. On the defensive, López Obrador found it necessary to repeat the phrase, "I'm not Chávez."[24]

In Costa Rica, what was supposed to be a walk in the park for former president and Nobel Prize winner Oscar Arias,[25] a socialist, turned into a nail-biting win by a few thousand votes when Chávez's candidate, Otton Solis, ran an anti-U.S. trade campaign that tied Arias to Bush, while Arias did not tie Solis to Chávez.[26] In four months, a 56 percent to 14 percent lead by Arias wound up in a tie at 41 percent, which demonstrated the power of his anti-American message (Costa Rica possesses the most successfully developed economy and democracy in Central America).[27]

In Peru, Chávez's actions have been more sinister. His candidate Ollanta Humala lost by only 4 percent to the socialist and former president, Alan García, whom Chávez deems insufficiently socialist and too pro-American. Chávez has not given up. Since the election, the Peruvian government has investigated three hundred pro-Chávez safe houses in Peru allegedly set up to foment violence, protests, and unrest. National polls in 2008 show that 73 percent of Peruvians think Chávez supports the FARC while 51 percent think he is interfering in Peru's politics on behalf of, and in concert with, Humala.[28]

Yet, bad as this is, it pales in comparison with what Chávez aids and abets in Colombia.

Proxy Warrior:
Chávez and the FARC

In the early hours of March 1, 2008, the Colombian army launched a missile attack about a mile into neighboring Ecuador that destroyed a secret encampment of the FARC, Colombia's dreaded narcoguerrillas. Killed in the raid was the guerrillas' second in command, chief strategist, and mouthpiece, Raúl Reyes. Reyes's computer was seized and the machine yielded 37,000 files, documents whose contents are still reverberating throughout the hemisphere. Colombian intelligence officials later divulged that they had been able to establish Reyes's coordinates because of a February 27 phone call between the guerrilla leader and the man who would soon be exposed as his chief patron: Venezuelan president Hugo Chávez.[29]

While Chávez—as ever—denies everything, documents seized by the Colombian government in the March 1, 2008, raid show that he has spent what is likely more than $300 million since 1999 supporting the FARC.

But more important, the evidence has shown conclusively that Chávez harbors sweeping ambitions for his alliance with the FARC. As *Washington Post* columnist Jackson Diehl explained it, Chávez created

> a breathtakingly ambitious "strategic plan" . . . with the initial goal of gaining international recognition for a movement designated a terrorist organization by both the United States and Europe. Chávez then intended to force Colombian President Álvaro Uribe to negotiate a political settlement with the FARC, and to promote a candidate allied with Chávez and the FARC to take power from Uribe. All this is laid out in a series of three e-mails sent in February [2008] to the FARC's top leaders by Iván Márquez and Rodrigo Granda, envoys who held a series of secret meetings with Chávez . . . [and who] outlined a five-stage plan for undermining Uribe's government, beginning with the release of several of the scores of hostages the FARC is holding.[30]

"The [FARC] email," Diehl continues, "dated Feb. 8, discusses the money: It says that Chávez, whom they call 'angel,' 'has the first 50 [million] available and has a plan to get us the remaining 200 in the course of the year . . . through the black market in order to avoid problems.'" It would thus appear that Chávez is giving as much money and military support to the FARC as the U.S. is giving to Colombia to fight its war against cocaine.[31]

In truth, many of these allegations had been circulating for years. As the president of the watchdog Human Rights Foundation, Thor Halvorssen, wrote in the *Washington Times*:

> The documentable ties between Venezuela and the FARC date back to August of 1999—just months into the Chavez presidency. Leaked letters signed by Ramon Rodriguez, a Chavez aide, revealed that the government had offered fuel, money and other support to the FARC. Mr. Chavez also ordered another henchman, Ignacio Arcaya (who later became ambassador in Washington), to give cash gifts to the FARC. Messrs. Arcaya, Rodriguez and Chavez denied the allegations despite eyewitnesses to the conversations.
>
> More evidence surfaced over the years tying Mr. Chavez and his government to the FARC. In one instance, the Colombian army seized hundreds of Venezuelan rifles in the hands of the FARC. Nothing came of it. On another occasion, Mr. Chavez included a FARC terrorist as a personal bodyguard on a state visit to Colombia. Despite photos and a local outcry in Colombia, the

rest of the world blithely ignored the incident. Meanwhile, FARC leaders were routinely welcomed in Venezuela and treated as heads of state. Prominent leader Olga Marin, for example, spoke on the floor of Venezuela's National Assembly, praising Mr. Chavez as a hero of the rebel movement.

Things got more complicated for the Venezuelan government when, on December 14, 2004, Ricardo Granda, widely known as the FARC's "foreign secretary," was arrested on the Colombian border. One of the most senior, well-connected and highly skilled political strategists in the FARC's history, Granda had been living in Venezuela's capital enjoying Venezuelan citizenship and even participating in a government-sponsored networking conference attended by Mr. Chavez. The capture of Granda had consequences: the military officer in charge of Venezuela's anti-terrorism unit, Humberto Quintero, was arrested, horrifically tortured and now sits in a maximum security prison for the charge of treason. Still, Venezuela kept denying its support of the FARC.[32]

The evidence brought to light has, at this writing, prompted a movement in the U.S. Congress to designate Venezuela a state supporter of terrorism—which, if officially enacted, would make Venezuela the hemisphere's second country to be so designated (Cuba made the list in 1982).[33] Chávez does not take the threat lightly. In response, he had his ambassador to the United States, Bernardo Álvarez, warn darkly of "very grave economic consequences. . . . Just think about the $10.2 billion lost in U.S. exports to Venezuela, 230,000 manufacturing jobs tied to exports and 1.58 million barrels of oil a day from Venezuela."[34]

WHAT IS THE FARC?

The Revolutionary Armed Forces of Colombia (Fuerzas Armadas Revolucionario de Colombia, or FARC) is one of the oldest and largest guerrilla movements in Latin America. It traces its origins back to the peasant self-defense groups organized with help from Moscow in the 1940s; but its modern form was launched in the 1960s as the military wing of the Colombian Communist Party, with the aim of fomenting a revolution in Colombia.

Hopes of revolution died out with the establishment of the National Front government—a collation of liberals and conservatives that put an end to La Violencia, a roughly ten-year period of partisan violence.[35] The FARC refused to give up, however, and was relegated by its own request to a demilitarized zone, a Switzerland-sized swathe of mountains, jungle, and grasslands on the fringes of the Amazon basin. To this day, the FARC controls much of the Colombian interior.[36]

As Colombia's urban economy progressed during the 1970s and 1980s, the FARC remained stuck in feudal poverty. Moscow abandoned the group, and its outdated social agenda, but the FARC pushed on as a guerrilla force, locked in the worldview of Fidel, Che, and the radical 1960s.

In the 1980s, the FARC tried its hand at the ballot in an attempt to remain relevant, but won only a discouraging 4.5 percent of the vote in the 1986 presidential election. Frustrated, the group, under its leader Manuel "Sureshot" Marulanda, began rearming and returned to the jungle with the intention of taking power by force.[37]

It also found a new revenue stream to replace Moscow's withdrawn largesse. In the 1990s, spurning the central government's peace talk overtures, "the FARC got into the drug business in a big way, as well as extortion and kidnapping," as Michael Reid records in his book *Forgotten Continent*. "By 2001, the best estimates were that it was making $250 million to $300 million a year from drugs," transforming the former revolutionary army into an organized crime syndicate—but one with as many as 20,000 armed soldiers, all up to their elbows in plunder and cocaine.[38]

Since turning unabashedly criminal, the FARC has imported arms, exported drugs, recruited minors, kidnapped thousands for ransom, executed hostages, hijacked airplanes, planted land mines, operated an extortion and protection racket in peasant communities, committed atrocities against innocent civilians, and massacred farmers as traitors.[39] Although most of the estimated 100,000[40] victims of these atrocities are Colombians, in March 1999 three U.S. activists working for indigenous rights in Colombia were killed by the FARC—whose operatives assumed them to be CIA agents. In 2003, the FARC captured three Americans when their plane went down in the jungle. President Bush has called these three, who later were rescued by Colombian government forces, "the longest held American hostages anywhere in the world."[41]

A long-held ambition of the FARC's leadership is to have the group officially recognized as a belligerent force, a legitimate army in rebellion. Such a designation—conferred by individual nations and under international law—would give the FARC rights normally accorded only to sovereign powers.

But two events scuttled that dream, at least for the foreseeable future. First, three Provisional Irish Republican Army bomb experts were arrested in Colombia in the summer of 2001 and later prosecuted for training FARC guerrillas in bombmaking. Since their arrival in the country was followed by a dramatic increase in fatal bombings in Colombia, the FARC's reputation plummeted.[42]

Second, the group's long history of criminality and terror—mostly ignored by other nations—finally caught up with it after the September 11 terrorist attacks on the United States. The FARC was quickly declared a terrorist organization by the United Nations, the European Union, and the United States.[43] Hugo Chávez's was a lone voice of protest; he insisted—as he continues to insist—that the FARC be granted belligerent status.

THE COLOMBIA-U.S. ALLIANCE

If the FARC's unreconstructed Castro-Guevara ideology, frozen in amber from the 1960s, were not enough to attract Hugo Chávez to their cause, in the 1990s the Colombian government gave him another reason.

The FARC's campaign of terror took its toll on Colombia. When the country began to collapse from the violence and chaos, many believed that Colombia was on the verge of becoming a failed state. In 1998, Colombians elected a new government determined to do something about this. Andrés Pastrana, a former TV news anchor turned conservative politician, came to power in Colombia at the same time that Chávez took over in Venezuela.

Pastrana turned Colombia around with two bold and seemingly contradictory moves: first, he opened peace talks with the FARC; second, he forged a strategic alliance with the United States.[44]

Allying with the United States was a courageous move for Pastrana. Throughout the 1990s, Latin American nations—and Latin American people—increasingly turned away from the U.S. political and economic model, and America's influence in the region waned.

While Colombia's peace talks with the FARC went nowhere—the guerrillas were committed to war, not peace—U.S. aid would prove to be decisive in shoring up the Colombian government. "Plan Colombia," begun under President Clinton in 1999 and continuing to 2008 under the Bush administration, has provided Colombia with some $6 billion in aid—mostly for military helicopters, equipment, and training. Intended to squeeze the

FARC's finances by fighting drugs on the ground, it has largely succeeded. By 2002, Pastrana had restored order to urban Colombia, reduced the business of the drug cartels (and thus the FARC and paramilitary forces), and reoccupied much of the demilitarized zone.[45]

Pastrana was succeeded by Álvaro Uribe Vélez, a liberal governor from the Medellín area whose father had been kidnapped and murdered by the FARC. Uribe, a calm and soft-spoken attorney, set out methodically to finish what Pastrana had begun. If Pastrana was the FARC's headache, Uribe was its brain tumor. Uribe was in the fight to win it by a knockout.

With the United States solidly behind him, Uribe added 60,000 skilled troops, 20,000 peasant soldiers, and 20,000 policemen to Colombia's modernizing forces; occupied most of the key passageways and rural posts the FARC needed for its criminal businesses; and created mobile forces to conduct rapid surprise sorties that keep the FARC off balance.[46] As a result of Uribe's success, the FARC was driven deeper into the jungles of Colombia and also across the borders of Venezuela and Ecuador to safe havens, and its forces were depleted to 12,000 or fewer by 2006. Some estimates put the numbers down to 6,000 in 2008.[47]

Uribe also unleashed a massive U.S.-backed program to spray coca fields, reducing them by half, which hurt the FARC's cocaine business bottom line; the murder rate was cut in half and the kidnapping rate to one quarter, further reducing the FARC's income and military options.[48] In 2006, Uribe was easily reelected with 62 percent of the vote, whereupon he resolved to finish off the FARC.

But by this time, the FARC could boast of a powerful ally: Hugo Chávez's Venezuela. When, in 2008, Uribe attacked a FARC safe haven across the border in Ecuador, Chávez leapt to defend the FARC and threaten war with Colombia.[49] To Chávez, any friend of the United States is his enemy, and any enemy of a friend of the United States is his friend—even a terrorist organization working to destabilize one of his country's most important neighbors.

CHÁVEZ'S DOUBLE LIFE WITH THE FARC
Hugo Chávez's relationship with the FARC is at once long-standing and well hidden. Early in his presidency, in 1999, Chávez declared himself "neutral"[50] in Colombia's war against the FARC, and thereafter he many times denied any military, political, and criminal collaboration with the FARC

terrorists in their struggle to take power by force in Colombia. But the 37,000 files from the laptop computer of Raúl Reyes, the FARC's number two leader, found after the March 2008 raid, tell a different story.

When Colombian helicopter gunships pounced on the scene and, within minutes, grabbed Reyes's laptop computer, they handed over the entire contents to the government of Colombia and the Organization of American States, which asked Interpol to analyze them for authenticity.[51]

A trove of incriminating data was stored on the hard drive. The Reyes computer provides evidence corroborating what intelligence agencies and newspapers have been suspecting or alleging for many years about Chávez, the FARC, terrorism, kidnapping, and cocaine.[52] Dozens of the files were released by Colombia to the press and splashed across TV screens all around the world.

The relationship began more than a decade and a half ago, in the wake of Chávez's failed coup. In 1992, the FARC gave a jailed Chávez $150,000,[53] money that Chávez would use as seed funding for the political movement that launched him to the presidency.

As president, Chávez has returned the favor, sending millions of dollars to the FARC. The most recent alleged promise—in February 2008—totaled a staggering $300 million.[54] "This implies more than a cozying up, but an armed alliance between the FARC and the Venezuelan government," Colombia's police chief, General Oscar Naranjo, told the *New York Times*.[55] In fact, such payments are a violation of UN Security Council Resolution 1373, passed in the wake of 9/11, which forbids state-sponsored terrorism. Payoffs to terrorists also violate the OAS charter, of which Venezuela is an original signatory.[56]

According to intelligence compiled by analyst Ken Rijock of World check.com, Chávez offered the FARC an "oil allotment to sell outside the country, which would give us a juicy profit," or the option of "selling oil inside Venezuela," as two senior FARC commanders reported to its secretariat on February 8, 2008.[57]

The Reyes files show that Chávez also secured for the FARC $250 million to purchase weapons.[58] Whether he has given the FARC some of the 100,000 Kalashnikov assault rifles purchased from Russia in 2004 or the old military weapons those AK-47s replaced, or whether he has given the FARC the Iranian antitank or antihelicopter missiles he purchased since 2004, remains to be seen, and may become clear when all Reyes files are finally released and analyzed, a task that could take years.[59]

Closer to home, Chávez has provided military-protected safe havens for the FARC in Venezuela, housed FARC members who kidnapped hostages in Venezuela, given FARC leaders diplomatic passports and immunity, registered FARC guerrillas as citizens of Venezuela, provided wounded guerrillas with hospital and health services, provided the FARC with food and quarters, and made himself available to FARC leaders, including their head, Manuel Marulanda.[60] Most of this was known before the Reyes computer was found; the documents on the machine have corroborated all of it.[61]

Reyes's computer also amply corroborates Chávez's, and the FARC's, relationships with Hezbollah, Hamas, al-Qaeda, ETA, and the Iranian Revolutionary Guard Corps (all of which is detailed in subsequent chapters).[62] Indeed, the computer files contain "smoking gun" evidence proving the solid connections between Chávez, the FARC, and terrorists responsible for attacks in the United States, Spain, Britain, and the Middle East.[63]

THE DRUG CONNECTION
But perhaps the most sinister aspect to Chávez's relationship with the FARC is the help he has provided to maximize its cocaine sales to the United States and Europe. British journalist John Carlin, who writes for the *Guardian*, a newspaper generally supportive of Chávez, secured interviews with several of the 2,400 FARC guerrillas who deserted the group in 2007.[64] One of his subjects told him that "the guerrillas have a non-aggression pact with the Venezuelan military. The Venezuelan government lets FARC operate freely because they share the same left-wing, Bolivarian ideals, and because FARC bribes their people."[65]

Without cocaine revenues, the FARC would disappear, its former members assert. "If it were not for cocaine, the fuel that feeds the Colombian war, FARC would long ago have disbanded," Carlin noted; "yet it looks capable of surviving indefinitely as an armed force as a result of the income from its kidnapping, extortion and cocaine interests."[66]

The amount of cocaine going through Venezuela has skyrocketed under Chávez's rule. According to a London-based independent consultancy, the International Crisis Group, "Sources estimate that between 220 and 300 tons [of cocaine]—one third to close to one half of Colombia's estimated annual production—pass through [Venezuela] annually."[67] In 2004, the U.S. Drug Enforcement Administration (DEA) estimated that fifty tons of Colombian cocaine transited Venezuela[68]—so there has been a huge increase in cocaine transiting Venezuela since Chávez suspended the bilateral antidrug cooperation agreement with the United States that kicked the DEA out of Venezuela for spying.[69]

The U.S. government maintains that Venezuela's security services are riddled with corruption and extensively involved in the transshipment of Colombian cocaine. According to the State Department's most recent *International Narcotics Control Strategy Report,* "A permissive and corrupt environment in Venezuela, coupled with counternarcotics successes in Colombia, has made Venezuela one of the preferred routes for trafficking illicit narcotics out of Colombia. While the majority of narcotics transiting Venezuela continue to be destined for the U.S., a rapidly increasing percentage has started to flow towards western Africa and onwards to Europe."[70]

In 2005, Chávez dropped out of the Joint Interagency Task Force East, whose radars monitor flights and ships in the Caribbean and along the South American coast. Not content to detach himself, Chávez even refuses to receive the task force's intelligence reports.[71] The International Crisis Group concludes that his noncompliance with antidrug programs in the region derives from "Chavez's outspoken support for the FARC, an important part of whose financing comes from drug trafficking."[72]

Chávez's government also facilitates cocaine production in Colombia by delivering the oil used in its production. The International Crisis Group reports that "While official figures on seizures of chemical precursors are virtually non-existent [in Venezuela], they along with Venezuelan petrol are smuggled to Colombia in large operations. The petrol is used as an indispensable cocaine precursor and is not being controlled by the counterdrug authorities in Venezuela."[73]

The "tactical convergence between the FARC and the Venezuelan armed ¹rces" has forged a militarily protected cocaine business in Venezuela, ac-
·rding to the FARC guerrillas interviewed by Carlin for the *Guardian.*
·se sources also described "making bombs alongside elements of
·ez's militias," learning "how to detonate bombs in a controlled fash-
·ing mobile phones," and training to "put together different types
·mines."[74] Materials—including C4 explosives, grenades, rifles, and

bullets—were provided by Venezuela's military, sometimes right in Fuerte Tiuna, the Venezuelan equivalent of the Pentagon.

"A European diplomat who is well informed about the drug-trafficking business generally, and who is familiar with Rafael's[75] allegations," the *Guardian* reported, "made a comparison between the activities of the FARC in Venezuela and hypothetically similar activities involving ETA[76] in Spain: 'Imagine [the diplomat said] if ETA had a bombmaking school in Portugal inside camps protected by the Portuguese police, and that they planned to set off these bombs in Madrid; imagine that the Portuguese authorities furnished ETA with weapons in exchange for money obtained from the sales of drugs, in which the Portuguese authorities were also involved up to their necks: it would be a scandal of enormous proportions. Well, that, on a very big scale, is what the Venezuelan government is allowing to happen right now.' "[77]

The Chávez Hostage TV Show

In late 2007, Chávez put his master plan for subverting Colombia into high gear. Masquerading as a disinterested observer, he volunteered himself as a mediator to bridge the gap between Colombia's president Uribe and FARC's leader Marulanda, to make peace. Reminding everyone that Colombia and Venezuela were one country under Bolívar, Chávez claimed he was in a unique position to help negotiate the freedom of some of the estimated eight hundred hostages sequestered by the FARC, who included at least sixty-eight Venezuelans.[78] He said he had no agenda but to secure the hostages and to forge a peace agreement between the FARC and his "brother country," Colombia.[79]

Repeatedly, Chávez presented himself as a man of peace—his supporters lost no opportunity to remind everyone that Chávez had been nominated for the Nobel Peace Prize.[80] President Uribe cautiously accepted Chávez's offer, which was roundly endorsed by the United States, France, Britain, the European Union, Mexico, and the OAS, and praised by the international news media.

Chávez turned his hostage negotiations into a grand TV soap opera that ran for more than a month worldwide.[81] Almost daily, he made long, emotional, televised appeals to the FARC to heed his humanitarian call and release some political hostages as a show of good faith.[82] He asked

"Sureshot" Marulanda to contact him, to sit down with him, and to work sincerely for peace.[83] He said he would go anywhere, any time, to free the hostages and to forge peace in Colombia.[84] He talked to the families of the hostages and televised their desperate appeals to have their loved ones sent home.[85]

Often the showman, Chávez decided to take a helicopter into the danger zone. He invited the presidents of Argentina and Bolivia to join him on the ride. And to record the event for posterity, he was also joined by the Hollywood director Oliver Stone, who allowed that he was struck by Chávez's "courage," and proclaimed that "the FARC is heroic."[86]

During all this hype, the world got behind Chávez. The families of the well-known political hostages were elated, if not the families of the more than 750 lesser-known hostages held for big ransoms. Chávez was praised as he had rarely been praised; some considered him a genuine hero.[87] In the face of this publicity onslaught, Uribe had little choice but to support Chávez, though he did so cautiously, always emphasizing the need to see results.[88] President Bush and Secretary of State Condoleezza Rice even complimented Chávez and asked for his help in releasing the three American hostages taken in 2005.[89]

President Nicolas Sarkozy of France went further. As the French media ate up the human interest story, Sarkozy phoned regularly to get updates on Chávez's "valiant" efforts to save the most celebrated victim, Ingrid Betancourt, a Colombian politician who also has French nationality, and who was reported to be frail and dying after six years of being chained to a tree.[90] The world's heart went out to Betancourt, and to Chávez for trying to save her.[91]

What Chávez did not mention was that he had personally scripted the hostage TV soap opera with top FARC leaders, who were promised $500 million to play their parts.[92] The script called for Chávez to emerge as the peacemaking hero by saving a few well-known hostages offered up by the FARC. Uribe, by contrast, was intended to come out looking the goat for not trusting a peace-loving Chávez.

Then Chávez would become the official peacemaker in Colombia and move the international community to drop the "terrorist" designation against the FARC, which would be recognized under the Geneva Conventions as a legitimate belligerent at war.[93] Finally, under that cover, Chávez and the FARC would knock Uribe from power.

But as happens in TV shows, actors can botch their lines or speak out of turn. When it emerged that one of the first three U.S. hostages to be released was not only *not* in FARC custody but was in Bogotá being cared for by the government of Colombia, Chávez was surprised and embarrassed.[94]

Worse, when the other two hostages were released on January 10, 2008, Venezuela's minister of interior Ramón Rodríguez Chacín—on hand to oversee the occasion on Chávez's behalf—told the FARC that "President Chávez wishes that you know we pay great attention to your struggle. Keep up your fighting spirit and your force. You can count on us."[95] Suddenly, admirers of Chávez wondered why his government was publicly identifying with the kidnappers and not the victimized hostages.

Not to be upstaged, Chávez echoed his minister's impolitic comments on the same day. The "FARC are not terrorists but armies with a legitimate political posture," he maintained, and went on to say that the FARC possessed "a Bolivarian project that is respected here." Finally, he ended with a bombshell request: "I ask the European Union that their [FARC's] label of 'terrorists' be erased."[96]

Within hours, the European Union had rejected Chávez's request out of hand, agreeing with Uribe, who told the *Washington Post,* "The violent groups of Colombia are terrorists because they kidnap, place bombs indiscriminately, recruit and murder children, murder pregnant women, murder the elderly and use antipersonnel mines that leave in their wake thousands of innocent victims." The *Post* article corroborated Uribe's statement, noting, "These assertions [by Uribe] have been well documented by Western human rights groups that are otherwise hostile to Mr. Uribe's government."[97]

Uribe disavowed any further support for Chávez's role as a negotiator in the Colombia hostage crisis.[98] Undeterred, with Oliver Stone in tow to record history in the making, Chávez made the helicopter trip to meet the FARC leaders in the Colombian jungle. But the insurgents didn't show up. Chávez blamed Uribe and the United States for scuttling the deal.[99]

Two weeks later, Chávez and the FARC managed to produce three more hostages, but it was obvious by late February that Chávez's public relations momentum had been squandered. Public opinion crystallized against him rapidly, while polls in both Colombia and Venezuela showed his credibility crumbling.[100] In Colombia, a march of several hundred thousand people against Chávez and the FARC was organized in just a few weeks after a Facebook group called "A million voices against the FARC" signed up 261,236 virtual members nearly overnight.[101]

Sensing that circumstances had turned decisively in his favor, Uribe ordered the air strike against the FARC's Raúl Reyes that turned up Reyes's incriminating computer files.

Manufactured Outrage

To divert attention from the Reyes findings, Chávez angrily denounced the attack against the FARC in Ecuador as if it had been an invasion of Venezuela, though Venezuela's border with Colombia is some seven hundred miles away! He ranted on Venezuelan TV for hours, ordered ten tank battalions to the Colombia border as if an invasion were imminent, expelled Colombia's ambassador, ridiculed Uribe as a U.S. puppet, and threatened to block Colombia-Venezuela trade.[102] The saber rattling reached a high pitch when Chávez pledged to "send the Sukhois"—Chávez's new Russian jet fighters—"to Uribe."[103] WAR! read the Venezuela headlines.[104]

Presidents Rafael Correa of Ecuador, Evo Morales of Bolivia, and Daniel Ortega of Nicaragua—all of whom would soon be implicated by the Reyes files as FARC collaborators[105]—chimed in. Internationally, only the United States defended (in muted statements) Colombia's right to conduct search-and-destroy antiterrorist missions across a border.

Some cooler heads in Caracas, however, saw the crisis for what it was. "If anyone has to protest, it is Ecuador's government, as the military incident took place in Ecuadorean territory, not ours," the Venezuelan opposition leader Teodoro Petkoff noted in his newspaper, *Tal Cual.* "Venezuela has nothing to complain about."[106] Petkoff was right, but he didn't know what Chávez knew: that the FARC was secretly all over Venezuela. At all costs, Chávez had to keep Uribe not so much out of Ecuador as out of Venezuela.

By Friday, March 6, tensions had climbed so high that the OAS—hitherto silent—felt compelled to intervene. An emergency meeting was convened in the Dominican Republic to make peace between the would-be belligerents. The meeting was, on those terms, a success: Chávez recalled his tanks from the border and cooled his rhetoric toward Uribe, who for his part deftly apologized to Ecuador. But, most important for Chávez, the computer files of Raúl Reyes were not mentioned at all. The conspiracy of silence about the FARC continued.

There were many unspoken reasons why Chávez sought peace only a few days after threatening war with Colombia. First, Colombia would likely win decisively in any confrontation: Colombia's military is bigger, better equipped, and more experienced than Venezuela's. Colombia's 263,000 troops are organized into mobile strike forces trained by the United States and aided by technology such as that used to kill Raúl Reyes.[107] Venezuela's 100,000 troops are not well organized, trained, or tested on their mix of new weapons from Russia, Iran, China, and Spain.

Venezuela is also dependent on Colombian imports, especially food. Venezuela's food supplies are always teetering on the edge of empty, thanks to Chávez's command economy policies. Without Colombian imports, Venezuela would be starved in weeks.

And third, Chávez realized that Uribe may be wiping out the FARC. On the very day of the meeting, it was reported that Manuel Jesús Muñoz became the fifth FARC secretariat member to be killed in 2008. It would be unwise for Chávez to provoke a winning army—especially when so many of the men that army is looking for are being harbored and aided by Chávez himself.

Chávez: "I was framed"

To most Latin American leaders, the facts were impossible to ignore or deny any longer. "Chávez is putting money in the FARC," former Mexican president Vicente Fox concluded. But the dozens of Latin American leaders beholden to Chávez held their breaths, waiting for word from their leader.[108]

He did not disappoint. "The Reyes computer is a fraud," Chávez said boldly in a long TV rant, during which he asked for a moment of silence in solemn remembrance of "our revolutionary brother" Raúl Reyes.[109]

"The maneuver with the computer is a wicked, last-resort action of a decadent government, the government of George W. Bush, to make up a file against our country," Venezuela's minister for foreign affairs Nicolás Maduro said, echoing his boss. In fact, Maduro insisted, "We do not acknowledge as true the alleged existence of those documents"—which had, in fact, been delivered to him the week before.[110]

In France, as concern grew that Ingrid Betancourt would die in captivity and that Chávez's efforts to save her were backfiring, President Sarkozy announced a humanitarian mission headed by the Red Cross to rescue her. The FARC's Rodrigo Granda discouraged the mission as "inadmissible" and Sarkozy as "naïve" to go into the FARC's "dangerous" territory.[111] Never to be upstaged, "Chavez expressed a desire to help," the *Oakland Tribune* reported, "but he said the United States and Colombia should first stop trying to catch Ivan Marquez, who is a member of the FARC's secretariat"[112] and the man responsible for kidnapping Betancourt. Hence, Chávez's new proposal to Colombia amounted to this: you stop trying to catch the kidnapper, and only then will I help you rescue the hostage.

This unusual request was prompted by the fact that Márquez was one of the FARC leaders who had helped Chávez design the botched strategy against Uribe in the first place.[113] Apparently showing more concern for the kidnappers than their victims, Chávez told the Oakland paper, "We have information which indicates that agents from governments of Colombia and the United States are hunting Ivan Marquez . . . [using] very advanced technology . . . they have satellites and so on."[114] When Betancourt and the three U.S. hostages were freed in a surprise rescue, a shocked and chagrined Chávez said publicly, "We are overjoyed at the liberation of those people."[115]

That is the spin-doctor at work. As we have seen, Chávez's antics in Colombia—indeed, his interference throughout the region—cannot bear scrutiny. Whenever the spotlight shines on his transgressions—from arming terrorists to aiding drug trafficking to buying foreign elections with bags of cash—Chávez first denies everything, then quickly goes mum, hoping the scrutiny will pass.

But America can no longer afford to look the other way.

6

The Real Axis
of Evil

When President Bush, in his 2002 State of the Union speech, described Iran, Iraq, and North Korea as an "axis of evil," the response was a mixture of ridicule, disbelief, and derision. And his critics had a point. The Axis powers of World War II acted in concert through a formal alliance; the three nations in Bush's "axis of evil" have little, if anything, to do with one another. Indeed, two of them—Iran and Iraq—are historic enemies that in the 1980s fought one of the twentieth century's bloodiest wars.

Yet right under America's nose, a genuine axis of evil has been forming: a working alliance between two nations united by their hatred of the United States and determined to act on it. Those two nations are Venezuela and Iran, and they have adapted Bush's terminology as a badge of honor, calling themselves the "axis of unity."[1]

Historically, the nations of Latin America have not looked too far abroad for friends. The United States, of course, looms large in the hemisphere. Latin America's historic ties to Spain and, to a much lesser extent, Portugal and France, have ensured ongoing close relations with those countries. And, of course, during the Cold War, Communist Cuba, and Communist movements in other nations gained significant help from the USSR.

But beyond these examples, it is rare for a Latin American nation to seek close ties with nations in other parts of the world. When the part of the world in question is the Middle East, and the nation in question is one of America's most dangerous enemies, one would think that Washington would take notice. But despite Iran and Venezuela's very public courtship, America has turned a blind eye.

It is a blind spot we can no longer afford. Iran and Venezuela are working together to drive up the price of oil in hopes of crippling the American economy and enhancing their hegemonies in the Middle East and Latin America. They are also using their windfall petro-revenues to finance a simmering war—sometimes cold, sometimes hot, sometimes covert, sometimes overt—against the United States.

Robert Bottome, the publisher of the Caracas newsletter *VenEconomy Weekly,* argues—persuasively—that the Iran-Venezuela alliance is about common enemies rather than common values. "It's all part of Chávez trying to promote himself as a leader of the Third World. Venezuela and Iran are both against the imperialists." The leader of the imperialists, in their minds, is the United States.

Courtship: Khatami

From his first days as president in 1999, Hugo Chávez was determined to forge a friendship with Iran as the first step toward enlisting a new partner in his war against America.

Chávez made his initial approach in 1999 to Iranian president Moham-med Khatami through the most logical venue: OPEC. Both nations are members, and both share an interest in seeing oil prices climb as high as possible. But more so than the other nations in the room, Chávez's Venezuela and the mullah's Iran share a deep hatred for America. That, and not oil, would prove to be the lasting foundation of their new frienship.

The relationship got off to a good start. At the very first OPEC meeting Chávez attended, he and Khatami successfully pushed the cartel to reduce oil supplies—an action which more than doubled the world price, from $12 to $28 per barrel by 2000.[2] Iran, a powerful voice within OPEC, enthusiastically supported Caracas's bid to host OPEC's Second Summit, planned for 2000. The last Caracas Conference had convened in the 1970s to declare the oil embargo against Western nations supporting Israel in the Yom Kippur War.[3] Securing this historic event was a major coup for Chávez. From day one in OPEC's halls, Iranian support helped Chávez become a major player.

To prepare for the Second Summit, Chávez embarked on a tour of ten OPEC nations—beginning with Iraq, where he became the first head of state of any nation to meet with Saddam Hussein since the 1990 Gulf War. Eager for any chance to overcome his isolation in the international community, Saddam happily met Chávez and drove him around Baghdad in a Mercedes. "He's a very good driver," Chávez deadpanned.[4] Seven years later, after Hussein's globally televised trial and execution for genocide by an Iraqi court, Chávez boiled down Saddam's story for Venezuelans on his *Aló Presidente* TV program to two sentences: "This gentleman was the president of that country. They [the U.S.] invaded the country, they captured him, and they hanged him."[5] As Chávez told Venezuelans repeatedly, Saddam's fate was also what he feared for himself.

Chávez's shuttle diplomacy paid off. His lavishly prepared September 2000 OPEC Summit was a smashing success. OPEC's curious leaders ceremoniously descended from sleek jets to be pampered and deferred to by the Venezuelan president. They were obviously stunned by the beauty of this Latin city nestled in the lush Mount Ávila region, thousands of miles distant from the political turmoil and arid climate of the Middle East. There, OPEC agreed with Chávez to unify in common cause to increase the world oil price,[6] while Chávez took this opportunity to nurture his budding strategic alliance with Iran.

Written in the guestbook at Bolívar's birthplace on September 29, 2000, by the left-handed Chávez, then in his second year in power, is the following notation: "Venezuelans will be eternally grateful to our brother

President Khatami for his friendship. The peoples of Iran and Venezuela are bound together by the new paths of history."[7]

That same day, the Iranian president, upon receiving Venezuela's highest honor, the Order of the Liberator, announced grandly, "From my brother President Chávez . . . it [the Order] is an emblem of the closeness and friendship that represents the unity between both our peoples. . . . Venezuela and Iran stand firm towards any aggression that could emerge in the two countries. . . . [Chávez is] a tireless fighter for all the right causes in the world."[8]

Khatami would visit Venezuela two more times before leaving office: during the OPEC 15 Group Summit in March 2004, when the oil price was boosted again; and in March 2005, on an official three-day visit to sign bilateral cooperation agreements solidifying the Venezuelan-Iranian partnership.[9] Chávez reciprocated with three visits to Iran himself—May 18, 2001, October 20, 2001, and November 28, 2004—all to extend and implement those political and financial agreements.[10]

By 2004, Iran and Venezuela had initiated dozens of projects involving billions of dollars in investments in both countries, centering on such diverse industries as oil, mining, agricultural machinery, marine equipment, roads, banking, shipping, cement plants, manufacturing plants, and even a bus factory. Most of the facilities were located in Venezuela, operating with Iranian technology.[11]

This unprecedented—and in many ways counterintuitive—cooperation should have set off alarm bells in Washington. Given the geographic distances and cultural differences that separate the two countries, such close ties make little practical or economic sense. The two countries share one obvious common thread: oil. Too little attention has been paid to the other: anti-Americanism. Seen in that light, these otherwise inexplicable or at least inefficient economic development deals might have a hidden purpose. Yet, at the time, only one observer noted that one such unannounced joint project might be preparations for weapons of mass destruction: Ken Rijock of the political risk consultancy World-Check.[12]

Marriage: Ahmadinejad

Chávez would find his true soul mate in 2005 with the election of Mahmoud Ahmadinejad, mayor of Tehran, to the Iranian presidency. Like

Chávez, Ahmadinejad is a populist who has galvanized the rage of Iran's poor against American imperialism, and nostalgia for the loss of Islam's historical grandeur.[13] He seeks to unify the Muslim world against American hegemony in precisely the same way as Chávez wants to unify Latin America against American hegemony. The chemistry between the two presidents is perfect, as Rowan described in a column in *El Universal* in 2006:

> Although the border between their two countries stretches halfway around the globe, the presidents of Iran and Venezuela are brothers. Both are engaged in a religious quest to reverse the forces of globalization. Both reject modern times in favor of past glory. Both are fundamentalist revolutionaries standing against the evil of the material world. Both see the US as an imperial devil threatening life on earth. Both use oil as a weapon to scare their enemies. Both are preparing for war. Both call for the extinction of their enemies with vehement threats. Both seek to become regional and perhaps world leaders of a new moral order. Both abrogate treaties with absolute righteousness. Both are driven by messianic zeal. Both feel anointed by God for their mission on earth. Both rule failing economies miserable from poverty. Both want the price of oil to skyrocket. Both are monopolists. Both are concerned about their sovereignty but not the sovereignty of others. Both defend violence as a defense against violence. Both rule over increasingly bloody countries. Both expect to be sacrificed or assassinated. Both feel victimized by the world. Both are autocrats posing as democrats. Both view the world in moral terms, where they are right and others are wrong. Both are righteously intolerant. Both run closed and controlled countries. Both are belligerent. Both can be charming, humorous and glib. Both expect the battle of Armageddon. Both assume war is inevitable to achieve peace. Both see themselves as prophets. And while many think both are insane, both think the world is insane.[14]

Chávez first began rhapsodizing about Ahmadinejad before the latter was even elected—before, indeed, Chávez had even met him. In June 2005, on the occasion of delivering the National Prize of Journalism in Caracas, he described Ahmadinejad as "a very young man committed to his people and to the struggles for sovereignty and self-determination," and went on to praise Iranian voters for showing "faith in their revolution and in their democracy." [15]

In 2006 and 2007, the two leaders would visit each other's countries five times, as Chávez became the only outspoken foreign defender of Iran's nuclear program, while Iran cleared the path for closer relations between Chávez and the nations of the Middle East and China.

NUCLEAR DIPLOMACY

One of the first specific issues around which Venezuela and Iran found common cause was Iran's budding nuclear ambitions. Chávez is attracted to Iran's anti-Americanism, and needs Iran to further his oil strategy. To buy Iranian support, he is only too eager to provide what Tehran most wants in the international arena: diplomatic cover for its quest for nuclear weapons. And Chávez has delivered.

In February 2006, Venezuela, Syria, and Cuba were the only countries on the thirty-five-member board of the UN's International Atomic Energy Agency (IAEA) to vote against reporting Iran's nuclear activity to the Security Council.[16] The IAEA had urged sanctions against Iran for not disclosing its technology or intentions to produce nuclear weapons, and the UN Security Council agreed.[17]

When Chávez visited Tehran on July 29, 2006, to counter intense international criticism of Iran's continuing nuclear program and support for Hezbollah terrorists,[18] President Ahmadinejad greeted him with an unusual welcome, saying, "In fact, President Chávez has come to his home." Chávez went right to the point, saying, "I assert that we will always stay by the Iranian nation at any time and under any circumstance. As long as we stick together, we will be able to resist and beat imperialism."[19]

Chávez was then presented with Iran's highest honor, the Higher Medal of the Islamic Republic of Iran, for "supporting Tehran in its nuclear standoff with the international community"[20] and for his strong condemnation of the February resolution by the UN's International Atomic Energy Agency.[21] Receiving the medal at a ceremony at Tehran University, Chávez condemned Israel for what he called the "terrorism" and "madness" of its 2006 attacks in Lebanon—Iran's position on the issue—and went on, "Let's save the human race, let's finish off the U.S. empire."[22]

As Ahmadinejad bestowed the medal on Chávez, he said, "Mr. Chávez is a kindred spirit, and my brother. He is a friend of the Iranian nation and the people seeking freedom around the world. He works perpetually against the dominant system [the U.S. and UN]. He is a worker of God and a servant of the people."[23] What was going on behind closed doors when these two presidents met was anybody's guess, but they were surely dancing a two-step on the world stage.

Two months later, in September 2006, Chávez reciprocated by awarding Ahmadinejad Venezuela's top medal, the *Order of the Liberator* (the same honor he had previously awarded to Khatami). At the ceremony, Chávez called his Iranian friend "a distinguished leader of a heroic people and of a sister revolution to the Venezuelan revolution: the Islamic revolution."[24] In Tehran and Caracas, this merger of revolutions by Khomeini and Bolívar did not go unnoticed, but still was ignored elsewhere.

After Ahmadinejad repeated his determination to pursue a nuclear program as Iran's sovereign right, and as the medal was bestowed on the Iranian president, Chávez said, "We support Iran's right to develop its energy with peaceful goals. It is essentially fair, honest, and logical what my brother Ahmadinejad has said."[25]

But the international pressure on Iran to fully disclose its nuclear program was becoming intense. When the UN Security Council pressured Iran to make its nuclear program transparent, a demand Ahmadinejad dismissed out of hand, his only defender was Chávez, who ridiculed "the threats against Iran and now the sanctions, unfair sanctions, no doubt, from the United Nations. Iran has the right to have its atomic energy for peaceful means as they have said."[26] But no one outside Iran could tell whether its program was for peaceful means—that was the UN's entire point.

One month later, in October 2006, Chávez delivered his infamous speech at the UN General Assembly in which he called President Bush "the devil" and pretended to smell the "sulfur of Satan" still hovering at the podium where Bush had previously spoken.[27] At the time, Chávez was campaigning for a nonpermanent seat on the Security Council, which he would lose after 45 ballots (nonetheless securing a hefty 77 of the 96 country votes he needed to win), and where his key issue was defending Iran's nuclear program and criticizing the UN's sanctions against Iran.[28] That Chávez could get so close to sitting on the UN Security Council every day did not appear to alarm U.S. officials, to the consternation of liberal democrats in Latin America.

DEEPER AND BROADER TIES

The nuclear issue is the essential link that ties Iran to Venezuela. But Chávez worked hard to broaden and deepen Iran-Venezuela relations. And he succeeded. All in all, Iran and Venezuela have signed 190 joint accords—some mundane, some sinister, but altogether worth an estimated $20 billion—since their alliance took shape.

In January 2007, Chávez welcomed Ahmadinejad to Caracas, where the Iranian president congratulated Chávez on his "landslide" reelection in December 2006, and announced a $2 billion fund to finance projects in both countries.[29] For his part, Chávez called for "an anti-imperialist military alliance against U.S. dominance. . . . The enemy is the same: the empire of the U.S. . . . Anybody who messes with one of us will have to mess with all of us, because we will respond as one."[30] By "us," Chávez made it clear that he was including Iran in his mutual defense pacts with Cuba, Bolivia, and Nicaragua.[31]

In July 2007, Chávez visited Tehran to launch a $700 million "joint petrochemical plant, strengthening the 'axis of unity' between two oil-rich nations staunchly opposed to the United States," as Reuters reported it.[32] "The two countries united will defeat the imperialism of North America," Chávez said, and added with a twinkle in his eye, "When I come to Iran, Washington gets upset." Iran's hard-line *Kayhan* daily said the two countries were riding on a "global anti-imperialism wave" which Chávez described as "the unity of the Persian Gulf and the Caribbean sea."[33]

Two months later, on September 29, Ahmadinejad visited Caracas for a day, where he was greeted the way he had welcomed Chávez in Tehran. His host said, "This is your home, Mr. President, yours and all Iranians."[34] On November 19, Chávez went again to Iran to repeat that almost two hundred agreements involving $20 billion of joint investment were being implemented by the two countries.[35] "Here are two brother countries, united like a single fist," Chávez said. "God willing, with the fall of the dollar, the deviant U.S. imperialism will fall as soon as possible, too."[36] Ahmadinejad tuned in, "I am working shoulder to shoulder with Chávez."[37] They were, indeed.

Under the logic of the new alliance, the two countries are not just helping each other; they are helping each other's friends as well.

Venezuela is constructing an oil refinery in Syria, Iran's closest ally in the

Arab world.[38] This project is often cited to justify the recently launched (March 2007) weekly service on Iran's national airline to and from Venezuela via Damascus.[39] Syria's transportation minister Yarub Suleiman Badr adds another justification, calling the flights (on a route with little commercial demand) a move to end the "harassment that Syrian, Arab and Muslim travelers are subjected to when they use other airports."[40]

Unsurprisingly, security standards on these flights are not tight. Individuals are free to carry contraband between Tehran, Damascus, and Caracas with impunity. Iranian nationals acting on behalf of their government can also freely and easily obtain multiple-entry visas at Venezuela's Tehran embassy, a privilege Venezuela extends to other strategic allies such as Cuba, Bolivia, and Nicaragua.[41] The flights are not covered by the extensive cooperation among the governments of developed countries to protect air travel. The ability of the United States or its allies to monitor who or what is being transported by Iran Air on these flights is close to zero. Given the fact that planes and ships going in and out of Venezuela are routinely found loaded with drugs, cash, weapons, and smuggled goods,[42] this development should have given pause to U.S. national security officials. And Pentagon officials reportedly voiced their concern to others in the administration, only to be ignored.

The obvious purpose of the flights is to bypass international and especially American scrutiny. The two countries have done something similar in the banking sector. Iran uses Venezuelan institutions to circumvent U.S. Treasury sanctions and international financial regulations. Most international banks won't deal with Iran, but joint banking operations avoid these restrictions because Venezuela still enjoys virtually unfettered access to the world financial system. Iranians used to work with banks in Dubai and UAE, but those governments, faced with renewed international pressure, are cracking down. Venezuela, on the other hand, welcomes Iranian business and scoffs at international sanctions. And, so far, neither the United States nor any other nation has put real pressure on Venezuela to change course.

Ahmadinejad returns the favor by looking out for Chávez's friends. On the day before his September 2007 visit to Caracas, he made a stop in La Paz to see Chávez's avid supporter President Evo Morales of Bolivia. Morales called the meeting "historic"—which it certainly was. Not only had no Iranian president ever visited Bolivia before, but the two countries did not even have diplomatic relations before the visit.[43] Heads of government do not typically inaugurate diplomatic ties, to say the least.

But kicking off formal relations was just the beginning. Ahmadinejad also pledged to invest $1 billion over the next five years to help desperately poor Bolivia—whose GDP is only $8 billion—to develop its vast gas resources.[44] Added to the billion dollars Chávez had given in 2006, Iran and Venezuela together gifted Morales with $2 billion—25 percent of Bolivia's GDP—and had virtually taken over the country's economy. Contrast that with American stinginess: only four years before, the United States had balked at providing a $50 million loan that might have saved the liberal democratic government that Morales helped destroy.[45]

ATTACKING THE GREENBACK

The Venezuela-Iran axis is also taking punitive diplomacy into uncharted territory. Chávez and Ahmadinejad have teamed up to aggressively attack the U.S. dollar in hopes of triggering a crisis in the American economy and financial markets.

Together, at an OPEC meeting on November 18, 2007, in Riyadh, Saudi Arabia, Chávez and Ahmadinejad provoked worldwide headlines when they called for dumping the dollar from international reserves and in OPEC transactions—something Iran and Venezuela had already begun. "The U.S. dollar has no economic value," Ahmadinejad said. Chávez, in turn, cackled and said, "The fall of the dollar is not the fall of the dollar—it's the fall of the American empire." Former Federal Reserve chairman Alan Greenspan and the distinguished economist Paul Samuelson, among others, predicted that such a run on the dollar was a distinct possibility and could produce a downturn as profound as that of the Great Depression.[46]

Chávez also warned that if the United States were "crazy enough to strike at Iran" or even his own country, oil prices would rise to $200 a barrel. And he proposed that OPEC should "get back to its militant and revolutionary roots" by "setting itself up as an active political agent." But cooler heads—sensing immediately the potential for greater uncertainty and instability in OPEC nations—prevailed.[47] Saudi Arabia's King Abdullah rebuked Chávez and Ahmadinejad, saying OPEC's goal was simply to produce prosperity. No action was taken, but the king's words were buried in the news reports, which focused on the Chávez-Ahmadinejad threat. The damage was done.[48]

Indeed, Chávez and Ahmadinejad had timed this attack on the dollar with precision: they understand the United States much better than American officials understand them. The U.S. trade deficit, the home mortgage crisis, the rising price of oil, and political instability, especially in OPEC nations, were combining to threaten a recession—a recession that a falling dollar would only hasten and deepen.[49]

It's impossible to know exactly how much effect the two presidents' threat had on the dollar's value. What's certain is that in the months following that OPEC meeting, the dollar fell, the stock market slid, and the United States teetered on the brink of recession. All of this was predictable—and predicted by some—but not prevented.[50] With American officials asleep at the switch, the media-savvy Caracas-Tehran "axis of unity" launched a swarming, small-country asymmetrical attack on the U.S. economy.

HOT WAR?

More recently, the two countries offered a grim reminder of how they could threaten not just American prosperity but the American military.

In early January 2008, five small, agile Iranian patrol boats in the Strait of Hormuz swarmed toward a U.S. naval vessel but backed off just before shots were fired. To retired Marine lieutenant general Paul K. Van Riper, that exercise looked like practice for a future attack by Iran against a U.S. carrier fleet—precisely the kind of attack he has long warned against. For years, General Van Riper was concerned about a 2002 Pentagon war game simulation he led in which a swarming strategy of suicide speedboats destroyed sixteen major U.S. warships, including an aircraft carrier. "The sheer numbers [of speedboats] involved overloaded their [U.S. team in the simulation] ability, both mentally and electronically, to handle the attack," General Van Riper explained.[51]

"It's clear, strategically, where the Iranian military has gone," Admiral Mike Mullen, chairman of the Joint Chiefs of Staff, told the *New York Times*. "For the years that this strategic shift toward their small, fast boats has taken place we've been very focused on that."[52]

Venezuela is now part of that focus. The same Iranian swift boats, missiles, rockets, and pilot trainers have been purchased by Chávez and might attack a U.S. carrier fleet in the Caribbean the same way.[53]

Indeed, the Defense Department is just about the only agency in the

U.S. government to treat the Venezuela threat with any seriousness. The Pentagon's Southern Command has been connecting the dots on Iran, the FARC, and Chávez since 1999, but it is virtually alone among U.S. institutions in making the links. After Saddam's weapons of mass destruction were not found and the link to al-Qaeda was assumed to have been overblown (despite the further corroboration that emerged in the wake of the invasion), the Pentagon's intelligence efforts lost credibility. To restore it, the department instituted tough new rules for corroboration[54]—rules that had the side effect of pressing SouthCom to hedge all warnings about Chávez's links to terrorism.

Yet in his most recent testimony, Admiral James Stavridis, the head of SouthCom, continues to correctly observe that "The connectivity between narcoterrorism and Islamic radical terrorism could be disastrous in this region [Latin America]."[55]

In May 2006, the United States suspended arms sales to Venezuela, warning that its arms buildup was destabilizing the region and citing "a nearly total lack of cooperation with the United States' antiterrorism efforts."[56] News stories circulated about Iran's looming presence in Venezuela[57] and Venezuela's collaboration in Iran as they might relate to oil, petrochemicals, and power, including uncorroborated claims that Venezuela was sending uranium to Iran in exchange for its nuclear technology; but few analysts connected the dots.[58]

NUCLEAR COOPERATION?

Chávez at a minimum is a stalwart supporter of Iran's nuclear ambitions in the diplomatic arena. But is there more to the story?

Before Ahmadinejad took power, Chávez had already raised the possibility of collaboration with Iran on nuclear energy research with Ahmadinejad's predecessor, in May 2005. Ahmadinejad would enthusiastically endorse the idea.

Iran's nuclear programs have long troubled American national security officials, who doubt Iran's insistence that it sought nuclear technology solely for energy production: Iran boasts the world's third largest oil reserves and second largest natural gas reserves. When Chávez began to argue that Venezuela—home to the world's eighth largest oil reserves and tenth largest gas reserves—needed nuclear power to diversify its energy supplies,[59] red flags finally went off in the U.S. intelligence community.[60]

For Chávez to make good on that threat, he would need significant help in acquiring the technology. And who better to help him than his friend in Tehran, who had spent the last decade building a covert nuclear program? "The fear was that both countries may be jointly developing nuclear weapons to use against the U.S.," under the pretext that the United States was about to attack them.[61]

In 2005, the Venezuelan and Iranian ministries for mining created a joint company in Venezuela for processing aluminum, iron, and metals smelting; there are suspicions that this company is really a cover for mining uranium for sale to Iran.[62] At the same time, $1 billion was co-invested in a bank to finance joint development projects, the details of which are all kept secret, raising more eyebrows in Washington.[63] In 2005, Iran also helped Venezuela to steer its oil exports to China and away from the United States, a slow process that by 2008 has China receiving about 150,000 Venezuelan barrels per day compared to 1.2 million for the United States.[64] Chávez has announced plans to be delivering 1 million barrels of oil per day to China by 2011, and presumably way less to the United States.

The consultancy firm World-Check, which provides political risk intelligence to corporate and financial investors worldwide, has been tracking Venezuela's links to terror for a decade. Kenneth Rijock, who has developed many confidential sources, leads World-Check's Latin American desk and has been consistently years or months ahead of breaking intelligence stories on Venezuela, Iran, and the FARC, among others. His analysis of the data—including the computer files seized from Raúl Reyes—yields some surprising and disturbing results.

According to Rijock, a number of factors strongly suggest that the Chávez regime is mining uranium covertly, in operations overseen by Iranian engineers, and shipping the product to Iran. First, after Venezuelan publications detailed the locations of the alleged aluminum mines, a senior Venezuelan government official announced that any unauthorized aircraft flights over regions where the mines are located would be strictly prohibited and straying aircraft would be shot down. It's hard to imagine such measures being taken to protect an aluminum mine.

Second, former Venezuelan government mining engineers say that, economically, they can see no reason for Iran to import aluminum. And yet the shipments continue, in Panamanian-flag vessels purporting to deliver legitimate goods. These engineers believe instead that Venezuela's state-owned aluminum company, ALCASA, is covertly mining uranium for export to Iran, under the cover of aluminum production.[65]

Colombia's ambassador to the Organization of American States, Camilo Ospina, agrees. In a 2006 speech entitled "Geopolitics in Latin America," he claimed that two clandestine uranium mining factories were operating in Venezuela: "If you were to go straight in the direction of Arauca, arrive at the border and penetrate about 400 kilometers beyond, you will find two factories," he said, "one is a bicycle factory and the other a motorcycle factory. These two factories are a façade for uranium production." [66]

Third, in 2006, Iran covertly shipped ballistic missiles to Venezuela. The weapons systems have now been assembled and installed in Venezuelan territory, with Colombia as their intended target. Eyewitnesses report that the missiles are under the direct technical supervision of Iranian nationals and are fully operational.[67] Technology transfers of this kind are a sign of a deep and serious alliance. It's hard to imagine that Iran would offer such a gift unless it were getting something more valuable than aluminum in return.

Chávez's choice to head ALCASA at this sensitive time is itself suspect. Carlos Rafael Lanz Rodríguez, a former guerrilla, reputed to be a sympathizer with the goals of terrorist organizations, was tapped in 2005 despite no background in mining or experience as a manager. His main qualification seems to be absolute allegiance to Chávez's vision of Bolivarian Revolution.

Most troubling of all, in March 2008, Colombian authorities (acting on information gleaned from Reyes's computer) discovered a cache of 66 pounds of uranium at a site outside Bogotá, Colombia. The material is presumed to belong to the FARC.[68] The uranium cache appears to have been mined in Venezuela.[69] Subsequent reports have alleged the material to be depleted uranium, and as such, unusable either for a nuclear weapon or a radiological "dirty" bomb. Some have speculated that the FARC was the victim of a scam, but at the time of this writing, too little is known to draw any conclusions.

ANTI-SEMITISM

Chávez has also adopted Ahmadinejad's virulent anti-Semitism—partly as a way of ingratiating himself with his friend, partly to appeal to radical Islamic anti-Americanism, and possibly (so far as anyone knows) out of genuine conviction.

Whatever the exact cause, the appearance of such anti-Semitism is surprising, given the country's tiny Jewish population and history of tolerance. That population numbered roughly 30,000 at the start of Chávez's rule. No one knows how much it has declined, but Jews have been leaving the country over the last decade and the community may today number fewer than 10,000.

And they have had good reason to leave. Since the beginning of Chávez's regime, many of his supporters have married their anti-Americanism with its logical cousin, support for Palestinian terror and anti-Israeli extremism. It began at the fringes. Demonstrators at pro-Chávez rallies would show up with signs and shirts bearing anti-Israeli and pro-Palestinian slogans. Visages of George Bush—always a target at pro-Chávez, anti-U.S. rallies—began to share the stage with Ariel Sharon, a man whose relevance to Venezuela seems tangential at best. Then radical journalists took up the cause, writing incendiary articles on the Middle East conflict and identifying Venezuela's situation in Latin America with the plight of the Palestinians.

Official affirmations soon followed. The government press adopted the rhetoric of the radicals, and even invented new modes of attack. One favorite was to call Colombia the "Israel of Latin America"; the FARC, by contrast, play the role of the beleaguered Palestinians. State-owned media also accused Jewish leaders of backing the alleged (but, as we have seen, phony) anti-Chávez "coup" of 2002, and of working against Chávez in his subsequent elections.

Chávez himself has gotten into the act, equating Israelis with Nazis and repeating the phrase "wandering Jews" as an epithet against his political enemies. Chávez denies that the phrase has anti-Semitic intent, maintaining it was used metaphorically. Harder to explain away is his repetition of the foundational tenet of anti-Semitism, the accusation that the Jews murdered Jesus. At a Christmas ceremony in 2005, he inveighed against "some minorities, the descendants of the people who crucified Christ, [who] seized the riches of the world."[70] He went on to blame the Jews for the failures of Bolívar: "[t]he world is for all of us, then, but it so happens that a minority, the descendants of the same ones that crucified Christ, the descendants of the same ones that kicked Bolívar out of here and also crucified him in their own way over there in Santa Marta, in Colombia. A minority has taken possession of all the wealth of the world."[71]

Far more troubling than any words have been the regime's actions. Twice, the Venezuelan government has mounted terrifying raids on Jewish institutions. In 2004—on the dubious pretext that Israeli agents had assassinated Danilo Anderson, a Venezuelan prosecutor—heavily armed secret police broke into a Jewish elementary school in Caracas, acting (they later claimed) on an anonymous telephone tip that equipment used in Anderson's killing was being hidden in the school. Police locked the children inside, and conducted a search of the premises, which they later admitted yielded no evidence.

Then, in December 2007—on the very day that Chávez's referendum bid to become president for life was being voted on—secret police raided a Jewish athletic and social club, also in Caracas. This time there was no pretext. That fact, and the timing of the raid, forced many observers to conclude this was an act of intimidation, pure and simple.

But beyond that, the purpose seemed as mysterious as ever. Venezuela's very small Jewish community is not particularly politically active, nor has it formed anything like the nucleus of an anti-Chávez movement. So what explains Chávez's anti-Semitism? Is he merely trying to please his new Islamist friends? Or has some of their irrational passion rubbed off on him?

On March 17, 2008, the renowned author Carlos Alberto Montaner presented an insightful analysis of the Chávez threat to America in a speech at the Center for Hemispheric Policy, at the University of Miami. We excerpt it here because it analyzes the strategic threat to the United States so succinctly, and because the process sheds light on the strategic purpose of Chávez's newfound anti-Semitism.

Montaner begins by citing the raids on Jewish institutions, Chávez's belief that Jews killed Jesus and caused most of the wars in history, and his view that Israel is a genocidal state[72] in his preface, and then leads into this analysis:[73]

Hugo Chávez's anti-Semitism and anti-Israelism do not have a theoretical base like the Nazis', but they serve as a cause to recruit allies for his political ends: the creation of an anti-West ideological axis that will replace the vision of the cosmos—a vision now vanished—held by the Soviet Union.

Why does a ruler who is historically and geographically distant from the dangerous Arab-Israeli conflict make such an effort to walk onto such an explosive stage? Simple. Anti-Semitism and anti-Israelism are the shortest way to recruit certain allies for the purpose of building a great international movement.

Iran, Libya, Syria and the most radical Palestinians from Gaza and the West Bank, especially the terrorist groups, are the natural collaborators for this new (and ancient) political project.

Chávez is trying to recreate the picture that existed during the Cold War, and those countries were some of Moscow's allies at that time. If Caracas is the 21st-Century Moscow, Chávez will try to do what the USSR did in the 20th Century.

The other component is anti-Americanism. Chávez often attacks President Bush with vehemence and vulgarity, and almost every time he refers to the United States he calls it "the Empire," convinced that anti-Americanism—along with anti-Semitism and anti-Israelism, in the absence of a coherent ideology—are the three signs of identity most relevant to what he pompously calls "21st Century socialism."

Once we're aware of this background, we can better understand what is happening in the Andean region, something that I have called the Palestinization of the Andes.

Hugo Chávez's first reaction after the attack on the camp of narcoterrorist Raúl Reyes was to accuse Colombia of behaving like Israel. "We're not going to allow an Israel in the region," he said.

Actually, the parallel is not far off. Like Colombia, Israel is a state that wishes to live in peace with its neighbors, but they insist on destroying it. Israel's fondest wish would be for the Palestinians to be capable of building a peaceful and prosperous nation with which Israel could establish normal relations.

Israel's burden is the fact that, on the Gaza Strip, Lebanon, Syria or faraway Iran . . . terrorist gangs have established headquarters from which they attack Israel or plan various types of atrocities. Every day, missiles launched by the terrorists fall on civilian settlements, killing innocent people.

Naturally, Israel responds militarily. What else can it do?

7

Chávez and
the Jihad

Chávez's ties with Iran are worrisome enough. His ties with Syria are more worrisome—and even harder to explain on any traditional diplomatic grounds.

We have seen through his support of the FARC that Chávez has no qualms about supporting terrorism. His support for terror doesn't stop with the FARC, nor does his support for Islamic radicals end with the regimes in Tehran and Damascus. At a minimum Chávez turns a blind eye to Islamist terrorism, refusing to help the international community take even basic steps to stop terrorist activity.

We have also shown that Chávez goes further than passive acquiescence. The air link between Tehran and Caracas allows for virtually unlimited movement of terrorist operatives in and out of the western hemisphere, and potentially into the United States. His bank deal with Iran allows terrorists to move money around the globe, evading U.S. and international sanctions.

In this chapter, we will demonstrate Chávez's record of support for various Islamist terrorist groups—most notably Hezbollah, once described by former deputy secretary of state Richard Armitage as the "A-team of Terrorists."[1] Such support goes well beyond mere friendship with Iran, and certainly has nothing to do with maintaining or improving Venezuela's position with respect to its neighbors. He can have only one goal: to harm the United States by any means at hand.

"Not Fully Cooperating"

Only one Latin American nation—Cuba—is officially considered to be a state sponsor of terrorism by the U.S. government. If one looks at Cuba's record, and compares Venezuela's, it is hard to see where the distinction lies. The first paragraph of the State Department's explanation for the Cuba designation reads:

> Cuba actively continued to oppose the U.S.-led Coalition prosecuting the global war on terror and has publicly condemned various U.S. policies and actions. To U.S. knowledge, Cuba did not attempt to track, block, or seize terrorist assets, although the authority to do so is contained in Cuba's Law 93 Against Acts of Terrorism, as well as Instruction 19 of the Superintendent of the Cuban Central Bank. No new counterterrorism laws were enacted, nor were any executive orders or regulations issued in this regard. To date, the Cuban Government has taken no action against al-Qaida or other terrorist groups.[2]

All of this could be said against Venezuela as well.

The Cuba designation goes on to cite numerous other examples of noncooperation with U.S. and international bodies, the country's close ties with other terror-sponsoring states—including Iran—and Havana's willingness to harbor terrorists and refuse extradition requests.[3] Just about the only activity mentioned in the Cuba citation that Venezuela has not also engaged in (so far as anyone knows) is a bioweapons program.

Still, after heated debate in the U.S. government in late 2007 and into

2008—which only intensified after the finding of the Reyes computer— officials declined to take the logical step and declare Venezuela a state sponsor of terror, thus invoking a host of sanctions and penalties. According to White House sources, cutting Venezuela oil sales to the American market stayed the administration's hand.

Whatever the cause for their caution, they instead took the unprecedented step of declaring the Venezuelan government to be "not fully cooperating" with global antiterror efforts without also naming it a state sponsor of terror.[4] Venezuela under Chávez has the dubious distinction of being the world's only regime so designated.

"Not fully cooperating" is a significant understatement. Venezuela is, by any measure, not cooperating at all.

The U.S. government has repeatedly attempted to persuade Venezuela to act responsibly, and repeatedly been rebuffed. Officials at the U.S. Embassy in Caracas—from the ambassador on down—have requested meetings with Venezuelan government officials responsible for counterterrorism on at least twenty occasions. No such meetings have ever been granted.[5]

American officials have also submitted some 130 written requests for basic biographical or immigration-related information, such as entry and exit dates into and out of Venezuela, for suspected terrorists. Not one of the requests has generated a substantive response.

Such information—as well as information on bank accounts and transactions, phone numbers, e-mail accounts, and other travel details— regarding terror suspects is routinely shared internationally, and not just among close allies but even among countries with few other formal ties. This information is considered essential to global efforts to fight terror; yet Venezuela conspicuously opts out of the sharing system that even U.S. critics routinely participate in. By doing so, Chávez has effectively turned his country into a terrorism black hole as far as the international community is concerned: no light escapes.

Or, rather, very little. Occasionally, glimpses emerge about Venezuela's ties to terror. For instance, in 2003, Rahaman Alan Hazil Mohammed— a thirty-seven-year-old Venezuelan citizen—was arrested in the United Kingdom after arriving at Gatwick Airport on a flight from Caracas, and found with a live grenade in his carry-on luggage.[6] He was subsequently convicted in a British court on terrorism charges. The government of Venezuela refused all British and American requests for cooperation before and during Mohammed's trial, and has rebuffed all requests for information since.

Hakim Mamad al Diab Fatah, another Venezuelan citizen, attended school with some of the 9/11 hijackers in New Jersey. Other members of his family in Venezuela have been alleged to associate with various Islamist extremist groups. Fatah was detained in the United States following the 9/11 attacks. All requests for information from the Venezuelan government were denied. Having little to go on, U.S. authorities deported him to his home country in early 2002. Later, when they sought him for further questioning, the Venezuelan government replied that he had left the country, and gave no indication of his whereabouts.[7]

Hezbollah in the Hemisphere

La Guajira Desert is a remote area of northern South America. The desert covers a peninsula that juts into the Caribbean Sea and straddles the border between Venezuela and Colombia. It is home to an indigenous people called the Wayuu, one of the few native South American tribes never conquered by the Spanish, and never fully integrated into the modern society around them. The Wayuu fought Spanish attempts to conquer them, rebelling several times throughout the eighteenth and nineteenth centuries. Spanish attempts to introduce Christianity similarly met with limited success, making partial headway only in the twentieth century and never achieving anything like universal conversion among the tribe.

Government control on both sides of the border has always been weak, which on the one hand helps the Wayuu preserve their unique way of life, but on the other hand makes the area a potential haven for those who seek to evade national and international authority—or worse. The border itself is virtually unprotected: Wayuu (and anyone else) can cross freely from Colombia to Venezuela and vice versa with no challenge from any authorities, and without the knowledge of the respective countries' military, police, or immigration officials.

Into this void has stepped the Iranian-backed Islamist terrorist group Hezbollah. Hezbollah operates openly in La Guajira. The branch there even officially calls itself "Hezbollah Venezuela" and has a website, with the logo of a fist raising an AK-47 above the name.

What they are doing, precisely, is hard to establish fully, since La Guajira—while not quite no-man's-land—is hardly ever visited by outsiders, much less the press. But reports have seeped out.

First and foremost, Hezbollah seems to be using the area as a base of operations, a foothold in the western hemisphere. In prelude to what? No one at this point can say. But given what Hezbollah has done with its main base of operations in Lebanon—bullied the Lebanese people and used the area as a base from which to project terrorism into Israel and against U.S. interests in the region—there is ample cause for concern.

Whatever their other goals, Hezbollah seems intent on establishing a long-term presence. Hezbollah's official propaganda attacks Venezuelan government corruption—a welcome message among the Wayuu, who have always distrusted Caracas—and savages the Venezuelan upper classes. The latter message is, of course, music to Chávez's ears, while the former must be mixed. Chávez himself has profited from campaigning against government corruption, but now that he has been in power for nearly a decade, such charges must inevitably reflect badly on his own administration.

More troubling for Chávez, presumably, should be Hezbollah's missionary activities. Incredible as it may sound, Hezbollah is succeeding where the Spanish friars failed: it is increasingly turning the Wayuu away from their ancient religion and toward Islam—and in particular to Hezbollah's radical vision of Islamic fascism fueled by terrorist violence.

In 2005, Chávez expelled from the area the Christian missionary group New Tribes of Venezuela, which translates scriptures into native languages and preaches the Gospel. Accusing them of spying and genocide, Chávez gave a fiery speech on Columbus Day—renamed "Day of Indigenous Resistance"—in which he announced the expulsion.[8]

Hezbollah, facing pressure from the governments of Brazil, Argentina, and Uruguay to vacate the so-called Tri-Border Area, filled the vacuum. There are signs that Chávez welcomed them to do so: he has openly met with Argentine Hezbollah leaders in downtown Caracas.[9]

La Guajira today is already a vastly different place. Wayuu women wear the Islamic veil in public, and children dress according to Islamic custom. Men walk the streets dressed and equipped like Middle Eastern terrorists, replete with the obligatory Kalashnikov rifles, and even pose for pictures wearing explosives-laden suicide belts. New recruits are tasked with spreading the Islamist message and recruiting their fellow Wayuu with the promise of a new Venezuela.

And that newness is not merely defined by attacks on government corruption or societal inequality. It is also defined in quasi-religious terms. Hezbollah propaganda attacks "the sex industry" (which it does not bother to define), "false idols," and "satanic cults." In case some have not gotten the point, it gets more explicit: their ultimate goal is to establish the kingdom of God in Venezuela by imposing a theocracy by force of arms. "The brief enjoyment of life on earth is selfish. The other life is better for those who follow Allah." [10]

Perhaps Chávez does not take this religious rhetoric too seriously. Or perhaps he feels he has no choice but to endure it so as not to alienate Hezbollah's chief patron and Chávez's great friend, the Iranian regime. Or perhaps he sees some broader strategic benefit in the Islamization of parts of his country.

Acquiescence, Complicity, or Partnership?

Whatever the case, it is undeniable that Chávez knows what is going on, and that his government supports the activity. La Guajira is hardly Hezbollah's only presence in Venezuela. Hezbollah actively recruits young Venezuelans of Arab ancestry all throughout the country. Many travel to Hezbollah training camps in Lebanon.

But such a journey is not necessary for everyone. Hezbollah operates at least five training camps in Venezuela, in the states of Monagas, Miranda, Trujillo, Falcón, and Yaracuy. At these sites, aspiring terrorists can learn to handle weapons, construct munitions, and run complex terror operations. And Hezbollah is not the only group that uses these camps. Hamas and even al-Qaeda have sent members to Venezuela to avail themselves of Chávez's hospitality. Chávez has transformed Venezuela into a nation that is, quite simply, the hub of Islamist terror in the Americas, and the vital bridge linking terrorists of all stripes to their brethren in other Latin American nations.

The hub of that hub is Margarita Island, a popular tourist destination in the Caribbean off the northern cost of the country, with a large Arab population. Known mostly for its beaches and resort hotels, the island is officially designated a free trade zone by the central government. In theory, this is meant to stimulate economic development. In practice, it means that the central government exerts scant control or oversight over what goes on.

Terrorist activity on Margarita Island is not new to the Chávez regime. The island has long been home to a large Lebanese expatriate population, and Hezbollah has had a foothold there for decades. In 1992, some of those Lebanese expatriates helped Hezbollah establish a cell in Charlotte, North Carolina.

While not a training center, the island is at or near the center of virtually all other Islamist terror activities in Venezuela and in the Americas. Its banks are integral to a network of financial institutions throughout the Caribbean that facilitate drug trafficking, money laundering, and terrorist fund-raising. It is home to several quasi-legal front businesses that funnel money overseas to terrorists as well as to outright illegal enterprises whose profits similarly get steered to Middle Eastern terror. The island has a thriving false-documents industry that provides phony passports, identification, and travel documents to terrorists and other criminals. And it is a transit center for terrorists and terror sympathizers, a way station for trips within the region and overseas to the Middle East.[11]

This activity is not going on under Chávez's nose, nor is it happening with his knowledge but only his tacit approval. All of it is in fact actively assisted by officials in the Venezuelan government.[12] The training camps, for instance, operate without interference from the Venezuelan Ministry of the Interior, which at the very least tolerates their continued existence and operation. There are also claims that the Venezuelan vice-minister of the interior, Tarek el Ayssami, is a sympathizer with Hezbollah.[13]

He is hardly alone. Ghazi Nasr al Din is a Venezuelan citizen and diplomat (with twelve known aliases) who has allegedly used his prominent positions, both in the government and as president of the Caracas-based Shi'a Islamic Center—ostensibly a charity and outreach group—to provide financial support to Hezbollah. His overseas postings have included stints as chargé d'affaires at the Venezuelan Embassy in Damascus, and director of political aspects at the Venezuelan Embassy in Lebanon—fertile ground for making and maintaining contacts with Islamists, radicals, and terrorists of all stripes.

And he availed himself of the opportunity. He has been tracked helping Hezbollah raise money, and even steering them donors, providing the latter with specific information on bank accounts to ensure that monies would be funneled directly to Hezbollah operatives. He repeatedly met with senior Hezbollah officials in Lebanon to discuss operational issues, and used his official position in the Venezuelan government to facilitate the travel of Hezbollah operatives to and from Venezuela. Some of those trips were fund-raising junkets; one was to open a Hezbollah-sponsored community center and office in Venezuela. Al Din has even arranged for Hezbollah operatives to travel to Iran to attend terrorist training courses.[14] How does that conceivably fit into the legitimate portfolio of a Venezuelan diplomat?

The lucky young men steered to camps overseas—typically in Southern Lebanon, but sometimes even Iran—often travel under the auspices of the Shi'a Islamic Center, whose personnel see to the details. There are tight links between the center and officials from the PUSV, the United Socialist Party of Venezuela, Chávez's political party that he formed in 2007. There is even evidence of students from the UNEFA, Venezuela's military academy, attending overseas training camps.

Official visas are granted frequently, regardless of the links or prior history of the recipients. At the time of this writing no fewer than three notable Hezbollah figures reportedly have visas that allow them to enter and exit Venezuela at will. There is the explosives expert Abdul Ghani Suleiman Wanked, right-hand man to Hezbollah Secretary-General Hassan Nasrallah. There is Rada Ramel Assad, a Colombia-born Hezbollah operative. And there is Abouchanab Daichoum Dani, who organizes tours of Caracas for visiting Hezbollah dignitaries.[15]

Islamist Ecumenicism?

Chávez's Venezuela welcomes not just the Shi'a friends of Iran, such as Hezbollah; its arms are also open to Sunni terrorists from Hamas and possibly even al-Qaeda.

On one of his many trips to the Middle East, Chávez met with Hamas's leadership in Damascus.[16] The meeting was Chávez's own idea: after Hamas's victory in the 2006 legislative elections in the Palestinian Territories, Chávez sent a note to Hamas informing the group of his upcoming visit to the region and asking them to meet him.[17]

Relations became warm enough that José Vicente Rangel, Chávez's vice president, announced that Venezuela would receive a Hamas delegation at any time "with pleasure" and expressed surprise that anyone might see something amiss.[18] As yet, Hamas has not availed itself of the offer, so far as is publicly known.

The most troubling allegation of all comes from Chávez's former pilot, a major in the Venezuelan air force who defected to the United States in 2003. Juan Díaz Castillo claims to have personally witnessed or overheard many shocking things in his time serving Chávez.

Most shocking of all: he claims that Chávez gave $900,000 to al-Qaeda in the wake of the 9/11 attacks, and $100,000 to Afghanistan's then ruling Taliban government. The money, according to Díaz, was passed to the Taliban through the Venezuelan ambassador in Delhi.[19]

Díaz also claims that Chávez considered sending Venezuelan troops to aid the Taliban, but decided against it only because he could see no way to get around the American air blockade then patrolling the skies around the country.

Sensational as these allegations are, it is important to remember that they have never been independently confirmed. Still, where there is—as we have seen—so much smoke indicating Chávez's alliance with Islamist terror, there just might be a fire somewhere behind these wisps as well.

American Action

The United States has finally begun to take the threat seriously. In 2006, the government appointed a dedicated official, known as a "Mission Manager" and only the third such ever appointed, to integrate intelligence collection and analysis on Venezuela and Cuba across the various agencies of the U.S. government.[20]

Through its Office of Foreign Assets Control, the Treasury Department has also designated Ghazi Nasr al Din and Fawzi Kan'an—and two travel agencies owned and controlled by Kan'an—as supporters of terror.[21]

Kan'an (who uses seven aliases) has no official role in the Venezuelan government. According to Treasury, he is an active fund-raiser for Hezbollah and frequently travels to the Middle East and throughout Europe to facilitate donations and advise on operational issues. While al Din has merely helped others get to Iran to avail themselves of terrorist training, Kan'an has allegedly attended the camps personally—bringing along other Hezbollah members to beef up the ranks.[22]

The Biblos and Hilal travel agencies—alleged Kan'an-owned "businesses" in Caracas—are, according to Treasury, in fact, front organizations whose real mission is to move money and people back and forth between Venezuela and the Middle East, and around the Middle East once in the region. The agencies are said to be significant couriers of funds from Latin America to Hezbollah's base of operations in Lebanon.[23]

Kan'an, naturally, denies everything. "These are all lies," he said at a press conference following the designation of his agencies as supporters of terror. But he confessed to, at a minimum, complete indifference about the character of the people who avail themselves of his services. "When someone walks in to buy a ticket I don't have the right to ask them what religion they are. I have all kinds of clients."[24] Indeed he does—including Hezbollah.

And that, so far, has been it. The designations may not sound like much, but at least they are a start.

8
Useful Idiots

seful idiots" is the phrase allegedly coined by Vladimir Ilyich Lenin to describe those Americans and other Westerners attracted or sympathetic to communism after the Russian Revolution of 1917, who defended the theory and practice of Bolshevism. As Lenin saw it, Western intellectuals were idiots because they didn't understand that communism posed a mortal threat to their societies and way of life. But they were useful because they defended communism to their fellow countrymen and convinced many in the West that the Soviet Union posed no threat.

Likewise, before World War II, Hitler had his own cadre of useful idiots. The America First Committee—led by Charles Lindbergh, and populated by influential figures including the publishers William Randolph Hearst and Robert McCormick, the diplomat Joseph Kennedy, and many prominent members of Congress—argued that America should isolate itself from the war in Europe, believing it to be irrelevant to America's interests.

Hugo Chávez, too, enjoys the support of useful idiots in the United States and throughout the West, people who believe he is leading a democratic revolution on behalf of the poor that presents no threat to U.S. interests or values.

But there is a significant difference between modern useful idiots and their ancestors. In the past debates over communism and Nazism, nearly all Americans had some knowledge of the regimes and movements in question. Many recent immigrants had direct experience. But few Americans today know anything of Chávez's Bolivarian Revolution. And they know even less about Chávez's asymmetric war against their country.

Into this vacuum of information about Latin America in general and Chávez in particular, stereotypes and ignorance—rather than knowledge and experience—have rushed in to shape America's political dialogue about Chávez, his actions, and his intentions.

To some extent, our ignorance is understandable. America is an open society, bustling with different commercial, political, and cultural interests, in which bold claims about distant issues and lands can go unchallenged. But these many preoccupations leave us vulnerable to Chávez's propaganda campaigns.

In 2008 alone, Chávez has spent an estimated $300 million[1] on a massive public relations campaign targeting the American people—more money than Senators McCain, Clinton, and Obama together spent on their 2007 to 2008 primary campaigns for the U.S. presidency through February 2008.[2] He has spent almost $1 billion on propaganda aimed at the United States and the West since 2004. His claims are simple: he is a proponent of peace, prosperity, and democracy; while the U.S. government responds to his benign intentions by trying to invade, overthrow, and assassinate him.

All of this is, of course, wholly untrue. Chávez, far from being an opponent of corruption, has become an enabler of it. The policies that he claims have helped the poor have in fact hurt them. And far from being a supporter of democracy, Chávez is exceeded only by Castro in the western hemisphere in his authoritarian zeal. America has no designs on Chávez's nascent empire; indeed, American policymakers continue to ignore the Chávez threat. Chávez is the abuser, not the abused.

Even the official statistics cooked up by Chávez's government show that no revolution has occurred in Venezuela.³ Half the population is still poor; one third lives in inadequate housing; and more than half work in the informal economy. There is no Social Security system and inflation has been the highest in Latin America throughout Chávez's tenure. Crime is out of control, with civilian death rates rivaling those in Iraq. Basic foods are missing from store shelves. Corruption is worse than under any of Chávez's predecessors. In Venezuela's prisons—the most dangerous in the Americas—many of the 21,000 inmates have conducted hunger strikes to protest years of incarceration without charges, trial, or conviction.⁴

Phony as it is, the picture of Venezuela painted by Chávez's propaganda is nonetheless effective. Gullible, naive, or worse, some very famous Americans have fallen for it—hook, line, and sinker.

The unvarnished truth is that Venezuela is still what it always has been: a very rich, government-enabled elite suppressing the freedoms of a multitude of poor, dependent people. That misery is nothing to brag about and certainly nothing to export. So why is it so attractive to the Idiot?

The Idiot's Creed

The renowned author Álvaro Vargas Llosa coined the term "Latin American Idiot" to describe the Marx-addled, would-be revolutionaries who for so long dominated political discussion in Latin America.⁵ His description is powerful, and worth quoting at some length:

> Throughout the 20th century, Latin America's populist leaders waved Marxist banners, railed against foreign imperialists, and promised to deliver their people from poverty. One after another, their ideologically driven policies proved to be sluggish and shortsighted. Their failures led to a temporary retreat of the strongman. But now, a new generation of self-styled revolutionaries is trying to revive the misguided methods of their predecessors.⁶
>
> Latin American Idiots have traditionally identified themselves with *caudillos*, those larger-than-life authoritarian figures who have dominated the region's politics, ranting against foreign influence and republican institutions. . . . Chávez is seen as the perfect successor to Cuba's Fidel Castro (whom the Idiot also admires): he came to power through the ballot box, which exonerates him from the need to justify armed struggle, and he has abundant oil, which

means he can put his money where his mouth is when it comes to champion-ing social causes. The Idiot also credits Chávez with the most progressive pol-icy of all—putting the military, that paradigm of oligarchic rule, to work on social programs.[7]

The Idiot's worldview, in turn, finds an echo among distinguished intellec-tuals in Europe and the United States. These pontificators assuage their trou-bled consciences by espousing exotic causes in developing nations. Their opinions attract fans among First-World youngsters for whom globalization phobia provides the perfect opportunity to find spiritual satisfaction in the populist jeremiad of the Latin American Idiot against the wicked West . . . [thus] propagating absurdities that shape the opinions of millions of readers and sanctify the Latin American Idiot.[8]

This worldview is today hardly confined to Latin America. A great many Americans and Europeans also hold these beliefs, and Chávez skillfully ex-ploits their ignorance.

All of his failures are placed on the shoulders of the West, where that blame finds a willing audience. In his 1998 presidential campaign, Chávez promised to eliminate poverty, inequality, and corruption in Venezuela.

Ten years after taking power, Chávez candidly admitted his many fail-ures but disingenuously spread the blame elsewhere. In his "state of the union" speech in January 2008, he asked:

Why is milk missing? Why in nine years has the revolutionary government been unable to change the dreadful situation in prisons? Why does personal insecurity continue to be such a serious problem in the streets, towns and slums? Why have we been incapable of solving the serious problems hitting people everywhere? Why is smuggling still so rampant and barefaced? What is the rationale behind impunity? Why are the mafias still embedded in state agencies? When are we going to put an end to permit-related blackmail? Why is it so expensive to produce goods? Why has corruption not been defeated?[9]

His answer in every case: American hostility.

To the Idiot, Venezuela and Chávez are *tabulae rasae*—blank slates—onto which Western grievances about our world can be projected. The Idiot's concerns are about himself, not Chávez. Chávez is no fool when it comes to fooling fools. He knows how to get Americans into "projecting their idealism, guilty consciences or grievances against their own societies onto the Latin American scene," as Vargas Llosa puts it. Americans with a grievance against President Bush, the war in Iraq, or U.S. power in the world project onto Chávez what they want, and Chávez is only too happy to accommodate them.

Idiots come in all shapes and sizes, and from all walks of life. But the most influential—and therefore the most dangerous—fall into four broad categories: intellectuals, activists, celebrities, and politicians. We will look at each in turn.

Intellectuals

Intellectuals are probably Chávez's most important source of support in the West. Though small in number and catering to a limited audience, they nonetheless exert an outside influence by giving theoretical heft and lending their considerable prestige to Chávez's propaganda.

Noam Chomsky is unquestionably the most prominent and the most influential. Long an opponent of U.S. global dominance, and virtually all American foreign policy since World War II at least, Chomsky routinely explicates the most negative possible interpretation of America's actions, and spins together implausibly complex conspiracy theories. Chávez is, understandably, a fan of Chomsky's oeuvre. In the infamous UN General Assembly speech in 2006 in which Chávez called President Bush "the devil," he also touted Chomsky's *Hegemony or Survival: America's Quest for Global Dominance* as a must-read for understanding America and the world. The book promptly jumped into the top ten in sales, and its publisher, Henry Holt, ordered a reprinting.[10] Afterward, Chomsky praised Chávez and his revolution—apparently not even having visited Venezuela.[11] The irony is that Chávez has never read Chomsky's book, but used it opportunistically only because it was written by an American attacking America.[12]

The Nobel Prize–winning economist Joseph Stiglitz is a gadfly in his profession who believes that nationalism and socialism are strategies equal to or better than free market democracy.[13] When Chávez nationalized and socialized major industries in Venezuela, Stiglitz wrote a *New York Times* column in support of Chávez's revolution in Venezuela.[14] About Venezuela's factual failure to improve the living standards of Venezuelans, Stiglitz makes no criticism. Adding the imprimatur of a Nobel laureate in economics to Chávez's command and control policies is a boon to the Caracas regime.

Victor Navasky—publisher emeritus of *The Nation,* a distinguished liberal journal in the United States—has at least visited the country. In January 2007, he made the journey to investigate Chávez's closure of Venezuela's oldest independent TV station, RCTV, which the president had shut down on the grounds that it opposed his revolution and supported the anti-Chávez "coup" of 2002. The shutdown created an uproar among human rights and democracy advocates worldwide.[15] After six days of investigating, Navasky concluded that Chávez's action against RCTV "would have a chilling effect on free expression." But he went on to provide this excuse: "but I shared Naomi Klein's view that it was 'absurd to treat Chávez as the principal threat to a free press in Venezuela.'" Navasky also found that RCTV was "probably" involved in the April 2002 coup against Chávez (whose account of which he took for granted to be true) and stated that Chávez's revolution was "still a fiction, but one to be nourished as an ideal to pursue rather than a policy to be mocked."[16] How he knew these things he did not say. Navasky remained completely silent on the Chávez government's takeover of most of the TV stations in Venezuela and his consolidation of the media.

Activists

A prominent apologist of Chávez who became a point of contention between John McCain and Barack Obama in the 2008 presidential race is William Ayers, the 1960s Weather Underground terrorist who is a professor today in Chicago. Ayers visited Chávez in 2006 to praise Chávez's indoctrination of schoolchildren with revolutionary thought.[17]

Chávez enjoys the widespread support of activists on the left in this country, who manage to convince their followers and rank-and-file that Chávez's official story line is true.

Brenda Stokeley, president of AFSCME Local 215 in New York City, is an ardent Chávez supporter who has even traveled to Venezuela to witness his "revolution" up close. In 2004, she addressed a rally in Caracas with generous praise for Chávez. "President Chávez is trying to provide poor people with health care, education and decently paid jobs. . . . Anyone opposed to that either has their head under a rock or has no respect for human beings that live in poverty."[18] A typical reaction to Stokeley's Caracas speech came from one Oakland, California, community organizer, Mamie Chow, who said: "You can't question what's happening here. It's so uplifting."[19] Millions like her believe everything they hear about Chávez's Venezuela.

Cindy Sheehan lost her son in the Iraq War and became media-famous for voicing a strong antiwar message and demonstrating against President Bush. She has since adopted virtually every left-wing cause imaginable, including embracing Hugo Chávez. In 2006, after a photo session with Chávez,[20] she urged the world to help bring down "the U.S. Empire," and said: "I would rather live under a president like Hugo who tries to improve living conditions in his country than someone like George who is demolishing our social structures and making the poor, poorer."[21]

Jesse Jackson, perhaps the most prominent activist in America over the last thirty years, visited Chávez in 2005 to promote the Venezuelan government's TV special commemorating Martin Luther King, Jr.'s "I Have a Dream" speech. The special unsubtly compared King's struggle to Chávez's, and linked Chávez to the great civil rights leader's struggle for racial and social equality. Chávez then invited Jackson to co-host a session of *Aló Presidente,* on which Jackson praised Chávez's work for indigenous rights, his aid to American victims of Hurricane Katrina, and his program of cheap oil for poor Americans.[22] Chávez basked in Jackson's praise and congratulated himself on leading a nonviolent revolution just like King.[23]

Celebrities

Many Hollywood stars and others in the entertainment industry are known for their left-of-center views, and are not exactly notorious for any rigorous analysis underlying those views. Hence it is no surprise that stars have flocked to Chávez's side. But their sheer number is nonetheless impressive.

Unlike intellectuals, and even activists, big stars reach millions of people, and the media often hangs on their words without question. Chávez is, naturally, grateful to have their support, and never misses an opportunity to welcome Hollywood royalty to Venezuela.

Music legend Harry Belafonte is perhaps Chávez's biggest booster in the world of show business. He led a delegation of Americans including the actor Danny Glover, the United Farm Workers union leader Dolores

Huerta, and the Princeton University scholar Cornel West that met with Chávez for more than six hours in 2006 and attended his *Aló Presidente* broadcast the next day. "There are many places in the world where they don't speak well of President Chávez or the efforts he is making for the Venezuelan people," Belafonte intoned. "We've decided to come to see what is really happening with our own eyes."

Naturally, he liked what he saw. Belafonte accused the American media of falsely painting Chávez as a dictator. "No matter what the greatest tyrant in the world, the greatest terrorist in the world, George W. Bush, says, we're here to tell you: not hundreds, not thousands but millions of the American people . . . support your revolution." [24] Chávez would use Belafonte's description of Bush many times thereafter, especially whenever he was accused of having links to terrorists. [25] Chávez's government subsequently contributed $100,000 to a Belafonte charity in California. [26]

Danny Glover told Chávez he was "excited to get back to the United States to talk about what is happening [in Venezuela], knowing that you are in a transformative stage and that you are the architects of your own destiny." [27] Glover's trip was also profitable from a business standpoint. He managed to secure $18.5 million from Chávez's *La Villa del Cine*—Caracas's response to Hollywood's colonialism, as Chávez calls it. [28] The money is to go toward the production of two films, both dreamed up by Chávez. The first is to be a biopic of Símon Bolívar; the second a study of the Haitian Toussaint L'Ouverture, whose slave rebellion uprooted French rule. [29] Chávez also appointed Glover to the advisory board of Telesur, [30] the Latin American TV network spouting Bolivarian "news" stories that Chávez created and funded to counter CNN and BBC news in the region. [31]

Chávez's interest in film has attracted other stars as well. Kevin Spacey visited Venezuela to praise Chávez's creation of a $13 million government-controlled film studio in Caracas. "I think every country should have this," Spacey ventured. [32] Spacey also listened approvingly to accounts of Chávez's plans to rewrite the 1999 constitution and to help negotiate the release of hostages held by the FARC in Colombia. He then flew to Cuba to see Fidel Castro. [33]

Actor Sean Penn visited Chávez "as a journalist," he said, "and so I owe it to that medium to wait until I've digested, fact-checked and finished my journey here" before saying more. [34] Yet Penn said enough. He took a look at Chávez's proposed constitution for Venezuela, which gives the president the power to rule by decree, and concluded that it was "a very beautiful document."[35] Penn also said, "I came here looking for a great country. I found a great country."[36] While standing beside Presidents Chávez and Ahmadinejad during his visit, Penn the journalist had no questions for either of them about terrorism, the FARC, nuclear proliferation, kidnapping, the drug trade, human rights violations, or the epidemics of murder and poverty in Venezuela—as Rowan recorded in a column for *El Universal* at the time.[37]

Supermodel Naomi Campbell also visited Chávez as a "journalist" to write a puff piece about him. Apparently a quick study, Naomi said, "I've been here for 24 hours and I'm amazed to see the love and encouragement for the social programs that you have here for women and children in Venezuela." She did not mention that poverty, inequality, malnutrition, and infant mortality among Venezuela's women and infants had worsened in the ten years of Chávez's rule.[38] Campbell, no stranger to Latin American dictators, holds a position with the Fund for Cuban Children, a charity set up by Fidel Castro.[39]

Oliver Stone, perhaps the most left-wing and certainly the most anti-establishment figure in Hollywood, is Chávez's natural ally. As we have seen, he accompanied Chávez on his January 2008 mission to airlift three of the eight hundred hostages held for ransom by the FARC in Colombia's jungles, calling it "a beautiful, great process"—despite the fact that the mission accomplished nothing.[40] Stone openly admires the FARC, notwithstanding it makes $300 million a year from cocaine sales, kidnapping, and extortion.[41] "I have no illusions about the FARC, but it looks like they are a peasant army fighting for a decent living," he told reporters. "And here, if you fight, you fight to win."[42] Chávez was impressed with Stone. "He's an anti-imperialist, Oliver Stone," Chávez mused. "He's a good man." Stone went one better, calling Chávez "a great man."[43]

Barbara Walters—a celebrity journalist almost as famous as the stars she covers—is known for giving her subjects the soft-focus treatment. Not one for tough questions, she was particularly soft on Hugo Chávez in her March 19, 2007, interview on ABC-TV, naming Chávez one of the "10 most fascinating people of 2007." Walters introduced the interview by saying that Chávez "was not what I expected. He was very dignified. He was warm, friendly. He likes the U.S. It's George Bush that he doesn't like."

Not all of Hollywood or the media elite fawn so shamelessly. Some bravely speak out about the abuses of Chávez's rule. Maria Conchita Alonso—Cuban-born, but also a former Miss Venezuela who starred in *Predator 2* (1990) and *Moscow on the Hudson* (1984)—takes issue with her fellow Hollywood stars. She lived in Venezuela and knows it well. She told TV's Hannity and Colmes in May 2007 that "Chávez is the biggest actor there, much better than Danny Glover, because he has a way of making people believe that he was elected democratically and that he cares for the poor."[44] To correct this misimpression, she is producing and starring in a film released in 2008, *Two Minutes of Hate,* about the events of the 2002 "coup," describing how Chávez crushed a peaceful protest march with violence.[45]

Similarly, not everyone in Venezuela's filmmaking community appreciates Chávez's Hollywood friends or his efforts to woo them. Claudia Nazoa, president of the Venezuela Chamber of Film Producers, has said that "What worries us is this trend for neo-colonialism by international figures who come to talk of their support for Chávez's government and then leave with money for their projects."[46] But dissent is rare, and most of it carries no weight in the one-man rule that is modern Venezuela.

Politicians

The American political class above all should know better than to excuse and encourage Chávez's actions. They are entitled to the latest intelligence, and—theoretically—are paid to keep up with what is going on in other countries. But they have not only failed to stand up for, or even understand, their own country's interests; some have actively—if unwittingly—worked to further the interests of an enemy.

Many prominent American political figures believed—or professed to believe—every word of Chávez's account of the so-called coup of 2002. John Conyers, the Democratic representative from Michigan, and fifteen other Democrats or members of the Congressional Black Caucus, sent a letter to President Bush after the "coup" complaining that the United States was not doing enough to protect Chávez from being overthrown by counterrevolutionary and antidemocratic forces in Venezuela.[47]

Senator Chris Dodd of Connecticut has long been hostile to the U.S. embargo against Cuba and long disposed to giving left-wing and anti-American regimes in Latin America the benefit of the doubt, to say the least. His was the most aggressive voice in Congress questioning the Bush administration's denial of any role in the so-called coup. He called for—and got—a federal investigation of U.S. involvement. When that independent analysis found that the Bush administration had nothing to do with the removal of Chávez, Dodd went silent on the matter. As information developed from 2004 to 2008 about Chávez's links to terrorism, the FARC, Iran, the drug trade, kidnapping, and money laundering, Dodd still believed the major problem the United States had with Chávez was that "we are losing the public relations war" in Latin America, as he put it in a 2007 presidential debate.[48] It is interesting to note that Connecticut is a major recipient of Chávez's oil discount program to poor families.

Dennis Kucinich, the Democrat representative from Ohio known for his quixotic presidential campaigns, is another stalwart Chávez defender. In 2004, he signed a letter along with Jesse Jackson, the actor Ed Asner, and the writers Howard Zinn and Naomi Klein, endorsing Chávez's reelection in the 2004 recall referendum and calling Venezuela "a model democracy."[49] The letter of course said not a word about Chávez's control of the voter list, the use of electronic voting machines to count the vote secretly, and fingerprint machines that could break the secrecy of the vote—all factors that if applied in America would generate a storm of human rights protest, not least from the very signatories to that letter.

Jimmy Carter:
In a Class by Himself

But by far Chávez's most prominent supporter in the United States is Jimmy Carter. It is impossible to overestimate the propaganda value of having a former American president repeatedly endorse Chávez's actions, validate his stolen elections, and assure the world that Hugo Chávez is a force for good. No doubt Chávez must marvel at his good luck, but he is not one to look a gift horse in the mouth.

After leaving the White House in 1981, Carter recounts, "Rosalynn and I searched our hearts for ways to help those less fortunate here in America and around the world. In an 'act of faith' we founded the Carter Center," for the purpose of "advancing peace and alleviating human suffering."[50] President Carter was best known for negotiating a peace agreement between Presidents Anwar Sadat of Egypt and Menachem Begin of Israel.

The Carter Center devoted itself to continuing that international work for which Carter himself is most acclaimed. In the years that followed, Carter Center teams were sent "to avert violence and foster peace" all over the world, prompting 750,000 Americans to "turn their faith into action by joining the Carter Center," where the prime rule is: *"First, our work must be non-partisan and non-political"* (emphasis in the original).[51]

However, whether Jimmy Carter followed his first rule in Venezuela is certainly open to question. In Carter's first trip to Caracas to observe the presidential election in 1998, he declared that he had witnessed "a democratic revolution" upon the election of Hugo Chávez, with whom he was obviously quite taken.[52]

Four years later, after the brief removal of Chávez in April 2002, and in the midst of a virtual civil war on the streets of Venezuela, the Organization of American States offered to mediate the impending civil war. But Chávez rejected the OAS, perhaps because it would include the United States (and Bush) in the deliberations.[53] Instead, on June 4, 2002, the government of Venezuela invited Jimmy Carter to "visit the country and facilitate a process of dialogue,"[54] an invitation Carter immediately accepted.

In fact, the entire episode appeared carefully orchestrated by Chávez and Castro. Only weeks before, Carter had taken a trip to Havana to meet with Fidel Castro.[55] Immediately afterward, Castro suggested Carter's name as the mediator in Venezuela's conflict.[56] One can only speculate but it is impossible to imagine that Chávez's mentor would have recommended anyone as a mediator who had shown an inclination to be objective. Could it have been a coincidence that Chávez's gratuitous rejection of the OAS offer to mediate occurred a day before his invitation issued to Carter? How did Chávez know Carter would instantly accept?

Unsurprisingly, on Carter's first mediation trip in July 2002—which was characterized by lengthy meetings and dinners with Chávez and his cabinet—the former U.S. president found that the opposition dismissed "Carter's claim to be an honest broker in their conflict."[57] Most wouldn't even meet with him.

Undeterred by the opposition's mistrust, Carter and Chávez pushed on as if joined in a coordinated campaign to counter them. On July 10, in Washington, Carter praised Chávez for creating "a pure brand of democracy"[58] while simultaneously in Caracas Chávez praised Carter's talks in

Venezuela as "historic" [59]—even though Carter had yet to talk to anyone. Both were irked by the recalcitrance of the opposition to enter negotiations in which Carter served as mediator, and Carter, who is known for his short temper, let the opposition know he was displeased that they had questioned his personal integrity.[60]

Chávez pushed hard for Carter as mediator. When Carter received the Nobel Peace Prize in October 2002, Chávez and his vice president were effusive in their public praise, and Chávez's minister of information, Nora Uribe, said she hoped the award would prompt the opposition groups to reconsider their refusal to negotiate, saying, "They [the opposition parties] have to understand that this prize is an affirmation of his work here in Venezuela." [61] Still, the opposition trusted Carter no more than Chávez, believing the two were in cahoots.

In December 2002, the opposition launched the national strike that crippled the country. The strike paralyzed the economy, created chaos on the streets, worsened the political impasse, and gave new life to Chávez, who could now pose as an advocate for law, order, and democracy.

On January 21, 2003, Carter presented his plan to end the strike. The centerpiece was a recall referendum on Chávez, which Carter described as a "peaceful and democratic solution." [62] Ironically, Chávez had written a recall provision into his 1999 constitution, never realizing that it might be applied to him. As the strike petered out a week later, the opposition—close to political death—reluctantly agreed to negotiate and accept Carter as the mediator.

As mediator, Carter was not hesitant to praise Chávez and criticize the opposition. To the latter's charge that Chávez was suppressing free speech and democracy, Carter replied, "In fact, under the Chávez government, in contrast to past governments of Venezuela, freedom of speech, assembly and association have been absolute. I believe that freedom of speech is as alive in Venezuela as it is in any other country I've visited." [63] By contrast, the Inter-American Press Association was complaining of abuses against free speech that put Venezuela almost at the bottom of the pile worldwide, close to Cuba and Haiti.[64]

While working to delay the vote as long as possible, Chávez plotted how to win it. In 2003, he created a dozen social initiatives—so-called Bolivarian Missions for the poor—and wound up spending an estimated $11 billion on them, equivalent to $1,000 per person among the 11 million poor in Venezuela's barrios at that time, before the referendum was finally held, in August 2004.[65]

While the opposition claimed Chávez was "buying votes" to thwart recall by the voters, Carter was exuberant about the spending spree. "Carter told me something wonderful," Chávez said in January 2004. "He told me that he met this morning—of his own volition—with people from the slums. I could tell by his voice that he was thrilled when he said that it had been one of the most wonderful meetings he has held in a long time, because he felt something miraculous was happening. . . . He was very impressed, and he even assured me that he will make sure the United States and the White House find out about his wonderful encounter with the poor of this country."[66]

Rather than talk to the chief economist Francisco Rodríguez, who could have informed Carter that independent audits of the spending showed Chávez was not improving the lives of the poor,[67] Carter depended on stories from individuals who may have been planted to influence him. This error would come back to haunt Carter's judgment on the night of the recall referendum in 2004; but its temporary success would also prompt a pleased Chávez to institute a visiting program for Americans susceptible to his charms.[68]

At the same meeting where Carter praised Chávez's slum spending, Chávez submitted a dossier to Carter containing what he said was evidence of the wrongdoing detected during the signature collection drive conducted by the voter's rights group Súmate or "Join Up." Chávez would force Súmate to collect 3.5 million petition signatures three times before finally agreeing to hold the vote. Shortly after the referendum, Chávez prosecuted the leaders of Súmate for treason—for being paid agents of the CIA—a case with no grounds that is still pending.[69]

The Carter Center is funded partly through U.S. government grants and partly through private donations—many of them from regimes not sympathetic to American interests. While the center reported no contributions from the government of Venezuela in relation to its 2002 to 2004 mediation work there, the OPEC Fund for International Development did send contributions in 2002, 2003, and 2004 (yet not before or afterward), which the center lists in the amounts of "$25,000–$99,000" for 2002, and "more than $100,000" for both 2003 and 2004. Venezuela is a member of OPEC—

an organization in which, we have seen, Chávez has much influence. The Carter Center has previously and repeatedly denied that any contribution from any foreign sources—much less OPEC—has had any impact on their work in Venezuela, or anywhere else for that matter.

We have already recounted the end of the story. Despite massive evidence that Chávez systematically manipulated the count, the Carter Center rejected the bulk of the allegations of electoral fraud, and Carter himself endorsed the final result of the recall. Questioned repeatedly about the many overlooked irregularities, Jennifer McCoy has allowed that we might never know the actual results of the recall. Carter himself has voiced no such doubt. He recently defended his conclusions without even trying to rebut the contrary evidence. "Our subsequent analyses showed a close correlation between the electronic returns and the paper ballot receipts that were required for substantiation of the results,"[70] Carter concluded, with no qualifications at all.

A grateful Chávez, naturally, simply pocketed his winnings, thanked the former president, and went on consolidating his power.

A few political leaders, initially seduced by Chávez, have come to see the light. Representative Dan Burton—a hard-line Republican from Indiana— has met with Chávez on more than one occasion. Burton at least had the sense to ask Chávez the right questions about his activities aimed at destabilizing the successful democracies in the hemisphere. And Burton has listened to the fears and concerns of Latin American democrats such as Colombia's Uribe.

Initially, Burton accepted Chávez's denials at face value. In a 2005 speech, he confidently stated that Chávez "assured me again that was not the case." Burton went on to say that he recommended to the State Department that "even though there have been some vitriolic statements made from Mr. Chávez, it's important that we try to open a dialogue with him."[71]

By 2006, Burton had changed his tune. At a hearing of the House International Relations Subcommittee on the Western Hemisphere, he said:

As this Subcommittee knows, I have tried to temper public remarks about Venezuela in the last twelve months, and I want to make it very clear that I wish to continue pursuing DIALOGUE with Caracas. Nevertheless, in recent weeks I have become increasingly convinced that the government of Venezuela is seeking to destabilize the region and dismantle the institutions of democracy within its borders and beyond them. Equally worrisome, in recent weeks President Hugo Chavez and Communist Dictator Fidel Castro of Cuba, along with other Latin American leaders, have begun reaching out to known Islamic terrorist organizations, such as Hamas, and cozying-up to renowned terrorist-sponsoring nations like Iran and North Korea. Any alliance between terrorist-sponsoring nations and leftist leaders in Latin America will be viewed as a serious and direct threat to the national security of the United States and our friends in the Hemisphere. When they cooperate with terrorist organizations such as Hamas, or cooperate with renowned terrorist-sponsoring nations like Iran or North Korea, President Chavez and the Cuban dictator are putting themselves and others at risk, and several world bodies will not long tolerate it.

Would that more American political figures had the sense and the courage to see that they have been wrong about Chávez, admit their mistake, and change course.

Buying Support with Oil Money

Chávez's appeal is not limited to leftist, anti-Bush, anticapitalist, or anti-American elements in the United States. As we have seen, Chávez has a lot of oil, which he uses to buy friends not just at home or in Latin America but in the United States as well. Those to whom he cannot appeal based on ideological conviction, he attempts to seduce with money. And he often succeeds.

Chávez's most ambitious effort is his so-called oil discount program, which provides low-cost and sometimes free oil to poor neighborhoods in the United States, in exchange for the (often eager) support of local politicians. The program costs Venezuela at least $250 million a year at 2008 market prices.[72] The TV and newspaper advertising budgets for the program alone are estimated at $50 million per year for 2008.[73]

Chávez is also a liberal contributor to those American philanthropic efforts that he judges will help his reputation, such as aid to the victims of Hurricane Katrina. This money, which is funneled through PDVSA, the state-owned oil company, and CITGO, its American arm, is estimated to vary from $10 million to $25 million per year since 2004.[74] The lobbying and legal costs alone are estimated at $3 million to $4 million per year since

2004.[75] When it's all added up, a conservative estimate is that Chávez has spent up to $300 million in the United States in 2008. But the real figure could be as high as $500 million.[76]

The public face of the oil discount program in America is, shockingly, a member of its most prominent and revered political dynasty. Joseph P. Kennedy II is the son of former Senator and presidential candidate Robert F. Kennedy and the nephew of President John F. Kennedy. Born in 1952, Kennedy founded the nonprofit Citizens Energy Corporation in 1979 to provide discounted home heating oil to low-income people in Massachusetts (the company has a market value of $58 million today).[77] After serving six terms in Congress, but losing a race for Massachusetts governor, he returned to Citizens Energy in 2002, the same year Chávez claimed he was temporarily overthrown by a U.S.-sponsored coup. It was then the two men began to talk.[78]

In 2003, Kennedy and Chávez agreed to have CITGO provide heating oil at about 40 percent below market prices to Citizens Energy Corporation customers in Massachusetts. The program expanded rapidly every year thereafter and has impacted an estimated 2 million American households in twenty-three states from Alaska to Maine, the District of Columbia, and a dozen Indian reservations.

The program is very popular with the American aid recipients who otherwise have seen their winter heating bills double or triple in recent years, as the New York Times found.[79] Ironically, the U.S. government–sponsored subsidy of low-income American households for oil heating was cut by the Bush administration just as the Chávez subsidy was coming on line, which gave Chávez's program added political potency.[80] Kennedy, who appears on TV ads for Chávez's program—intoning that the oil comes from "our Venezuelan friends" and that "help is on the way"—insists that the program is purely philanthropic and has no political agenda to legitimize Chávez's revolution.

While Chávez's support from American political figures comes mostly from the Democratic side of the aisle, that is far from universally true. Chávez knows the value of spreading his bets around, and he has netted three of the country's most prominent Republicans.

Jack Kemp was the Republican candidate for vice president in 1996 and for decades served in the U.S. House of Representatives. Kemp proposed a business alliance with Venezuela in 2002, trying to broker a sale of Venezuela's oil to the U.S. Strategic Petroleum Reserve via an intermediary company—Free Market Petroleum LLC—on whose board Kemp sits. Since joining the Board of Free Market Petroleum, Kemp has visited with Chávez and his ministers in Caracas.[81] After the phony coup of April 2002, Kemp did nothing to rebut Chávez's contention that the United States had tried to overthrow him and defended Chávez as "easy to control and not a threat to America" at a meeting of former members of Congress in Washington, D.C.[82]

When Kemp was publicly upbraided by the *Wall Street Journal* editorial board for shilling for Chávez (Kemp accompanied Venezuela's Ambassador Bernardo Álvarez to the editorial board meeting),[83] Kemp took a lower profile, but privately he continued to work with for Chávez. Kemp, who ran for the U.S. presidency in 1988 as a staunch defender of national security, has not said as much as he could have about Chávez's links to Iran, the FARC, or terrorism.

Mitt Romney, as a 2008 Republican presidential candidate, was critical of Chávez, but he also reported a large political contribution from Dutko Worldwide employees of $15,400 in 2007. Dutko, a lobbying firm in Washington associated in the past with Democrats, counts Chávez's CITGO as one of its major clients. CITGO pays Dutko an estimated $1 million per year—something Romney never explained. Nor did he disclose the business his former financial firm, Bain Associates, conducted with Chávez's government or national oil company.[84]

Rudy Giuliani, the former Republican mayor of New York and one-time presidential candidate, allowed his law firm, Bracewell and Giuliani, to lobby for Venezuela while he was running for U.S. president, presenting himself as the candidate with the most experience fighting terrorism in the Americas.

Bracewell and Giuliani received $60,000 in 2005 and 2006 to lobby in the Texas state government on CITGO's behalf, but Giuliani saw no conflict. "Mayor Giuliani believes Hugo Chávez is not a friend of the United States and his influence continues to grow because of our increasing reliance on foreign sources of oil," a presidential campaign spokesman told the *New York Times*.[85] Giuliani said he did not work under the contract himself and saw no direct connection between CITGO, which he called "an American company," and Chávez. He further defended his firm's work on behalf of CITGO as "protecting American jobs."[86]

The Chávez Propaganda Machine

To some extent, Chávez simply attracts the support of ideologically sympathetic figures without needing to exert any effort. These Americans ignore inconvenient facts about Chávez. Not much "fact-checking"—Sean Penn's words—appears to be going on. And that encourages Americans to think uncritically about him.

But Chávez is not one to leave things to chance. He has constructed an elaborate propaganda machine to ensure that he gets his hooks into as many potential fish as possible. Notwithstanding the efforts of Maria Conchita Alonso, the river of information about Chávez is still flowing his way. "Chávez is the piper leading the most strident anti-Americanism to parade through Latin America since the Bay of Pigs invasion," the Venezuelan writer Ibsen Martínez notes.[87] How Chávez accomplished this outcome is a tribute to his application of modern propaganda techniques, in particular: political tourism to Venezuela; the Venezuela Information Office in the United States; and, as we have seen, buying support with oil money. These three tools have combined to create the most powerful foreign national propaganda machine in the United States today.

Potemkin Tourism

Chávez has enlisted the U.S./Cuba Labor Exchange and its much larger partner, Global Exchange—the activist group that encouraged protests at the World Trade Organization meeting in Seattle in 1999[88]—to attract Americans to visit Venezuela in a packaged tour at a discounted price. Naturally, the itinerary and agenda of the tour are designed to promote Chávez's Bolivarian Revolution and his anti-American positions.

What visitors see and hear is planned down to the last detail, from the arrival at the airport to choreographed meetings at PDVSA headquarters, trips to selected ministries and government TV studios, visits to selected poverty missions and socialist cooperatives, visits to the election commission, and "spontaneous" meetings with real people. The whole whirlwind reminded one experienced European diplomat of the machinations of Grygor Potemkin, who impressed Catherine the Great by fabricating for her visit, the perfect (if imaginary) "Potemkin village."[89]

The Global Exchange advertising sales pitch which touts the "reality tour" for Americans reads: "Something remarkable is happening in Venezuela. The lives of millions of Venezuelans are improving, while past mistakes are being corrected. . . . Before, Venezuelan oil wealth benefitted a few. Now it benefits a few million. . . . We invite you to travel to Venezuela with Global Exchange to dig past the headlines and explore the changes occurring in Venezuela." [90]

In 2008, Global Exchange offered thirteen "reality tours" of Venezuela, lasting from ten to fourteen days, to show that the country was "at the center of a new, progressive model of socioeconomic development that is shaping Latin America's future." [91] Since 2004, thousands [92] of American visitors have experienced this Hollywood-set tour. And those tours have had their intended effect. Consider the effusive reaction of one young American man at the end of his visit: "The faith that they have in their government and the faith that the government has in them is something that is really beautiful and is something that I've never seen before and I didn't really know it existed." [93] Hundreds if not thousands of small-town newspaper articles and university or Internet blog letters have been produced by Americans who return from visits to Venezuela fully converted to the Bolivarian Revolution and the Chávez personality cult.

Big fish have also gone for Chávez's bait. Cornel West of Princeton, who is well known for denouncing the United States as racist and patriarchal, believes the Venezuelan reality tour is essential because "We in the United States have so many lies about President Hugo Chávez and the Bolivarian Revolution." He visited in 2006 "to see the democratic awakening taking place." [94] Needless to say, Professor West saw nothing else.

The Venezuela Information Office

The Venezuela Information Office (VIO)—clearly an oxymoron—was established in 2003 inside Venezuela's embassy in Washington. The VIO's activities involve TV, radio, print, and Internet message production and distribution on a massive scale in the United States.

As *The National Review* documented in 2004, the VIO moved aggressively by contracting with the lobbying and legal firm Patton Boggs, expanding the lobbying and communications activities of Dutko Worldwide, buying ads in *The Economist*, *The New Yorker*, the *New York Times*, and *Roll*

Call, hiring staff from Global Exchange, and retaining the communications consultant Michael Shellenberger, a proponent of "transformative, post-modern, anti-globalization politics."[95]

The VIO operates under an undisclosed budget, but what can be gleaned from U.S. reporting laws shows a multi-million-dollar annual lobbying effort.[96] Yet the VIO's budget is only the tip of a massive iceberg of funding used by Chávez to influence Americans to favor his revolution.

The Venezuelan government's official budget for 2008 included $250 million to finance pro-Chávez groups and "anti-imperialist" movements in the Americas and the promotion of solidarity "with sectors that have been excluded from the North American Society."[97] The official budget document states that the strategy for spending the $250 million is to "neutralize the actions of the empire [by] strengthening the solidarity and the public opening of organized social movements."[98] These funds have become increasingly difficult to track since no public review is permitted.

Chávez controls other funds whose sources are opaque, including an off-budget slush fund called Fonden that receives and distributes tens of billions of dollars per year,[99] plus PDVSA and CITGO spending that he can draw upon at will, with little or none of it exposed to public review. PDVSA has not reported its expenditures to the Securities and Exchange Commission since 2003.[100]

Chávez's Motivation

Why is Chávez spending so much on lobbying in the United States? Is his purpose to help the poor and protect Venezuela's oil sales to the United States, which are the two most common explanations he gives?[101]

If Chávez wanted to help the poor, he could do much better by spending his money in Venezuela, where there are far more poor people and where the poor are much poorer by any objective measure. An American family of four with an income of $24,000, though technically poor in America, would be rich in Venezuela: such a family is in the bottom 20 percent of American income but the top 20 percent of Venezuelan income. Half the population of Venezuela lives on $2 per day; virtually no one does so in America, not even the homeless. Venezuela's GDP per capita is 10 percent of America's. Poverty and inequality are right on Chávez's doorstep and they are worsening. It beggars credibility to suppose that Chávez is spending $300 million a year in America to solve a poverty problem that is orders of magnitude less intense than the one in his own country.

Similarly, if Chávez wanted to protect his oil sales in the United States, he wouldn't need to spend a cent to do so. The United States buys whatever he sells at the current market price. U.S. buyers gave $29 billion to Chávez for his oil in 2007 alone.[102] Far from seeking to expand his U.S. market share, Chávez is reducing his sales to the United States for political reasons. He would rather sell to geopolitical allies like China. Since 1999, Chávez has reduced oil sales to the United States by 25 percent,[103] and he has threatened a total oil cutoff of the United States at least a hundred times.

The truth is: Chávez is spending his money to buy credibility and legitimacy for his revolution against American economic and political influence in the world. When push comes to shove, he relies on his Idiots to back him up in America. "He's not the crazy man we've heard about," Barbara Walters told her ABC viewers prior to her 2007 interview. "This is a very intelligent man, a passionate man, a dignified man. He sang to me!"[104] She's at least partly right: he's not crazy, he is passionate, and he is intelligent.

We cannot say the same about his American supporters and apologists.

9

Chávez as
Spin Doctor

His speeches can be highly entertaining, but it is sometimes difficult
to know if he means what he says or has simply been carried away by
his own oratory.

—Jon Lee Anderson, "Fidel's Heir," a profile of Hugo Chávez,
The New Yorker, June 23, 2008

It's impossible not to note the irony in a photo of Hugo Chávez published widely during 2008's summer of outrageous oil prices. Here is the infamous Latin American leader, clad in a bright red workshirt, riding a bicycle on one of his weekly TV broadcasts of *Aló Presidente.*[1] He looks almost comical perched above the high-tech handlebars. Had the state limo run out of gas? Chávez was ostensibly promoting a deal with an Iranian company to produce 100,000 such green vehicles in a Venezuelan-based factory. Yet his ulterior motive went deeper than simple hype for a joint business venture. In one of his regular pokes at the United States, he offered a bike to President Bush. The underlying message was clear: *without my oil, you may need one of these!*

The inscrutable version of Hugo Chávez in 2008 is something to behold. Chávez is a talker, a voluble one. According to his own Ministry of Information, he has spent forty hours per week on TV (including replays) since 1999 (imagine watching a show for forty hours a week if you can), explaining everything from what to name babies to how to raise chickens on the tin roof of your shack. He has also declared war, fired and hired vice presidents, played illegal tapes of phone calls, sung songs, painted pictures, played baseball, and made billion-dollar investments on TV.

To gain credibility for his narrative, Chávez controls or has destroyed information about his government and Venezuelan society. Official numbers and words have been redefined, changed, or have disappeared with Chinese precision. The media are almost totally in his control (while he overtly pleads they are traitors or CIA stooges). In August 2008, Chávez proposed a new law to control the Internet. Only the Catholic Church and private education have escaped his grasp—although he has started up a loyal branch of the Catholic Church with *chavista* bishops, and his Bolivarian schools outnumber all the private schools in the country.

Some days he's serious, even somewhat logical, if not exactly truthful; other days he's outrageous, loud, and threatening. We've come to heed his actions either way because he's a very unpredictable and potentially dangerous man indeed. To know him is to fear him. As Chávez began his frightening quest to communize Venezuela's young democracy, U.S. ambassador John Maisto warned, "Watch what he does, not what he says." *The Economist* wondered in a June 2008 headline whether Chávez was a "Master Tactician or Failing Bungler?"[2] Can there be any doubt?

Let's not forget that in the summer of 2008, Chávez was busy making deals with his allies, including a trip to Russia where he met with Putin and Medvedev to secure a $1 billion-plus agreement to buy arms.[3] The quid pro quo was getting the Russians to use their vast oil and gas exploration resources to look for more reserves in Venezuela. Chávez is intent on stockpiling energy and defending himself from what he calls the Evil Empire. He's also ensured that Cuba would benefit from his vast oil cache. In return, Raúl Castro would provide medical aid to Venezuela in what has been called a "doctors for oil" deal.

The trip also sowed the seeds for a potentially more formidable agreement. Witness the startling news on September 8, 2008, when Russia decided to join Chávez for a first-ever joint naval drill with Venezuela. Russia has not held maneuvers in the Caribbean since the Cold War, and now it will be sending the most heavily armed nuclear cruiser on earth for a war games exercise that could lead to anything but games.

In his weekly television address, President Chávez said: "Russia's naval fleet is welcome here. If it's possible, we'll stage an exercise in our Caribbean waters." Anticipating criticism from Washington, he taunted his northern neighbor, saying, "Go ahead and squeal, Yankees."[4] And after the warships landed in the Caribbean, Chávez proclaimed boldly on Venezuela TV that "the Yankee hegemony is finished."[5]

Why is this potentially such a threat? As of May 2008 more than a quarter of our oil imports came from Latin American and Caribbean nations that use Caribbean waters. Add Canada, which ships some of its oil through Panama to the Gulf, and it's 47 percent. We heavily rely on the shipping lanes and access routes in the area where Russian warships, along with a thousand Russian troops, will be headed to Caracas for simulated battles.[6]

The Russians, Venezuelans, and Cubans are circling the wagons.

All this is going on while Chávez appears to be softening his image and playing up to his rivals. Let's take a look at his latest olive branch, extended to Colombia.

Anyone with a modicum of interest in Latin American affairs has to wonder about the relationship between Colombia's Álvaro Uribe and Hugo Chávez. According to the Reyes files, Chávez aided and abetted the FARC. He has steadfastly clung to his dream: a socialist empire—indeed, even a coalition of Latin America's struggling, like-minded nations—inspired by the liberator Simon Bolívar and the Communist Fidel Castro. President Uribe's Colombia, which is allied with the United States against the narcoterrorist guerrillas of the FARC, stands as a huge obstacle to Chávez realizing those dreams for power.

Uribe has every right to wonder about the intentions of Chávez. As we have previously reported—in 2008 alone, Chávez called for international political recognition of the FARC but also for its disbanding altogether; Chávez called Uribe his "brother" but also planned to overthrow Uribe in favor of the FARC; Chávez threatened to send jet fighters to attack Uribe, but also said he wanted to make peace with Colombia; and Chávez sent tank battalions to his border in preparation for war with Colombia but also got the FARC to release seven hostages to Uribe.

It's difficult to trust anything Chávez says nowadays. He plays the spin doctor as well as any propagandist with a worldwide agenda. The Chávez of 2008 has systematically confounded many of the world's political strategists and leaders. Every time he is called out for his draconian ruling tactics or bombastic pronouncements, he seems to temper his strident behavior to appeal to potential allies and mainstream critics. He is a master at pivoting or reversing course at the drop of a hat.

He's backed off other major positions, besides his support of the FARC rebels in Colombia. On June 10, 2008, he recalled his initiative to start a major domestic intelligence-gathering program that would have turned the Venezuelans into spies against themselves (dubbed the "Gestapo Law").[7]

The revamped Venezuelan law would have required citizens to spy on one another and turn in those disloyal to Chávez's agencies—a policy akin to that practiced by the Stasi, the German secret police, before the Berlin Wall was torn down. The penalties were severe, including prison terms up to four years. Human rights activists, political opponents, and the Roman Catholic Church all expressed concerns about turning the citizenry into a nation of snitches. (Opposing pundits in Venezuela substituted *Getsapo* for *Gestapo,* which is a wonderful play on words: *sapo* or "frog" means "tattle-tale" in colloquial Spanish, so the Gestapo Law was literally a law to snitch or go to jail.) "Even within the Bolivarian movement, this would officialize Soviet- and Cuban-style purges, accusing dissidents of being spies, traitors or agents of the imperialist enemy," *El Nacional* said in an editorial. "This is revolting."[8]

Chávez also withdrew an idea for a socialist-inspired school curriculum because Venezuelans of all political stripes opposed Chávez teaching his revolutions in the schools. Student demonstrations successfully blocked a move to abolish university entrance requirements. When Chávez charged private TV stations exorbitant fees to use clips from his state channels, the industry refused to pay so he dropped it. Amid a barrage of protests, he shelved a proposed increase in bus fares. But when Human Rights Watch published the truth about Chavez's rights violations, his police raided the hotel of its spokesmen and dragged them to the airport for the first flight out of the country.

In a December 2007 referendum (as we have seen), Chávez apparently lost his bid to be president for life. It was his first election defeat in eleven outings since winning the presidency in 1998. But the real story was not

Chávez losing the majority vote in the elections—that happened in 2004, in our view. The revelation was that General Raúl Baduel and the university students prevented Chávez from rigging the vote count in his favor with his tricked-out machines by threatening a civil war.

Chávez's proposal to lift term limits, specifically allowing the president to be reelected indefinitely, was especially unpopular. At one large demonstration attended mostly by university students, the Caracas police used tear gas and water nozzles to disperse the crowd; at a later demonstration it was reported that *chavistas,* the president's supporters, wore masks and fired guns into a crowd of students. But all of Chávez's fire power didn't stop them. The students, like General Baduel, were fearless.

Let's not forget that Chávez hasn't abandoned his agenda or his approach. His main concern is keeping himself in office, so he can continue to spread havoc among nations sympathetic to his views. Yet he certainly looked the part of a conciliator after Colombian commandos rescued fifteen hostages, including Ingrid Betancourt and the three American defense contractors, from six years in captivity in FARC prison camps. (Colombian senator Betancourt, the dual French/Colombian citizen, was a long shot candidate for president in 2003 when the FARC kidnapped her. As Betancourt became a world cause célèbre, the FARC used her as a bargaining chip to get international recognition as a belligerent force.) The effort to release the hostages and reach out to his peers in Colombia only signifies a temporary strategy of appeasement.

Chávez was dangerously weakened by the 37,000 files captured upon the killing of the FARC's number two guerrilla leader, Raúl Reyes. While he fumed that the files were fabricated by the CIA—even after Interpol had found them to be authentic—three events corroborated their accuracy, as we have previously reported: thirty kilos of nonenriched uranium were confiscated in Bogotá; $450,000 of FARC drug money was found in a FARC safe house in Costa Rica; and one of Chávez's military was found selling AK-47 munitions to the FARC in Colombia. All three of those incidents were tipped by the Reyes files, which have been only partially released.

The bluster of Chávez declaring war against Colombia for attacking the FARC camp in Ecuador where the Reyes files were confiscated appeared to be a classic Chávez cover-up. Chávez needed to create a problem he could solve and distract people from the real story. A few weeks later, he made peace with Uribe in the Dominican Republic as if it was a big deal, inviting a *New Yorker* writer into the meeting secretly—the journalist went in as part of his presidential delegation, of all things—where Chávez played the peacemaker.[9]

Returning to Caracas, Chávez called on the FARC to surrender to Uribe. It took expert spin-doctoring because Chávez had to deny something he had done covertly but repudiated overtly for over a decade: supporting the FARC with money, weapons, oil, and cocaine transit. Chávez once again came off in the press as the peacemaker, while Uribe stood by and tacitly endorsed these heroics by saying nothing.

After the Reyes files were exposed, Chávez ordered the military to prepare for war with Colombia—and the United States if necessary—but there was a small problem. There were eight hundred to one thousand objecting generals and officers whom he had relieved of their commands and put on temporary home leave. This fact went largely unreported in Venezuela but was confirmed by sources who called dozens of the objecting officers and found that they were assigned to home duty. Almost all of these military officers were openly opposed to revolutionary indoctrination, and especially to Chávez's mandated daily salute, "Fatherland, socialism or death!" which some retired soldiers have likened to "Heil Hitler."

In the age of the cell phone, having that many potential military "coupsters" at home plotting against him was something Chávez understood but could not tolerate. The national security edict he issued was intended to stifle military conspiracy talk by making any government employee liable to four years in prison for not reporting counterrevolutionary conversations. Chávez simply wanted to muzzle his soldiers. Going further, the edict declared that any citizen could be imprisoned for two years for the same offense.

Chávez can probably only be counted on to remain consistent when it comes to wielding his oil dipstick. In June 2008, he predicted that light, sweet crude prices would reach $200 a barrel if the United States or Israel were to strike against Iran's nuclear facilities. Soaring prices have fueled Venezuelan government spending, and Chávez confidently shrugged off the possibility of a downward draft in oil prices. He said his nation could stand a 33 percent decline, claiming that $100 a barrel would still provide plenty of profits for Venezuela. (The oil price dropped to under $70 a barrel when the financial crisis toppled global markets in October 2008.)

On July 10, 2008, when oil tipped to a record $145 per barrel, Chávez repeated his mantra: Americans are paying high prices for gas because of dwindling reserves, a weak U.S. dollar, the conflict in Iraq, and Washington's "threats" against Iran. Three days later, he was at it again, intensifying the rhetoric. He threatened to stop oil shipments to the United States if ExxonMobil succeeded again in freezing the financial accounts of Petróleos de Venezuela, S.A. overseas. "If they freeze us, there's no more oil for the United States, and the price of crude will go to $300 a barrel," Chávez told the participants of the Petrocaribe V summit.

This is all taken from a page in the Chávez playbook, where he assumes center stage whether he is attacking his enemies or appeasing the undecided. Listen to his stance when he's addressing so-called neutral nations, as he did earlier in the summer of 2008: "They want to blame us: the Arabs and Venezuela. We are not to blame. Withdraw the troops from Iraq and you'll see how oil prices will drop," Chávez told visiting delegates from countries belonging to the Non-Aligned Movement. (The Non-Aligned Movement is an international organization of states considering themselves not formally aligned with or against any major power bloc. It was founded in April 1955; in 2007, it had 118 members.) "Stop the threats against Iran and Venezuela, oil-producing countries, and you'll see prices will tend to decline." Does anyone really believe this?

Again, let's not forget who he really is, even when he appears to behave like a responsible leader. Recall Chávez's ties to Hezbollah and Iran—which includes $20 billion committed to over two hundred joint military, political, and economic ventures that threaten U.S. national security. Chávez is a vociferous advocate of Iran's nuclear ambitions, Hezbollah, insurgencies in Iraq and Lebanon, Hamas, and also Iran's desire to wipe Israel off the map. You might think that his oil and financial support to the Middle East would raise red flags in Washington.

Hezbollah, the radical Shiite militia sponsored by Iran, has a new base of operations in the Americas: Venezuela. Western intelligence officials told the *Los Angeles Times* that President Hugo Chávez has formed "a strategic partnership" with Iran, and that Hezbollah is exploiting the new ties. The group intends to create a special terrorist cell to kidnap Jewish businessmen in Latin America and take them back to Lebanon, the intelligence officials said. Another danger, they say, is that Hezbollah could use Venezuela as a base from which to insert terrorists into the United States."

As we have previously reported, Chávez and Ahmadinejad have already created the bank and airline that could facilitate Hezbollah operations.[10]

In July 2008, the Bush administration fingered Chávez for providing cash and protection to the militant Islamist group Hezbollah of Southern Lebanon. (Iran and Syria are Hezbollah's primary sponsors in the Middle East.) But this revelation barely received any press. According to a report in the *Washington Times*, the U.S. Treasury Department's Office of Foreign Assets Control (OFAC) named the Venezuelan attaché Ghazi Nasr al Din and the Venezuelan-Arab businessman known as Fawzi Kan'an as those who provided a connection between Venezuela and Hezbollah. The Treasury Department also froze the assets of both men and banned them from conducting business in the United States or with American residents. The Treasury's actions came after an investigation of Venezuelan-registered businesses that were suspected of being money-laundering fronts for Hezbollah. The agency's report alluded to even more startling charges, including Kan'an's planning of "possible kidnapping and terrorist attacks" and of "traveling with other Hezbollah members to Iran for training." Ka'nan denounced the accusations.

Adam Szubin, the political affairs director of OFAC who suggested it was "extremely troubling to see the government of Venezuela employing and providing safe harbor for Hezbollah facilitators and fund-raisers,"[11] should be more than extremely troubled. This was not the first rumbling of a serious link between Chávez and the militant Middle East.

Though Chávez has denied any connection between his government and Hezbollah, it's fairly certain that he is actively forming alliances with Iran, Syria, and Lebanon to buttress a political bloc that can oppose the United States, Israel, and its allies. Chávez is smart enough to know that Iran will continue to be a craw in the throat of American politics well after the November elections, whether a Democrat or Republican enters the White House. Even if the constant saber rattling about Iran and its development of nuclear weapons has primarily been an attempt by the United States to distract the public from the arduous, seemingly endless conflict in Iraq, Ahmadinejad's Iran wishes only ill for the United States.

If you are worried about Chávez's expanding powers, then you should be worried about the effect he's having on the Iranian government. Chávez and Iranian president Mahmoud Ahmadinejad already have exchanged cordial state visits and agreed on more than $20 billion worth of joint ventures in energy, mining, and various industrial projects. In 2007, Ahmadinejad gave Chávez his nation's highest honor, a medal signifying his solidarity in standing by Iran in its standoff in the international community over nuclear development inspections. The two are working strategically for the same end against America.

While Chávez may be a favored son in Tehran, he has nominally overestimated his sway in neighboring South American nations. His Iranian alliance may be overshadowed by the losing chess game he is playing out with both Colombia and Brazil.

Chávez's power may ultimately be weakened because of the political and economic resurgence now occurring in both of those countries. He had to make overtures to Uribe because of the relevations of the Reyes files. According to the *Financial Times*, "He spent precious political capital in succumbing to Uribe's government. Mr. Chávez's conciliatory rhetoric and Mr. Uribe's enhanced international prestige are a sign of the sharp reversal in the fortunes of the two leaders. The shift may in turn presage a broader rebalancing of the neighbouring countries' rival claims to influence in the region—especially if Mr. Uribe's *coup de théâtre* translates into lasting victory over the FARC." [12] Perhaps Chávez is regretting the moments when he referred to the Colombian president as a "pawn of imperialism" and a "mafia boss."

Now he must make similar peace offerings to Brazil's Luiz Inácio Lula da Silva, because of business; not a political crisis. It's all about business, and it's not personal. Whereas Venezuela's economy has shown signs of sputtering, Brazil's has been quietly expanding what has been a traditionally strong portfolio of businesses. Brazil recently has made new discoveries of offshore oil reserves, and this has blunted Chávez's most potent bargaining tool. Lula da Silva has taken advantage of a number of positive trends, broadening the nation's industrial base, and turning Brazil into an attractive trade partner. Brazil houses a huge and diversified market that is seven times the size of Venezuela's. Lula has soybeans and sugar-based ethanol to sell, while Venezuela remains a single-item exporter. Brazil has a trade surplus with the eleven other countries that form the Latin American Integration Association. In 2002, Lula da Silva's nation was exporting $1.7 billion more in goods than it imported. Five years later, the trade surplus jumped to $16 billion.

"While Chávez grabs the headlines, the debate over whether Brazil is becoming a regional power is moot," says Kenneth Maxwell, a historian at Harvard University and a columnist for the Brazilian newspaper *Folha de São Paulo.* "Brazil has actually made it to that level but in a very non-bombastic way."

On the other hand, Chávez must now concentrate on coping with an inflation rate of more than 30 percent and shortages of basic commodities. He's trying to stir up investment by reaching out to businesses leery of the nationalization or confiscation of all oil and gas, electricity, aluminum, steel, cement, telephone industries, and some banking, television, and food businesses. In short, Latin Americans are seeing that Chávez's brand of socialism is not working in a region that has a lot of room to expand.

Riding bikes on his national TV show is not going to cut it.

Whether Chávez wins or loses most of the state and city elections of November 2, 2008, is a moot issue. He is a master at rigging the results in voting booths using subtle tactics—yet even if he lets some opposition candidates win their elections, Chávez loses not a drop of power or money in Venezuela. Even if he lost most of the local elections, the iron fist of Chávez will still grip the executive, legislative, judicial, military, and PDVSA, and most of the private sector.

Chávez is a realist only when he faces military opposition. Like Mao, he believes power comes out of the muzzle of a gun. In 1992, he surrendered to the military gun pointed at him, but through an astonishing media flourish—his *"por ahora"* TV statement—was able to enter jail not just politically alive but a popular hero. In 2002, he surrendered to the military gun again, but again by a media flourish and a big lie—blaming the coup on the United States—was able to stay alive politically. And in 2007, he basically surrendered to the military once more, but to the retired and unarmed General Baduel this time, who forced Chávez to allow a referendum loss of 1 percent to be reported when he had actually lost by about 12 percent.

Baduel prevented Chávez from using his tricky electronic voting machines in 2007, but the president will surely be back with that referendum before he has to vacate Miraflores in 2013. When Chávez is down, he's at his most dangerous.

In the local elections of 2008, Chávez (who is not on the ballot) is once again running against Americans, calling them *pitiyanquis* this time, which probably amuses the Venezuelan military. We find it interesting that the *New York Times* reporter Simon Romero has adopted Chávez's false explanation for his anti-Americanism, as this sentence in his story indicates: "Mr. Chávez has stepped up his confrontational tone with Washington ever since the Bush Administration tacitly approved a coup that briefly toppled him [in] [sic] 2002."[13] Only a few weeks later, Chávez expelled the U.S. ambassador Patrick Duddy on the preposterous charge that he was conspiring to assassinate and overthrow Chávez. That was a day after Bolivia's President Morales had expelled his U.S. ambassador on the same groundless charge there. But Chávez went even further, promising to finance a subversive guerrilla war in Bolivia if Morales is removed from power by Bolivians. To all but the dense, it has become fully obvious that all these charges against America are intended to distract Venezuelans from their real problems of poverty and insecurity so that Chávez can stay in power indefinitely.

Clearly, Chávez's control of Venezuela is based on the price of oil. If it stays high—$100 or more—Chávez will have all the money he needs to solidify and extend his rule. If the oil price falls to the $60 range, which is where it is at this writing, or if Chávez can't sell his oil for whatever reason and thus can't pay his bills, which are enormous, he is vulnerable to a revolt by his own military. A nation's overall health can be measured by the level of desperate measures its citizens take to survive. According to the *CIA World Factbook,* "Venezuela is a source, transit, and destination country for men, women, and children trafficked for the purposes of commercial sexual exploitation and forced labor; Venezuelan women and girls are trafficked within the country for sexual exploitation, lured from the nation's interior to urban and tourist areas; child prostitution in urban areas and child sex tourism in resort destinations appear to be growing; Venezuelan women and girls are trafficked for commercial sexual exploitation to Western Europe, Mexico, and Caribbean destinations."[14]

The week before Venezuelans go to the polls for local elections on November 23, 2008, Russia's President Medvedev is to visit his number one military client in the world to review Russsian nuclear bombers and warships coursing through Venezuela's airspace and waters. Russia is happy to help distract Venezuelans from Chávez's failures by reheating the Cold War from the Soviet Union's salad days. Whether Venezuelan voters will be fooled to vote for "21st century socialism" as a result of such sword-rattling against America remains to be seen.

10

The Alliance of the Americas: A Strategy to Thwart the Threat

T he big lesson Hispanic Americans teach is that they can produce five times the GDP per capita of their home countries within our system. So why can't it work there? If the 550 million Latin Americans were as productive as the 45 million Hispanic Americans in the United States in 2006, Latin America would not have produced $2.4 trillion in GDP as it did but a whopping $12.1 trillion—a trillion dollars more than the United States that year. Had that happened, a $12.1 trillion economy in Latin America would have driven up the standard of living of its prime trading partner, the United States. That wealth creation would also change dramatically the equation of world politics in the United States. It could compare favorably or exceed what Europe can do with its investments in Eastern Europe, the Middle East, or Africa; or even what China can do (and is doing) with hegemonic investment in Asia. The way for America to compete with Europe and China in the next fifty years is in its own backyard: Latin America.[1]

It is certainly possible for Latin American countries, especially Venezuela, to prosper despite the inflexible and often destructive leadership of Hugo Chávez. It will take a major effort, however, to thwart his tactics.

According to a report released by the Council on Foreign Relations in 2008, "U.S.–Latin America Relations: A New Direction for a New Reality":

> The anti-U.S. policies of President Chávez should be taken seriously by U.S. policymakers. It is important that the United States keep a close watch on Venezuela and that Chávez's potentially destabilizing policies within Latin America be carefully monitored. At the same time, a good deal of Venezuela's international support is limited to the concrete benefits that Venezuela provides, such as financial support, subsidized oil, and infrastructure investments. Thus, according to the most recent *Latino Barametro* poll of Latin Americans, President Chávez's leadership ranks at the bottom, only slightly above lowest ranked Fidel Castro.

The report continued:

> In addition, a Pew 2007 Global Attitudes Project indicates that "nearly three-quarters of Brazilians, Peruvians, and Chileans doubt that Chávez is 'doing the right thing' in world affairs. This suggests the United States must temper its vigilance with a careful assessment of Chávez's real interest in the region."[2]

Today, it is difficult to accurately assess what's behind Chávez's "official position" on any important political issue. We cannot trust what he says because he's constantly lunging, parrying, and at times retreating. In January 2008, he announced that the FARC guerrillas in Colombia should not be treated as terrorists but as an "insurgent force" with international rights under the articles of war. Six months later, he did an about-face, surprising the world by calling on the guerrillas to give up their forty-year struggle to overthrow the government and to release their eight hundred hostages. He all but said that guerrilla warfare in Latin America had to end. (In July 2008, when several of the hostages were rescued in the dramatic mission led by Colombian commandos, Chávez tried to position himself as some kind of contrite champion of liberty.)

In the past he's pointed to the trade and pipelines he promoted with Uribe's government in Colombia, but when he was accused of promising $300 million in support of the FARC guerrillas to overthrow Uribe's government—including a cache of underpriced oil they could sell for a profit—he sloughed off the accusation by saying, why would he give to both causes? This is precisely the kind of behavior we've come to expect from Chávez.

Chávez has certainly made his mark in the social realm of Venezuela. Most Americans are unaware of the structural poverty he has let fester in the region for far too long. Much of this poverty has led to violent crime, an issue that half of Venezuelans consider the principal problem affecting their lives.[3] Since he took over as the nation's leader, Venezuela's homicide rate has tripled, according to Chávez's own statistics. The true figures may be considerably higher, as many killings never make it into the ledger, including those who are "resisting arrest" and those murders that occur in jails.[4]

Jon Lee Anderson, a *New Yorker* writer who recently visited Venezuela, noted that "Caracas is, in many respects, a failed city, and it looks and feels like a place that has spun out of control." He went on to report on the city's "shockingly high" crime rate and the legions of homeless and poor who were living along a "sewage trough of a river." This hardly describes the result of competent government.[5]

A prosperous Latin America would enhance U.S. security, stabilize immigration, and promote economic growth in the Americas for the long term. In order to secure this, America's future response to the Chávez regime must be swift and clearly thought out. And it should involve both a short-term strategy to thwart his oil extortion tactics and a long-term plan to unravel his influence and reverse the wave of populism, anti-Americanism, and hostility that is emerging in Latin America.

The short-term strategy should entail four elements:

- A significant reduction of U.S. dependence on Venezuelan oil imports;
- Sanctions against Venezuela as a state sponsor of terrorism, drugs, and crime—as warranted by the evidence;
- Support for Colombia's worthy free trade agreement and its effective anti-drug war;
- And, finally, an expanded arms embargo of Venezuela.

The long-term strategy should combine the spirit of John F. Kennedy's Alliance for Progress with the financial commitment of Truman's Marshall Plan. The strategy is to create a vigorous public-private partnership—it could be called the "Alliance of the Americas"—that invests in the tools of wealth creation for the 200 million poor people in Latin America. A carefully wrought plan could help many of the suffering masses, who could easily become newly productive, proud members of society. Such an alliance would enhance Latin America economically, lessen the pressures of millions of poor trying to enter the United States illegally via our porous border with Mexico, and alleviate the root grievances behind the rise of belligerent populists like Chávez: poverty and inequality.

The Historic Relationship of Inequality—And What to Do About It

To understand the present, we must look to the past. The culture and history of the region cries out to be understood. Latin Americans have experienced three centuries of Spanish or Portuguese colonial conquest followed by the century of U.S. corporate and military dominance after the Spanish-American War. Many Latinos think of themselves as "subordinated." Populists like Chávez feed off the rage against historic slavery and the resentment of unrealized aspirations, which in turn shapes the "savage discourse" so resonant in the region today.[6]

It may be difficult for Americans to realize, but the memory of U.S. military intervention in a handful of Central American and Caribbean nations during the Cold War still lingers in the minds of Latin Americans today. The legacy of the United Fruit Company—the firm that created the banana republic—branded that dominance for American corporations. And the "dependency" theory provided leaders like Chávez a way to explain Latin America's failures as the result of external Western abuse.

President Kennedy attempted to overcome these huge obstacles by creating the Alliance for Progress, but the nuclear missile crisis in Cuba, the Bay of Pigs invasion, his own assassination, the Vietnam War, and the proxy wars with the Soviet Union in El Salvador and Nicaragua effectively subjected Latin Americans to unilateral or hegemonic U.S. actions.

In the 1990s, the government of Carlos Andrés Pérez was overthrown in Venezuela, eventually leading to Hugo Chávez; the government of Gonzalo Sánchez de Lozada was overthrown in Bolivia, giving rise to Evo Morales; and Argentina went through four presidents in a financial crisis that threatened the entire region, finally putting the populists Néstor and Cristina Kirchner in power.

U.S. dominance and Latin American subordination are still perceived today in treaties, markets, trade, finance, investment, and multilateral organizations such as the World Bank, the International Monetary Fund, the World Trade Organization, and the Organization of American States, which many Latin Americans see as a U.S.-run coalition for exploitation and thus part of the problem, not the solution. Americans are also largely unconscious of the cultural arrogance communicated by imported U.S. TV programs and advertising, movies, the Internet, consumer products, corporations, and the English language itself. We are largely unaware of how Latin Americans at home feel about our government's overbearing influence.

A post–Cold War, post–Monroe Doctrine relationship of equality with Latin Americans can only make the United States a better nation. Latin America has been trying for a half century to work with us—with respect, equality, and dignity—to create wealth. A few leaders have succeeded, many more are trying, and still too many are failing. We must encourage success and discourage failure in Latin America with an active, respectful voice.

Latin America's main challenge in the coming years is widespread poverty. In 2006, there were 550 million Latin Americans,[7] of whom 200 million were poor, meaning 36 percent of the population lives on $2 per person per day or less.[8] The gap between the rich and poor is wider in Latin America than anywhere on earth.[9] As anyone with experience there can attest, the sharp contrast between the few rich and the many poor is visible throughout the entire region—in every country, every city, even the larger neighborhoods.

The solution can only be wealth creation through a fair, free market economy, which gives the needy a chance at becoming productive, the proverbial rising tide that lifts all boats.

If any nation knows how to do this, the United States does. From 1820 to 1992, the gross domestic income per capita[10] of today's poor countries increased by 5.4 times while that of today's rich countries—and we were the pacesetter—increased by 19 times, a disparity unique in human history.[11] The causes of this astonishing growth rate include technology, in-novation, law, and trade—the industrial and then information revolutions. That global explosion of prosperity permitted the earth's population to grow from an already unprecedented 1 billion to more than six billion, un-raveling the doomsday prediction of Thomas Malthus.[12] From the year 1000 to 1820, the GDP per capita in both rich and poor countries of today was low and flat: virtually all humans living in that eight hundred year pe-riod would be classified poor in today's terms (living on $2 per person per day or less).[13]

Not only has the planet endured, but it has survived, with some collec-tive dignity, to feed its hordes, despite the seemingly endless political unrest and insurgencies among developing nations. We have proven we can lift ourselves to a higher standard of living, and there is no reason why we should not provide the tools by which Latin Americans can do the same.

U.S. foreign policy needs to be redirected to give Latin Americans a chance.

Putting the Short-Term Plan into Effect

Chávez's influence is buttressed by our purchase of Venezuelan oil—$35 billion in 2006 alone.[14] This absurdity arises from the nonsensical en-ergy policy operating in the United States, which one expert, Peter Schwartz of Global Business Network, summarizes as: "Maximize de-mand, minimize supply and buy the rest from people who hate us the most."[15] The first step in reducing America's vulnerability to Chávez's asymmetric attack is to *reduce* the amount of oil America purchases from him. Oil is the key to his money and money is the key to his power.

If Venezuela remains determined to be a safe haven for or state sponsor of terrorism, the FARC, or Iran's nuclear weapons program—sanctions are automatically required by UN Security Council Resolution No. 1373[16] and U.S. law.[17] If Chávez is determined to be a sponsor of or money launderer for illicit drugs, sanctions must be applied under laws penalizing known drug kingpins, one of which might be the government of Venezuela itself.

Let's put Chávez's oil production and America's oil consumption in the proper context. The world guzzles about 85 mbd (million barrels per day) of oil; the United States uses about 21 mbd of that, including 10 mbd for its vehicles.[18] Chávez produces about 2.4 mbd,[19] of which 1.4 mbd[20] is sold to us, and importantly, half of that (about 700,000 barrels per day)[21] is heavy oil that can be refined almost exclusively in America's Gulf Coast facilities. We're his principal customer and refiner. American consumers paid Chávez $37 billion in 2007 alone.

If Chávez were to refine his heavy oil elsewhere, it will take *four to five years* and billions of dollars to construct new refineries. This is not a short-term option for him. Of the 307 billion barrels of oil reserves Venezuela claims to have,[22] nearly 90 percent is heavy oil,[23] which needs high-technology, specialty refining that is centered at the moment in the United States. Thus, for now, we hold a very valuable trump card.

If Chávez's oil supplies to us were cut for whatever reason (he has made this threat numerous times in the past), the 700,000 barrels per day of heavy oil could not be refined or sold but would have to be stored, and Venezuela has limited storage capacity in-country or in the Caribbean. He can continue to export 900,000 barrels per day elsewhere if sanctions do not apply—Europe might join in the sanctions if it responds strongly to Iran's nuclear weapons program—yet most of his non-U.S. export oil is already committed at discount prices to the countries he's calling his allies (and our enemies). His remaining 800,000 barrels are then committed to the Venezuelan market,[24] where his price subsidies (a gallon of gas costs about 20 cents in Caracas) are digging Chávez an endless hole. Selling gasoline cheaply is considered a birthright in Venezuela. When President Pérez attempted to rationalize an increased price for gas in 1989, a riot broke out, followed by Chávez's coup attempt three years later. Again, when Chávez talked about raising the price of gas in 2008, the public outcry quickly squelched the idea.

If Venezuelan oil flow to the United States were interrupted, Chávez's cash flow would be reduced to a fraction of what it is today. Effectively, the $37 billion provided in 2007 by U.S. consumers could be replaced by half that or less in spot-market export sales or contracts. But since 2002, Petróleos de Venezuela has been very badly managed. Bottlenecks in production, pipelines, storage, refining, and shipping are likely to interrupt PDVSA's operations in an emergency, further reducing its income.

The result would then cause a crisis in Venezuela's international economic standing. There would be an immediate loss of confidence in the nation's capacity or willingness to pay its international bank debts, which

Chávez has quadrupled during his time in office. Credit could erode or even disappear overnight. A cash crunch could occur very rapidly, forcing Chávez to curtail foreign spending and switch gears into an emergency mode. He'd have to worry first about paying his 3 million government employees, a million in military reservists, another 100,000 in the regular army, the 100,000 in PDVSA, and the untold tens of thousands who work in state enterprises that are losing money. Then there's the near-certain cut he'd have to make in social spending to his barrio supporters. He would have to dip into his Central Reserve Bank to just make payroll.

The money he's spending on the FARC, Iran, Cuba, Belarus, Russia, China, Bolivia, Nicaragua, and on arms purchases would suddenly be unavailable. And the cash shortfall would force him to deal with an irate political party and military, who would quickly realize that Chávez's behavior is what caused the sanctions and that changing his behavior would remove them. With Chávez's approval rating at 35 percent[25] (America's is at 70 percent among Venezuelans),[26] Chávez will have a difficult time explaining to his party and military how they should continue to sacrifice revenue from America for "Fatherland, socialism or death." A financial squeeze would distract Chávez from his near-hysterical posturing toward the United States.

Because the nation's biggest export is oil, playing hardball with Chávez would create hardship for all Venezuelans. But PDVSA could be producing 5 to 6 mbd if it was well run. If Venezuelan oil was not available, America would have to account for a shortfall of 700,000 barrels per day of oil and refined products from the supply or demand side of the equation.[27]

We can understand all this by taking the following measures:

On the demand side, research indicates that if the conservation savings proposals were *all* enacted, up to 30 percent of our oil demand could be replaced by other fuels or cut out altogether. Not all of those savings could be realized immediately, but a 30 percent reduction in demand is the equivalent of 6.3 mbd, of which Venezuela's 700,000 barrels per day represents only 11 percent.[28]

On the supply side, we can expand the Strategic Petroleum Reserve (SPR) in anicipation of a cutoff of Venezuela oil, as Representative Connie Mack (R-Fla.) suggested to President Bush in March 2007.[29] We can also draw down on the 90 million barrel SPR as needed in the event of a Venezuelan oil cutoff because that's exactly why the emergency reserve exists. Finally, we can request that our three major suppliers—Canada, Mexico, and Saudi Arabia—increase allocations during the time when Venezuela's oil will be unavailable.

Removing 700,000 barrels per day—or more if PDVSA collapsed—would raise the price of oil for the short term. If Venezuela turns off the spigot, the world oil price may increase in the short term, yet it could be rolled back by a larger amount thereafter. (A similar situation occurred over two months during the 2002–03 national strike in Venezuela.)

But after several months of turmoil, if PDVSA returned to market with competent management, Venezuela could get on track to produce 5 mbd or more in the short term. If Chávez was not around to artificially up the oil price with daily threats and political risks, speculation would subside; the political risk premium in the current oil price would be markedly reduced; and Iran would lose its foothold in Latin America, and maybe Russia as well.

From a price perspective, the downstream benefits far outweigh the short-term loss to the oil market of PDVSA's 700,000 barrels per day of heavy oil. With the price of oil fluctuating dramatically, it may never be convenient to make the cut, but we cannot allow the price to prohibit necessary actions in defense of America's security.

The Colombia Free Trade Agreement

It's hardly surprising that America's interests are identified with the path Colombia is leading in Latin America, as opposed to that of Venezuela. Colombia is a large country, with a vibrant democracy and a robust free market. It has made considerable economic progress in the last decade, going from near collapse to a model for recovery. Colombia is winning the war against the narcoterrorists in the FARC and ELN, or the National Liberation Army—Colombia's other predominant rebel group; it has disarmed almost all the paramilitary forces; and it has maintained steady economic growth with more freedom than any of its neighbors can boast.

Venezuela is a smaller country with a failed democracy and a monopolized, corrupt market. Its measurable "progress" in the last decade is associated with terrorists, Iran, the FARC, and the drug trade. Its economic growth is totally dependent on driving up world oil prices. Inflation, disinvestment, unemployment, corruption, and homicide are its major features. Caracas is a case study of a cosmopolitan city allowed to go to seed.

Venezuela is the problem. Colombia is the solution. This is eminently clear. But unfortunately, our lawmakers refused in April 2008 to even vote on the U.S.-Colombia Free Trade Agreement because of misguided politics. International trade agreements do not normally enjoy political support on Capitol Hill when American companies are exporting good jobs to China and India. But the main objection of the Democrats to the bill was that labor union murders there are still high, when in fact the homicide rate for all civilians in Colombia is higher than that for all labor union members in Colombia. We are now in an election year in the United States and many Democrats (including presidential candidate Barack Obama) are loath to oppose the activist Democratic labor union constituency. The Democrats would do well to show some independence and vote for the U.S.-Colombia Free Trade Agreement as soon as possible. Anything less will send a huge, negative message to pro-U.S. market democracies in Latin America.

Not coincidentally, Chávez also opposes the U.S.-Colombia Free Trade Agreement and has lobbied vigorously in Washington to kill the treaty. He also hopes to defeat the U.S. drug interdiction program in Colombia, which reduces the income of the FARC. If Chávez wins and Colombia loses this debate on trade in Washington, America's next president will face even greater challenges to improve our relationship with friendly Latin American countries.

Beyond a trade agreement looms another option: sanctions. We can strengthen the strategic arms embargo of Venezuela that was imposed in 2005 when Venezuela was upgrading its U.S.-made jet fighters and making disproportionately large arms purchases that alarmed the United States and Colombia, among other nations. That embargo has been costly and inconvenient for Chávez; but he circumvented it by spending approximately $5 billion for arms purchased from Russia, Belarus, China, Iran, and elsewhere.

This may be the period in history where Chávez is more vulnerable to a domestic rejection than he thinks. The Pew 2007 World Survey of sixty nations showed that no population in the region is more pro-American than Venezuelans: it is only the Chávez government that is anti-American.[30]

"The greater the ties to the West, the greater the degree to which the elite is educated in the West and has career prospects in the West, then the greater the likelihood the coalition behind the regime will crack," says Steven Levitsky, professor of government at Harvard, who studies the conditions under which autocracies crumble.[31] Those conditions exist in the military, entrepreneurial, and cultural character of Venezuela, but Chávez is working to extinguish them all.

In any case, extending the arms embargo on Venezuela will set a good example of the kind of leadership the United States can exert in Latin America. Just as African states have been hesitant to rein in Zimbabwe's Robert Mugabe on their own, Latin American states are hesitant to rein in Venezuela's Hugo Chávez, who is buying a lot of their compliance as well as their silence. That is precisely the space the United States must occupy in the face of a despot.

Chávez may be infecting a lot of Latin Americans, but he is not yet in control of the region. The United States must support a reasonable alternative to Chávez's twenty-first-century brand of socialism, take the moral high ground, stand by the law, continue its antidrug efforts, support free and fair trade agreements, promote democracy, and most important, work for equality in the region. By announcing a summit of the Americas to *cocreate with Latin Americans* a strategy for regional economic growth and equality, we can take the first step toward a policy that will work long term.

The choice is to continue our ineffective Latin America policy or change it. Our current laissez-faire, unilateral, and interventionist policies will only invite more populism, anti-Americanism, and hostility from Latin Americans. It is fairly obvious to realistic American policymakers that we need to alter our policy to prevent the situation from deteriorating further—with or without Chávez.

We need to change *what* we're doing a little and *how* we're doing it a lot. We need to ratify our relationship to Latin Americans so that it reflects equality. We need to help Latin Americans in their quest, their way of life, rather than dictating a way of thinking. We only need to decide to do these things.

Modern Hispanics and Wealth Creation

Today, the rich nations account for only 15 percent of the world's population but well over half of its GDP and purchasing power. The United States, with only 4.6 percent of the planet's population, accounts for 28 percent of the world's economic output. In just a few hundred years, the global economy has shifted from total dominance by agriculture to one where production derives from services (68 percent), industry (28 percent), and agriculture (4 percent).[32] We have not fully adapted to this tectonic shift.

Latin America, with 8.8 percent of the world's population, has produced only 5.8 percent of the world's GDP in 2006.[33] As a region it is somewhere between struggling and failing. Since 1970, Latin America's economic growth has lagged at 2 percent a year, reducing the population in poverty by only 7 percent (from 43 percent to 36 percent) in over three decades; by comparison, since 1970 Asia grew by 6 percent annually and reduced the population in poverty by 31 percent (from 50 percent to 19 percent).[34] Africa, which surely has its share of political unrest and health tragedies among certain populations, is also growing faster than Latin America.[35]

What do the Asians and Africans know that the Latinos don't?

Hispanics can succeed at wealth creation. The table on page 177 identifies the gross domestic income per capita of those living in the Americas by nation of residence. It reveals both the problem and the solution to poverty. Fifty million Hispanics can show how 550 million others can achieve some degree of economic prosperity.

There are 126 million Latin Americans living in ten poor countries (see group B in the table) with GDP per capita incomes ranging from $2,000 to $6,000 a year (from 5 percent to 15 percent of the United States' GDP per capita), which spells poverty, misery, and unrest by any economist's analysis. At the moment, we can view this as "Chávez country." From the bottom up, these ten nations are Bolivia, Cuba, Honduras, Nicaragua, Ecuador, Guatemala, El Salvador, Paraguay, Venezuela, and Peru. Peru narrowly escaped inclusion in the Chávez camp by electing Alan García in the close presidential election of 2006.[36] The historically pro-American Honduras joined Chávez's anti-American ALBA camp in August 2008 to get his oil discounts.

The average person in these countries is in his or her early twenties. Global research shows that countries with young populations are the most

THE WEALTH OF NORTH AND LATIN AMERICA[37]

GDP per capita	Country	Population	Median Age
U.S. $70,000	Bermuda	100,000	36
40,000	USA	297 million	36
30,000	Canada	32 million	39
25,000	Puerto Rico	4 million	33
22,000	USA—Hispanic Americans only	45 million	n/a
16,000–20,000	Aruba, Curacao, Bahamas, Barbados, Virgin Islands	1 million	34
Group A 13,000	Argentina	39 million	29
12,000	Trinidad & Tobago	1 million	29
11,000	Chile	16 million	31
10,000	Mexico	105 million	25
9,000	Costa Rica	4 million	26
8,000	Brazil	181 million	27
7,000	Colombia	45 million	25
7,000	Dominican Republic, Guadeloupe,* Belize	10 million	23
Group B 6,000	Peru	28 million	24
6,000	Venezuela	26 million	25
5,000	El Salvador, Paraguay	13 million	22
3,000	Ecuador, Guatemala	26 million	21
3,000	Bolivia, Cuba,** Honduras, Nicaragua	33 million	20

Source: This table is drawn from The Economist online, World in Figures, 2007, and refers to data from 2006.
*Guadeloupe median age is 34.
**Cuba median age is 34.

violent on the planet.[38] Indeed, war, conflict, or high murder rates plague half of these countries today. Several of them are failed or failing states. Most of them have produced large out-migrations to the United States: Haiti, Cuba, Honduras, Nicaragua, Guatemala, El Salvador, and recently Venezuela.

All of them fall into what has been called the "bottom billion"— economically, the worst-off people on earth—yet all of them have the highest birth rates in the hemisphere. In fact, 90 percent of the anticipated population growth from 6.7 billion to 9 billion people by midcentury is expected to come from the poorest countries.[39] Left unattended, these countries are likely to double the number of poor people who reside in them, producing anti-American Chávez look-alikes unless the economic picture improves.

Though Chávez would like to unify Latin America, he has no wealth creation solution for the hundreds of millions of poor Latin Americans (or for poor Venezuelans either). What he does give them is a voice for their resentment, rage, and misplaced revenge; he is more of a channel for hate than hope. These countries are the top priority challenge the United States faces in the coming decades. Provided the tools of wealth creation, there is no reason why struggling Latinos cannot realize their aspirations and become productive. The United States must help them escape from the trap they find themselves in, or else face the immigration, violence, and terrorism that desperate people can turn to when there's no hope in sight.[40]

There are ten nations with a total population of 401 million people (see group A in the table) that are producing GDP per capita incomes ranging from $7,000 to $13,000. These countries are beginning to improve but need us as a partner to spur economic growth. Two of the largest, Brazil—a potential economic powerhouse that occupies a huge piece of the continent—and Mexico, have been key Latin players. Mexico is already part of a trade agreement with the United States and Canada: NAFTA.

Both low-cost imports from and U.S. exports to Latin America (especially in the service industries) already produce significant improvements in the U.S. standard of living.[41] We are the most convenient and efficient trading partner for almost all the locations in Latin America. The wealthier that Latin American consumers become, the better the economy will be for typical working- and middle-class American families.

We must begin to countervail the significant progress Chávez has made with his antitrade, antiglobalization, anti-American messages. Brazil is run by socialists walking a fine line between America and Venezuela. Mexico may appear identified with the United States because of the NAFTA treaty, but in the 2006 presidential race, the Chávez-backed socialist anti-American candidate lost by less than 1 percent. The same result occurred in Costa Rica, a big supporter of CAFTA (the Central American Free Trade Agreement), where a Chávez-backed anti-American candidate came within a percentage point of defeating the Nobel Peace Prize laureate and former president Oscar Arias, a socialist.

In Chile, considered the poster child for development and democracy following our model, the United States has a free trade agreement. That nation is run by socialists who are market-wise to today's international economy. Argentina may be an aberration. In Argentina, the Kirchner family has occupied the presidency—first Néstor and now Cristina—who are Perón-style populists identifying with Chávez. Sensing their weakness, Chávez has purchased $6 billion of Argentina bonds since 2004 and showered the Kirchners with personal gifts, making Argentina the only successfully developing country in Latin America squarely in Chávez's corner. And in Colombia, the best ally of the United States from a free market democracy or anti–drug trade perspective, Chávez is working with the FARC to overthrow the government while the United States hesitates on signing a trade agreement (for petty political reasons already outlined) that would be a win-win deal for both nations.

Finally, let's consider the more successful Latin nations. There are the 50 million Hispanics, who produce a GDP per capita equal to 50 percent or more of the U.S. total. These are models for all of Latin America. They include the 4 million Puerto Ricans who live on that island and the 45 million Hispanic Americans who live in the United States, albeit 12 million illegally. Many Americans think of Hispanic Americans as an economic problem, but in fact—like all historical immigrants to America—they are a solution to America's continued prosperity. This is an ongoing controversy that we will not attempt to debate here.

With no competitive resource advantage over five neighboring island countries, why is Puerto Rico's GDP per capita eight times Cuba's, double that of Trinidad and Tobago (which has abundant natural gas), and triple that of the Dominican Republic? The answer is that since 1952, when Puerto Rico was as poor as its neighboring islands, it cocreated with the United States a commonwealth relationship. That relationship entails the application of U.S. law and courts in Venezuela, the use of U.S. currency, U.S. military protection and service, citizenship for Puerto Ricans, no income tax for Puerto Ricans, the provision of education, unemployment, and food stamp benefits for Puerto Ricans, and tax breaks to American corporations that invest there.

That combination of policies accounts for Puerto Rico's economic improvement, which is equivalent to what Singapore, the worldwide pacesetter for island development, has achieved. Singapore's 4.3 million island people have a GDP per capita of $28,000, compared to Puerto Rico's

4 million islanders, who have a GDP per capita of $25,000. Interestingly, Singapore has developed with similar policies for law, private property, investment, and universal education.

Puerto Ricans have mixed feelings about their political status. Since the 1960s, about 45 percent want full statehood; 45 percent want to maintain the commonwealth relationship that exists; and 10 percent want Puerto Rico to become an independent country.[42] In sum, 90 percent of Puerto Ricans living and voting in Puerto Rico want the current or a stronger relationship with us, and for obvious reasons.

If Puerto Rico serves as a model, the small tourist islands of the Caribbean can do so as well. Why do Bermuda, Barbados, Aruba, Curacao, the Bahamas, the Virgin Islands, and others produce such high GDP per capita economies—some soaring above the United States—while islands controlled by mainland Latin American countries (for example, Margarita, which is part of Venezuela) demonstrably do not? Is not the difference explained by law and systems borrowed from the British, Dutch, or French colonial powers? The residue of colonialism for plunder is useless for development by a liberated colony. But the legacy of colonialism that implanted institutions for law, private property, and education is very useful for wealth creation by a liberated colony. That's what the stories of the Caribbean Islands and Puerto Rico tell us.

An even grander success story comes from the 45 million Hispanic Americans. They produced $1 trillion of income in 2006 while 550 million Latin Americans were producing $2.4 trillion.

Why such a disparity? Hispanic Americans have assimilated into our system (without losing their identity), which is very efficient and effective at economic expansion and inclusion, while the rest of Latin America does not have an efficient wealth creation system. Most Hispanic immigrants to our shores came from the poorest Latin American countries or the lower portion of the economic pyramid of another country. There was nothing special, different, or unusual about these immigrants other than that they were so desperate for work and income they simply had to leave home, many of them risking their lives in the process. It's the U.S. system of opportunity that attracted them, and it's our way of life that made them productive. They made the right move toward us and we should think about making the right move toward them and their homelands.

Hispanic Americans are making a positive difference for Americans. They do all kinds of work at low wages that few nonimmigrant Americans want to do: agricultural crop picking, gardening, unskilled labor, inside and outside home maintenance, and so on. Because they're young and working, they contribute to Social Security, while few receive such benefits—they contributed up to $150 billion to the retirement system in 2006 alone. And finally, they sent $63 billion in remittances to their Latin American families in 2006. The Hispanic American immigrant is today's Horatio Alger for America, lifting up himself (and his or her family back home) by the bootstraps.

The U.S. Economic Engine

The United States has led planetary growth for a century. The World Bank measures us first in global competitiveness, first in infrastructure, first in business environment, first in innovation, third in information technology, second in e-readiness, and first in attracting foreign direct investment.[43] This system is the one the World Bank believes developing nations should imitate, the current financial crisis notwithstanding.

Since World War II, every nation that became wealthy did so by exchanges with the U.S. market system, including Europe, Japan, South Korea, the Asian "Tigers," and India and China today. From 1980 on, China has lifted 300 million people from poverty and India has lifted more than 100 million poor by exchanges primarily because of U.S. trade. A renewed effort is needed to connect the American market to Latin America, starting with its 200 million indigent, who are largely without access to the tools for creating wealth: law, private property, enterprise, credit, education, and technology as the main engine parts.

Our legal system—our Constitution—allowed us to became the world's wealthiest nation, according to the Nobel laureate economic historian Douglass North.[44] Understanding how reliable institutions can support markets has led to dramatic improvements in the economic performance of many societies.[45] Law, regulation, and competition that break monopolies and mitigate institutional corruption are essential to markets.[46] The rule of law can improve the prospects of almost all nations.

Latin Americans are struggling to create, and more important, enforce, the laws that promote competitive economic systems. The World Bank and International Monetary Fund are trying to help. If these efforts are massively supported by our public and private sectors, Latin America can emerge from the curse of monopoly and corruption.

Just 150 years ago, today's rich nations were teeming with black markets, pervasive mafias, widespread poverty, and a flagrant disregard of the law, as Latin America is today. The conversion to wide-scale individual private property ownership allowed economies to soar, vast wealth to be created, and large middle-class populations to emerge.

Fifty years ago, Alaska's indigenous peoples—the Eskimos, Indians, and Aleuts—were living on $2 per person per day, and two thirds were unemployed. Today, most are in the middle class and unemployment is down in the 10 percent range. One reason for this is that indigenous shareholders now own enterprises, including the largest zinc mine in the world, an oil company that earned $1.3 billion in 2006, a half-billion-dollar global investment firm, as well as fishing, timber, tourism, and service firms with hundreds of millions of dollars of annual earnings each. Alaska's two hundred indigenous enterprises have also created partnerships with American oil and mineral firms that Latin Americans falsely believe are the enemy.[47]

Alaska's indigenous enterprises were made possible by the U.S. government's $960 million enterprise capitalization for a land claims settlement in the 1970s. Tribal members own, direct, manage, and may work for their enterprises, which are like any other in U.S. law except for the ownership restrictions. Each tribal member received equal shares in the enterprise that could not be divested. The United States offered incentives to invest the capital in wealth creation ventures in Alaska and elsewhere. In thirty years, Alaska's homegrown enterprises have produced close to $40 billion in corporate earnings, a 40-to-1 return on investment—unprecedented in the annals of development.[48]

In Mexico, Central America, and the Andean nations, there are 50 million indigenous people living in poverty similar to that of the Eskimos of 1960. Minimal efforts have been made to create and finance homeland enterprises so they can help themselves. But if a maximum effort *were* made, the people of Latin America could use these enterprises just as their northern cousins did to adapt and prosper in a modern, global economy. This is the way to cope with poverty. It's about partnerships, not welfare. Fishermen don't need fish but nets.

Here's another example of how creative thinking on the micro level can have a vast impact on a population. A private entrepreneur, Muhammad Yunus, created Grameen Bank in Bangladesh to provide credit for micro-businesses run by poor people, most often women. His loans ranged from only $100 to $250 in most cases. The borrower became a shareholder in Grameen Bank by virtue of the loan amount (a variation on the Alaska enterprise). Yunus also gave away cell phones to facilitate his customers' businesses.

Yunus built a relationship of trust with his borrowers (and shareholders) that yielded fruit—only 1 percent of his loans were not repaid. After a few years, millions of small loans were working, Grameen had $7 billion of new capital in Bangladesh, poverty was being ameliorated by wealth creation, three hundred micro-credit programs worldwide were imitating his success, and Yunus received a well-deserved Nobel Peace Prize. In 2008, Grameen Bank opened a branch for the poor in the financial capital of the world, New York City. It works anywhere.

In yet another example, closer to our area of concern, a private entrepreneur decided to shift his successful appliance sales business from Brazil's wealthy suburbs to the slums. He hired local slum residents to sell appliances to customers who had no credit. Buyers with zero credit could take the appliance if they agreed to pay 20 percent on the day of sale and 20 percent on that date for each of the following four months. The result? He had only 2 percent bad bills compared to 20 percent for credit cards in the rich suburbs of Brazil. Because his customers loved him for extending them credit based solely upon trust, he became a billionaire in just a few years.[49]

The field is ripe for more innovative entrepreneurs and lenders in both the public and the private sectors of Latin America. We just need a massive effort to connect them to poor, productive wealth creators.

Education Is Still Paramount

At its core, education is the ultimate tool for uplifting the poor and disadvantaged, allowing all other tools to function. Universal education has more to do with America's success than any other factor. After World

War II, the G.I. Bill stimulated a decade of middle-class prosperity in the United States. Japan, just one generation after the war, virtually eliminated poverty by universalizing education from the bottom up.

In Latin America, free education is traditionally provided from elementary school through the university degree. While the system sounds unimpeachable, the net effect is that half the educational funds get directed to the small percentage of students who make it to college—most of them privileged to begin with. The schools do not perform well at the elementary and secondary levels, and so most of the students drop out.

However, this is beginning to change. Progressive Latin American countries have adjusted their priorities to keep people enrolled and performing in all grades. Mexico and Brazil provide a stipend of about $100 per month to the parents (usually mothers) of poor children upon presentation of proof that their children attend school regularly and visit a health clinic monthly. While intended as a long-term investment in the children, the programs had an unexpected impact in reducing overall poverty by several percentage points. Mayor Michael Bloomberg of New York City has been imitating this Latin American innovation since 2007.

The growth of modern technology has enhanced education, as well. Television and the Internet are fabulous tools for distance learning. The cell phone has been instrumental in the success of micro-enterprises, as it was with Grameen Bank's customers in Bangladesh.[50] With a small investment in technology, poor families anywhere can leap the digital divide and lift themselves from poverty. If public funds and private philanthropists worked together to offer access to the tools for wealth creation, Latin America could decrease its poverty and inequality dramatically.

IN HIS twelve-minute commencement address at Harvard on June 5, 1947, George Marshall articulated a strategy for global wealth creation that rebuilt Europe and Japan while eventually rendering America the world's major superpower.

After World War II, the devastated countries of Europe had no choice but to buy American imports, which exhausted their capacity to rebuild much-needed wealth-creating infrastructures. Europe was caught in a cycle of poverty and debt. "The United States is the only country in the world today which has the economic power and productivity to furnish the needed assistance," Marshall said, noting that the resulting economic growth would benefit America as much if not more than Europe and Japan—which it has. "We have learned that we cannot live alone, at peace; that our own well-being is dependent on the well-being of other nations, far away."[51]

The key to world success, as Marshall saw it, was not dominance by the United States as in a Pax Americana but in alliance of equality with Europe and Japan. That is precisely what is needed in Latin America today. The Marshall Plan was not imposed on Europe but created with Europe as an ally. In fact, the Alliance of the Americas is a version of the Marshall Plan, which was open to any nation for reconstruction; Latin America simply was not approached. President Kennedy made overtures to Latin America with his Alliance for Progress, but it was shelved because of the Cold War.

Well, the Cold War is long over. It's time to reread what George Marshall said—and do it. "Our policy is directed not against any country or doctrine but against hunger, poverty, desperation and chaos," Marshall said sixty-one years ago.[52] What would Venezuelans think if a U.S. president said that to them?

While the United States has been focused on the Middle East, Eastern Europe, Russia, and Asia, Chávez has used his oil money to assemble a loose anti-American alliance of several countries on four continents with a total population of 220 million and a GDP per capita averaging only $4,208, half the world average (see the table on page 186).[53] The Chávez alliance is a collection of globalization's losers, plagued by poverty and inequality, violence, and rage against the United States and Western civilization. It includes the countries that want a nuclear weapon—Iran, Syria, and North Korea—and the countries that ally with revolution, instability, and terror around the world.

If he were alive today, how would George Marshall deal with this problem?

Marshall would certainly address the immediate military threats as he saw them. But just as certainly he would repeat what he said in 1947 at Harvard: "Any government that is willing to assist in the task of recovery will find full co-operation, I am sure, on the part of the United States. Any government which maneuvers to block the recovery of other countries cannot expect help from us."[54] That is the solution to both Hugo Chávez and world poverty, as we see it.

THE CHÁVEZ GLOBAL ANTI-AMERICAN ALLIANCE[55]

Country	GDP ($ billion)	GDP per capita	Population	Median Age
Belarus	23	$7,000	10 million	38
Bolivia	9	2,700	9 million	21
Cuba	33	2,900	11 million	36
Ecuador	30	4,000	13 million	24
Iran	163	7,500	70 million	23
Libya	29	8,400	8 million	24
Mali	5	1,000	13 million	16
Nicaragua	5	3,600	6 million	20
North Korea	40	1,800	23 million	31
Syria	24	3,600	18 million	21
Venezuela	110	6,000	26 million	25
Zimbabwe	5	2,000	13 million	19
Above twelve countries	$476 billion	$4,208 per cap	220 million	24.8 years
World	$41.3 trillion	$8,920	6.4 billion	28.1
USA	$11.7 trillion	$39,680	297 million	36.1

Source: This table is drawn from The Economist online, World in Figures, 2007.

In 1960, presidential candidate John F. Kennedy gave a speech in Tampa, Florida, while on the campaign trail. He pointed out that our Latin American neighbors were "drifting away" because we did not support our democratic friends. He rightfully claimed that "our major failure in that area has been to assist these people in achieving any kind of economic existence." Kennedy emphasized that we needed to stand up to those "exploiting domestic distress and unrest, encouraging growing dislike of the United States. . . ."[56]

He could have been speaking specifically about Venezuela. And his words are just as relevant today as they were half a century ago.

Acknowledgments

We are extremely lucky to have had the help of many different people in many different areas to guide and assist our research. We would like to thank our friends and colleagues at *El Universal Daily* and *VenEconomy* magazine in Caracas for all their help in providing research and guidance in framing and structuring the manuscript. We have also benefited from the advice and judgment of the following people: Diego Arria, Daniel Benveniste, Nelson Bocaranda, Toby Bottome, Alec Boyd, Richard Brand, Bob Carr, Sol Castro, Gustavo Coronel, Eric Ekvall, Carolina Ferrero, Francis Gibbs, Luis Giusti, Phil Gunson, Parag Khanna, Connie Mack, Damian Merlo, Eduardo Penate, David Punchard, Maria Ramirez Ribes, Otto Reich, Kenneth Rijock, Hernando de Soto, Jack Sweeney, Gerver Torres, and Andy Webb-Vidal.

In additional, we would like to thank John Buntin, Doug Garr, and Eve Kessler, who provided research and guidance in making the manuscript much better than it would otherwise have been. All gave selflessly of their time and effort and we are very grateful for their help. In addition, Michael Anton provided much-needed work in helping to structure and refine our arguments. We benefited from his counsel, as well as that of Dan Gerstein, a trusted friend and source of wisdom. Our final thanks go to somebody who literally guided all phases of the work: Carly Cooperman. Carly worked with a wide range of researchers, analysts, advisers, consultants, and advocates of the endeavor to make this an incomparably better book.

Her influence can be found on every page, and it is our good fortune that she was as committed to this work as we have certainly been. Needless to say, what we have written is ours and ours alone, but what we know about the story has been greatly augmented by the input we have received from the people listed above, as well as many others who wanted to remain anonymous.

Notes

Introduction

1. Hugo Chávez to Jan James of the Associated Press, September 23, 2007.
2. Otto Reich in an interview with the authors, February 22, 2008.
3. Francisco Rodríguez, "An Empty Revolution: The Unfulfilled Promises of Hugo Chávez," *Foreign Affairs* (March/April 2008).
4. Chávez in interview with Robin Lustig, BBC, October 2005. Video can be downloaded at http://news.bbc.co.uk/2/hi/americas/4359924.stm. Also: www.worldofradio.com/dxld5184.txt.
5. Chávez in a joint TV broadcast in Caracas with President Lula da Silva of Brazil, April 10, 2007.
6. Chávez speaking at Tehran University, RCTV News, July 30, 2006.
7. *Gringos* or "green goes" refers to the U.S. military uniform color. Chávez on the TV interview show of Carlos Croes in Caracas, April 1, 2005.
8. Amy Chua, *World on Fire, How Exporting Free Market Democracy Breeds Ethnic Hatred and Global Instability* (New York: Anchor Books, 2003), 230. While 4 percent of the world's population is American, 28 percent of the world economy is American; Chua writes that "America dominates every aspect—financial, cultural, technological—of the global free markets we have come to symbolize."
9. "Chávez Decorated in Iran; Initials Cooperation Pacts," *El Universal*, July 31, 2006.
10. Nasser Karimi, "Chavez, Ahmadinejad to Work Against U.S.," AP, November 19, 2007.
11. Ibid.
12. José de Cordoba and David Luhnow, "Colombia is Criticized for Raid into Ecuador," *Wall Street Journal*, March 6, 2008, A4.
13. Christopher Toothaker, "Chávez Defense of FARC Rebels Angers Columbia," *The Star*, January 11, 2008.
14. Michael Fox, "Defining the Bolivarian Alternative for the Americas—ALBA," Venezuelanalysis.com, August 4, 2006.
15. Marc Frank, "Analysis: Cuban-Venezuelan ties boom under Raúl Castro," Reuters, July 21, 2008.

16. Anne Barnard, "Russia and Venezuela will coordinate on energy," *New York Times*, July 23, 2008.

17. Benedict Mander and Daniel Dombey, "Russian exercises off Venezuela stir cold war ghosts," *Financial Times*, Sept. 23, 2008.

18. "Chávez, China Agree to Build Oil Refineries," *Wall Street Journal*, Sept. 24, 2008, A25.

19. Arthur Herman, "Petro-Tyrants of the World United," *New York Post*, September 26, 2008, www.frontpagemag.com/articles/Read.aspx?GUID=B7B44505-307A-49FF-A8CE -4B2EB6237393.

20. "Democrats warn Chavez: Don't Bash Bush," CNN.com, Sept. 21, 2006. http://www .cnn.com/2006/POLITICS/09/21/chavez.ny/index.html.

21. Francisco Rodríguez, "Venezuela's Empty Revolution," *Real Clear Politics*, March 6, 2008, www.realclearpolitics.com/articles/2008/03/venezuelas_empty_revolution.html.

22. Mark Lifsher, "Venezuelan Government to Use Marketing Group to Sell Its Oil," *Wall Street Journal*, June 2, 2003.

23. Fernando Báez, "On the Road with Bush and Chávez," *New York Times*, March 11, 2007.

24. "Visit by Bush Fires Up Latins' Debate Over Socialism," *New York Times*, March 9, 2007.

25. "Bush and Chávez Spar at a Distance," *New York Times*, March 10, 2007.

Chapter 1: The Origin of the Threat

1. Cristina Marcano and Alberto Barrera Tyszka, *Hugo Chávez: The Definitive Biography of Venezuela's Controversial President* (New York: Random House, 2007), 13.

2. Ibid., 10.

3. Ibid.

4. Rosa Miriam Elizalde and Luis Báez, eds., *Our Chávez* (interviews with family, friends, and leaders of the Bolivarian revolution) (Havana, Cuba: Abril Publishing House, 2004), 17. (ISBN 959-210-375-5.)

5. *Hugo Chavez: 1954–President*, http://biography.jrank.org/pages/3045/Ch-vez-Hugo-1954-President-Childhood-in-Farming-Village.html (note: Ch-vez [sic]).

6. Johann Hari, "An audience with Chavez, the man with the most powerful enemies in the world," *Independent*, May 16, 2006, www.independent.co.uk/news/people/an -audience-with-chavez-the-man-with-the-most-powerful-enemies-in-the-world-4784 03.html.

7. Elizalde and Báez, *Our Chávez*, 52.

8. José Sant Roz, "Falleció el historiador J.E. Ruíz Guevara, maestro del Presidente Chávez," www.aporrea.org/actualidad/n81238.html, July 24, 2006.

9. Marcano and Barrera Tyszka, *Hugo Chávez, Definitive Biography*, 23–26.

10. Bart Jones, *Hugo!: The Hugo Chavez Story from Mud Hut to Perpetual Revolution* (Hanover, NH: Steerforth, 2007), 32–34.

11. Marcano and Barrera Tyszka, *Hugo Chávez, Definitive Biography*, 32.

12. Richard Gott, *Hugo Chavez and the Bolivarian Revolution* (London: Verso, 2005), 110.

13. Peter Gribbon, "Brazil and CIA," *CounterSpy* (April–May 1979), www.namebase.org/ brazil.html.

14. Elizalde and Báez, *Our Chávez*, 339.

15. Ibid., 322.

16. Ibid., 333.

17. Ibid., 361.

18. Ibid., 338.

19. Ibid., 349.
20. Ibid., 350.
21. Ibid., 342.
22. Jones, *Hugo!: Hugo Chavez Story*, 38–40.
23. Elizalde and Báez, *Our Chávez*, 85.
24. Ibid, 86.
25. Ibid, 362.
26. Marcano and Barrera Tyszka, *Hugo Chávez, Definitive Biography*, 39.
27. Carlos Andrés Pérez, or CAP, was first elected president in 1973 for one five-year term. He won the presidency again in 1988. Rafael Caldera was also elected president twice, in 1969 and 1993. Under the constitution of Venezuela before Chávez, a president could not succeed himself in office.
28. Marcano and Barrera Tyszka, *Hugo Chávez, Definitive Biography*, 4.
29. Ibid., 52.
30. Norman Gall, *Braudel Papers*, Fernand Braudel Institute of World Politics, No. 40, 2006, 1.
31. Ibid., 2.
32. Hari, "An Audience with Chavez."
33. Jones, *Hugo!: Hugo Chávez Story*, 56–75.
34. Gall, *Braudel Papers*, Nos. 39 and 40; Marcano and Barrera Tyszka, *Hugo Chávez, Definitive Biography*, 43–53; Richard Becerra Jiménez, "Douglas Bravo Interview," *Seminario La Razon*, No. 491, June 6, 2004, www.soberania.org/Articulos/articulo_1138.htm.
35. Gall, *Braudel Papers*, No. 40.
36. Elizalde and Báez, *Our Chávez*, 352.
37. Jones, *Hugo!: Hugo Chávez Story*, 66–80.
38. Chávez replaced Bolívar's words *the Spanish throne* with *the powerful*, which included oligarchs, capitalists, and imperialists. See Elizalde and Báez, *Our Chávez*, 354, for Chávez's detailed telling of this event.

Chapter 2: *Por Ahora*—"For Now"

1. Marcano and Barrera Tyszka, *Hugo Chávez, Definitive Biography*, 52 (see chap. 1, n. 5).
2. The 1961 constitution of Venezuela bars the military from voting.
3. Elizalde and Báez, *Our Chávez*, 337 (see chap. 1, n. 4).
4. Ibid., 201.
5. Marcano and Barrera Tyszka, *Hugo Chávez, Definitive Biography*, 51.
6. Elizalde and Báez, Our *Chávez*, 256.
7. Ibid., 356.
8. Marcano and Barrera Tyszka, *Hugo Chávez, Definitive Biography*, 53.
9. Elizalde and Báez, *Our Chávez*, 39.
10. Marcano and Barrera Tyszka, *Hugo Chávez, Definitive Biography*, 49–50.
11. Ibid., 56.
12. Ibid., 57.
13. Ibid., 59.
14. Ibid., 68–71.
15. Ibid., 64.
16. Ibid., 64–68.
17. Personal communication of Pérez's military aide to one of the authors, 1996.
18. Elizalde and Báez, *Our Chávez*, 202.

19. In 1999, when Chávez's military took over PDVSA, they also faced technical obstacles with its computers, which have stunted oil production to this day.

20. Marcano and Barrera Tyszka, *Hugo Chávez, Definitive Biography,* 67–72.

21. Ibid., 69.

22. Ibid., 71–72.

23. Ibid., 72–73.

24. Ibid., 73–74.

25. Ibid., 74–75 (italic emphasis added by authors). Also: "Por ahora no hemos logrado controlar el poder," February 5, 1992, 1–17.

26. Elizalde and Báez, *Our Chávez,* 227. Also: www.voltairenet.org/article120084.html.

27. Ibid.

28. Marcano and Barrera Tyszka, *Hugo Chávez, Definitive Biography,* 76, 108, 115.

29. Elizalde and Báez, *Our Chávez,* 124.

30. Marcano and Barrera Tyszka, *Hugo Chávez, Definitive Biography,* 95–96. Also: Richard Gott, "The Failed Coup d'état of Admiral Gruber, November 1992," in *Hugo Chávez and the Bolivian Revolution* (London: Verso, 2005), 71–76. Also: *El Universal:* "Dominada la rebelión militar"; *El Universal:* "La Guardia Nacional puso fin a la toma de VTV"; *El Universal:* "Suspendidas garantías constitucionales"; *El Universal:* "Miraflores se convirtió en un campo de guerra"; *El Universal:* "Enfrentamientos, saqueos y quema de vehículos"; *El Universal:* "Cronología de la subversión."

Chapter 3: The Democratic Dictator

1. www.cartercenter.org/documents/297.pdf.

2. As a military cadet, Chávez met General Velásquez in Lima in 1974; and upon release from jail for his coup attempt of 1992, Chávez met Fidel Castro in Havana in 1994. See Elizalde and Báez, *Our Chávez,* 371–375.

3. "Homeland, Socialism or Death,"www.reuters.com/article/worldNews/idUSN114258 0120070511; *El Universal:* "Presidente Chávez plantea reordenamiento militar. 'Patria socialismo o muerte,'" January 11, 2007, 1–2.

4. The FARC gave Chávez $150,000 while he was jailed in 1992, according to the Colombian government's release of Raúl Reyes's computer captured in Ecuador on March 1. See also Mary Anastasia O'Grady, "The FARC Files," *Wall Street Journal,* March 10, 2008, A14.

5. Elizade and Báez, *Our Chávez,* 374.

6. Ibid., 375.

7. Ibid., 117.

8. "Venezolanos queman una bandera estadounidense y bloquean temporalmente al embajador de EE.UU," Voice of America online, Mar. 23, 2006, www.voanews.com/spanish/archive/2006-03/2006-03-23-voa5.cfm.

9. The Fourth Republic included all the presidents elected since democracy began in 1958 and the Fifth Republic included him, according to Chávez.

10. Richard Brand in a personal conversation with one of the authors, January 2008. Brand is an investigative journalist who unearthed Chávez's scandalous connections to the electronic voting machine company that counted Venezuela's votes in the recall referendum of 2004 and afterward.

11. Michael Rowan, *Getting Over Chávez and Poverty,* (Caracas: El Nacional Books, 2006), 122. Also: Jennifer McCoy and David Myers, eds., *The Unraveling of Representative Democracy in Venezuela* (Baltimore: Johns Hopkins University Press, 2004), 276.

12. Marcano and Barrera Tyszka, *Hugo Chávez, Definitive Biography,* 3 (see chap. 1, note 5). Also: http://74.125.45.104/search?q=cache:9_MTL2s-QasJ:www.analitica.com/va/internacionales/opinion/1165174.asp+visa+chavez+98&hl=es&ct=clnk&cd=3&gl=ve&lr=lang_es.

13. Evo Morales of Bolivia also got a similar upswing in election polls during the 2005 presidential campaign when the U.S. ambassador made a similar attack against him.

14. Rowan, *Getting Over Chávez and Poverty,* 126–130.

15. Ibid., 128.

16. Michael Reid, *Forgotten Continent: The Battle for Latin America's Soul* (New Haven: Yale University Press, 2007), 160.

17. "Chávez took advantage of the change by holding new elections in July 2000, this time winning 59 percent of the vote," www.foreignaffairs.org/20011101faessay5775/kurt-weyland/will-chavez-lose-his-luster.html. Also: www.mci.gob.ve/noticias-prensa presidencial/28/11615/presidente_hugo_chez.html.

18. Michael Rowan, "The Democratic Revolution" (essay), *Caracas Daily Journal,* October 22, 1999. Also: *TIME,* Aug. 24, 1999, www.time.com/time/magazine/article/0,9171, 29947-3,00.html.

19. Marcano and Barrera Tyszka, *Hugo Chávez, Definitive Biography,* 136–37.

20. Gabriel Loperena, "Chávez's Charade: Democracy in Venezuela," *Harvard International Review,* vol. 25 (summer 2003).

21. "The Rise of the 'Boligarchs,'" *The Economist,* August 11, 2007.

22. Fabiola Sanchez, "Venezuelan lawmakers investigate Chavez brothers for allegedly acquiring ranches," Associated Press Worldstream, March 27, 2008. http://democracy inamericas.org/caracasconnect/March27=2. Venezuela's National Assembly has opened an investigation into how two of Chávez's brothers acquired seventeen ranches in Barinas State, where their father is governor. The accusations have been made by an opposition candidate for governor. Also: *El Universal:* "AN investigará denuncias contra hermanos del presidente Chávez," March 26, 2008, 1–4. Also: www.iht.com/articles/2007/02/18/news/venez.php.

23. In an interview by one of the authors in 2001.

24. Juan Forero, "Venezuelan Thrives on Seeing Threats From 'Mr. Danger,'" *New York Times,* October 11, 2005, www.nytimes.com/2005/10/11/international/americas/11 venezuela.html.

25. "The Sickly Stench of Corruption: Venezuela—A Campaign against Sleaze Raises More Questions Than Answers," *The Economist,* March 30, 2006.

26. Simon Romero, "A clash of hope and fear as Venezuela seizes land," *New York Times,* May 17, 2007.

27. Ibid.

28. "Carnicerías pequeñas afectadas por actuales precios regulados," *El Universal,* March 2, 2007; "Se requiere cambiar el control de precios para reducir escasez," *El Universal,* May 28, 2007; "Gobierno descarta medidas adicionales para frenar precios," *El Universal,* August 3, 2007; "Persiste explosión de consumo pero con alto desabastecimiento," *El Universal,* August 4, 2007; http://broward.el-venezolano.net/articulo.asp?id=4649 &edition-173; www.tendenciaeconomica.com/inflacion/la-economia-venezolana-el-talon-de-aquiles-de-chavez.html.

29. Casto Ocando, "Food shortage sparks Cuba-style rationing," *El Nuevo Herald,* February 25, 2008, http://cubadata.blogspot.com/2008/02/food-shortage-sparks-cuba-style .html.

30. Chris Kraul, "Hard row to hoe for farmers," *Los Angeles Times*, September 22, 2007, C1.

31. David J. Lynch, "Venezuelan consumers gobble up U.S. goods despite political tension," *USA Today*, March 28, 2007, www.usatoday.com/money/world/2007-03-27-venezuela-economy_N.htm. Also: www.guia.com.ve/noticias/?id=8910.

32. Economist Intelligence Unit survey of April, 2006.

33. www.radiosantafe.com/2008/01/28/chavez-propone-crear-fuerza-armada-conjunta-con-nicaragua-bolivia-cuba-r-dominicana-para-enfrentar-a-eu-y-colombia/; and www.abn.info.ve/go_news5.php?articulo=118202&lee=16.

34. William Lowther, "U.S. could intervene as Chavez prepares for war on Colombia," March 2, 2008, www.dailymail.co.uk/news/article-524314/U-S-intervene-Chavez-prepares-war-Colombia.html. Also: "President Hugo Chavez Threatens Colombia With War," March 1, 2008, www.liveleak.com/view?i=29d_1204429349. Also: "Chávez envía tanques y tropas a la frontera con Colombia," *El Universal*, March 3, 2008.

35. Phil Gunson, "Chávez's grip on media getting stronger," *Miami Herald*, March 26, 2008.

36. "IPI Watch list: November 2004 Update," International Press Institute, www.freemedia.at/cms/ipi/watchlist_detail.html?country=KW0032.

37. Steven Dudley, "La 'ley mordaza'obliga a la prensa venezolana a autocensurarse," *Miami Herald*, October 13, 2005. http://web.sumate.org/democracia-retroceso/Prensa/LeyMordazaobliglaAutocensurarse-MiamiHerald.htm.

38. Chávez is the number one client of every bank in Venezuela except for one small bank, which refuses as a matter of principle to buy government paper (Bánco Venezolano de Crédito).

39. Iain Bruce, "Venezuela Sets Up 'CNN Rival,' " BBC News, Caracas, June 28, 2005.

40. Rowan, *Getting Over Chavez and Poverty*, 134–140.

41. Francisco Rodríguez, "Venezuela's Empty Revolution," *Foreign Affairs*, April 2008.

42. Francisco Toro's "Three days that shook the nation," *VenEconomy*, April 2002, is one of the best efforts at authentic journalism covering this much-maligned story.

43. "April 11: Setting the record straight," *VenEconomy Weekly*, April 11, 2007.

44. Venevision TV, April 11, 2002; or "Hugo Chávez", 175, which includes the following story: At midnight the evening of April 11, Chávez called Monsignor Baltásar Porras, president of the Venezuelan Episcopal Conference, and said, "After three hours and a lot of consultation, I have decided to relinquish my power and am willing to sign if you can guarantee that they will let me out of the country."

45. "Profile: Hugo Chavez," BBC News, December 3, 2007. http://news.bbc.co.uk/2/hi/americas/3517106.stm.

46. Ari Fleisher's full statement on the morning of April 12, 2002, is at www.whitehouse.gov/news/releases/2002/04/20020412-1.html.

47. Condoleezza Rice on NBC's *Meet the Press*, Sunday, April 14, 2002.

48. See the transcript for ABC's *Nightline*, September 16, 2005. Chávez denied supporting the FARC; denied not cooperating with the U.S. against cocaine smuggling; denied reducing exports to the U.S.; and he promised to provide proof of U.S. plans to invade Venezuela and to provide proof that the U.S. supported the "coup" of 2002. None of these claims were true and none were followed up by ABC or in a subsequent interview by Barbara Walters.

49. "The Untold Story of Venezuela's 2002 April Crisis," *Caracas Chronicles*, April 14, 2004, http://caracaschronicles.blogspot.com/2004/04/untold-story-of-venezuelas-2002-april.html.

50. Several of the signatories have disavowed Chávez since signing the letter in his support.

51. www.fpif.org/commentary/2004/0404nedven.html. Also: http://kucinich.house.gov/Issues/Issue/?IssueID=1563#Venezuela; Also: "Jesse Jackson, Naomi Klein, Zinn, Kucinich, others express support for Venezuela's Chávez," *Venezuelanalysis*, August 13, 2004; available at www.venezuelanalysis.com/news/633; Also: www.rethinkvenezuela.com/downloads/08-12-04solidarity.htm.

52. Marcano and Barrera Tyszka, *Hugo Chávez: Definitive Biography*, 186.

53. "The Systematic Annihilation of the Right to Vote in Venezuela," Venezolanos por la Transparencia Electoral, July 16, 2007, 4–5, www.esdata.info/pdf/right-to-vote.pdf.

54. Ibid., 6–7, 13.

55. http://muse.jhu.edu/journals/journal_of_democracy/v016/16.1mccoy.html. Also: http://aceproject.org/ero-en/regions/americas/VE/Venezuela.pdf/view. Also: www.humanrights.uio.no/forskning/publ/nr/2004/13.pdf. Also: www.rnv.gov.ve/noticias/index.php?act=ST&f=2&t=5970.

56. "CNE intenta descongestionar centros de votación," *El Universal*, June 18, 2005, 1–6; "CNE concretará control sobre registro civil en 2007," *El Universal*, December 22, 2006, 1–4; "Denuncian doble cedulación que involucra a 'el Boyaco,'" *El Universal*, June 19, 2005, 1–6.

57. See alderman Edward Burke's stories at www.chicagoist.com/tags/hugochavez. Also: "Smartmatic de Venezuela enfrenta investigaciones federales que incluyen presuntos pagos en Venezuela de comisiones millonarias no declaradas," Casto Ocando, *El Nuevo Herald*, November 30, 2006, http://baracuteycubano.blogspot.com/2006/11/smartmatic-de-venezuela-enfrenta.html.

58. www.vcrisis.com/index.php?content=letters/200508141135. Also http://vcrisis.com/index.php?content=letters/200610301338. Also www.nytimes.com/2006/10/29/washington/29ballot.html.

59. "Caso Smartmatic," *El Universal*, July 18, 2005.

60. Both the authors were associated with Súmate in 2004.

61. Chang-Tai Hsieh, "The Price of Political Opposition: Evidence from Venezuela's *Maisanta*." Edward Miguel, Daniel Ortega, and Francisco Rodríguez, September 2007. www.yale.edu/polisci/info/conferences/Venezuela/papers/PriceOfPoliticalOpposition.pdf.

62. Juan Forero, "Foes Press Audit of Venezuela Recall Vote," *New York Times*, Aug. 18, 2004, http://query.nytimes.com/gst/fullpage.html?res=940DE6DC113FF93BA2575BC0A9629C8B63.

63. "Audit Confirms Chávez Victory in Recall," *New York Times*, August 22, 2004.

64. Ricardo Hausmann, "Cornered in Caracas," *Wall Street Journal*, Review and Outlook section, September 9, 2004. Also: "Dos ligaditos sumando para la abstención," June 16, 2006, http://resteados.blogsome.com/2006/06/16/dos-ligaditos-sumando-para-la-abstencion/. Ricardo Hausmann and Roberto Rigobon, "Harvard's Hausmann & MIT's Rigobon speak out about Venezuela's electoral fraud," http://vcrisis.com/index.php?content=letters/200409061610.

65. www.cartercenter.org/documents/2021.pdf. English version: www.cartercenter.org/documents/2020.pdf.

66. As noted by Rowan at the Inter-American Dialogue, Washington, DC, meeting of September 7, 2004. Also: www.cartercenter.com/news/documents/doc1826.html.

67. "A Technical Analysis of an Exit Poll in Venezuela," www.zonalatina.com/Zldata373.htm.

68. Both authors have worked for Zulia state governor Manual Rosales.

69. http://goliath.ecnext.com/coms2/summary_0199-6023689_ITM.

70. PSB poll conducted for the Rosales campaign (in file of author).

71. Andy Webb-Vidal, "Opponent takes pot shots at unassailable Chávez," *Financial Times*, September 29, 2006. www.ft.com/cms/s/0/364df65a-4f9a-11db-9d85-0000779e2340 .html?nclick_check=1.

72. http://ipsnews.net/news.asp?idnews=42484. Also: www.laregioninternacional.com/ noticia/30424/Ourense/Venezuela/emigrantes/gallegos/inseguridad/secuestros/ase sinatos/. Also: http://archivo.eluniversal.com/2008/08/21/opi_art_perder-caracas_ 986634.shtml. Also: http://jrestrepo.wordpress.com/2008/06/20/caracas-entre-las -ciudades-mas-peligrosas-del-mundo/. Also: www.noticias24.com/actualidad/?p=15788.

73. "Entre el azul y el rojo," *Producto*, vol. 276, November 2006, www.producto.com .ve/276/notas/portada.html.

74. "Chavez: New 'defeat for the devil,'" CNN.com, December 4, 2006, www.cnn .com/2006/WORLD/americas/12/04/venezuela.election/index.html. Also: "Smart-matic-Sequoia opuesta a que sus máquinas sean auditadas," www.tecnologiahecha palabra.com/sociedad/politica_economia/articulo.asp?i=2268, March 24, 2008.

75. *VenEconomy* editorial, May 30, 2007. Note: The publisher of *VenEconomy*, Robert Bottome, is the brother of RCTV's chairman, Peter Bottome.

76. www.nytimes.com/2007/11/10/world/americas/10venez.html; Also: *El Universal:* "Radio Caracas TV quedó en silencio," May 28, 2007; *El Universal:* "Existen presiones para evitar que salgamos por cable," May 28, 2007, 1–6; *El Universal:* "Para editores la medida es parte de una estrategia global," May 28, 2007, 1–6; *El Universal:* "Manifesta-ciones en numerosas regiones a favor de la televisora," May 28, 2007, 1–10; *El Universal:* "Preocupa a la SIP persecución a RCTV," July 31, 2007, 1–2.

77. Phil Gunson, *Miami Herald*, March 26, 2008, 1.

78. *El Universal*, October 10, 2007.

79. Simon Romero, "Students emerge as leading force against Chávez," *New York Times*, November 10, 2007.

80. Ibid., "Venezuela general likens Chávez's proposals for constitution to a coup," *New York Times*, November 6, 2007.

81. Tim Padgett, "Chavez Tastes Defeat Over Reforms," *Time* magazine, December 3, 2007, www.time.com/time/world/article/0,8599,1690082,00.html?xid=feed-cnn-topics.

82. "Cardenal denuncia a Chávez en Roma," *El Universal*, November 24, 2007, 1–4. Also: www.guardian.co.uk/world/2007/dec/03/venezuela.rorycarroll.

83. www.ibtimes.com/articles/20071127/chavez-warns-business-group.htm.

84. Credible legal and news sources who wish to remain anonymous to avoid recrimination provided this information to the authors in 2008.

85. Castro Ocando, "Chávez popularity cools amid push for socialism," *El Nuevo Herald*, July 18, 2007, http://canadiancoalition.com/forum/messages/23957.shtml.

86. "Si no se aprueba la reforma habría que pensar en mi relevo," *El Universal*, November 24, 2007, 1–6; http://www3.wsvn.com/news/articles/world/MI69009/.

87. John Otis posts at http://freerepublic.info/focus/f-news/1932723/, *Houston Chronicle*, November 30, 2007. Also: "Si no se aprueba la reforma habría que pensar en mi relevo," *El Universal*, November 24, 2007.

88. Simon Romero, "Chávez ready to rule until 2050," *New York Times*, November 29, 2007. Also: *El Universal:* "Chávez cerró campaña con amenazas," December 11, 2007; *El Universal:* "Chávez cerró campaña con amenazas," December 11, 2007.

89. CNN.com, www.cnn.com/2007/WORLD/americas/12/03/venezuela.referendum/.

90. Enrique Andrés Pretel, "Poll says Chavez loses Venezuela referendum lead," November 24, 2007, http://freerepublic.com/focus/f-news/1929935/posts.

91. Economist.com, www.economist.com/world/americas/displaystory.cfm?story_id=1025 1226; Also: www.finlay-online.com/tomasromay/medcubext2.htm.

92. Jorge Castaneda, "Attempted Theft," *Newsweek*, December 7, 2007, www.newsweek .com/id/74230.

93. www.timesonline.co.uk/tol/comment/columnists/david_aaronovitch/article3031178 .ece. Also: "Chávez anuncia "segunda ofensiva para aprobar reforma," *El Universal*, December 6, 2007.

Chapter 4: Oil Is His Most Potent Weapon

1. David Ebner, "Oil Prices Too High, Saudi minister says," *The Globe and Mall*, November 14, 2007.

2. Gustavo Coronel, "Corruption, Mismanagement and Abuse of Power in Hugo Chávez's Venezuela," Cato Institute, Development Policy Analysis No. 2, November 27, 2006, 13. Also: www.analitica.com/va/economia/tips/9362309.asp.

3. Juan Forero, "Venezuela Says Oil Industry to rebound Soon from Strike," *New York Times*, February 18, 2003. Also: Gustavo Coronel, *The Nationalization of the Venezuelan Oil Industry* (Lanham, MD: Lexington Books, 1983), 257.

4. David I. Lynch, "Has CITGO Become a Political Tool for Hugo Chavez?," *USA Today*, January 13, 2006.

5. Gregory Wilpert, "The Economics, Culture, and Politics of Oil in Venezuela," VenezuelaAnalysis.com, August 30, 2003, www.venezuelanalysis.com/analysis/74. Also: "Audiencia en caso Exxon—Pdvsa prosigue en tribunal británico 5 de marzo 2008-09-11," *El Universal*, 1–4. Also: www.elnuevodiario.com.ni/internacionales/8225.

6. Nikolas Kozloff, *Hugo Chavez: Oil, Politics, and the Challenge to the U.S.* (New York: Macmillan, 2007), 13. Also: www.soberania.org/Articulos/articulo_1242.htm.

7. "Memorandum of Determinations," Overseas Private Investment Corporation (OPIC), July 12, 2004, www.opic.gov/insurance/claims/report/documents/INTESAMoDv7_ FINAL.pdf.

8. Otto Kreisher, "Venezuela Rips Ruling Against its Oil Company in SAIC's Favor," *San Diego Union Tribune*, July 22, 2004, www.signonsandiego.com/uniontrib/20040722/ news_1b22saic.html.

9. Gustavo Coronel, "Corruption, Mismanagement and Abuse of Power in Hugo Chávez's Venezuela," Cato Institute, Development Policy Analysis No. 2, November 27, 2006, 14, www.cato.org/pub_display.php?pub_id=6787. Also:"Restablecidas operaciones en refinería Cardón," *El Universal*, 1–20; "Operativo otra vez el craqueador catalítico de Puerto La Cruz," *El Universal*, 1–18, November 23, 2007; "Superada emergencia operativa al haber 141 taladros en el país," *El Universal*, November 23, 2007, 1–18. Also: www .aporrea.org/trabajadores/a22698.html; www.guia.com.ve/noticias/?id=26598. Also: www.venezolanosenlinea.com/index.php?option=com_content&task=view&id=175 08&Itemid=64. Also: www.analitica.com/va/sintesis/nacionales/6141431.asp. Also: www.venelogia.com/archivos/1062/; Also: http://penzini2.blogspot.com/2007/11/ riesgo-pais-se-dispara-accidentes.html; Also: www.ecoanalitica.net/newsite/uploads/ im_2006_12%20es.pdf.

10. Cesar J. Alvarez and Stephanie Hanson, "Venezuela's Oil-Based Economy," Council on Foreign Relations, backgrounder, June 27, 2008, www.cfr.org/publication/12089/. Also

El Universal:"Expediente: PDVSA suicida," May 22, 2005; *El Universal:* "La OPEP reju-
venece y Venezuela envejece opinión," June 18, 2005. *El Universal:* "Exigen al gobierno
informe real situación contable de PDVSA," July 31, 2007; and www.ecoanalitica.net/
newsite/uploads/im_2006_12%20es.pdf.

11. Juan Forero, "Venezuela Set to Assume Control of Its Oil Fields," *Washington Post,* May
1, 2007.

12. All three American oil companies reported earnings and asset losses in the billions in
2008 as a result of Chávez's nationalization of their properties.

13. Kirza Janicke, "Venezuelan State Oil Company to Challenge Asset Freeze in the Nether-
lands," Venezuela Information Centre, London, www.venezuelanalysis.com, April 22,
2008. Also: Marianna Parraga, "Court Unfreezes PDVSA'S Oil Assets," *El Universal,*
March 19, 2008, http://buscador.eluniversal.com/2008/03/19/en_eco_art_court
-unfreezes-pdvs_19A1445483.shtml.

14. Venezuela's heavy crude oil, which is like a tar sludge, must be sent abroad to make it
into useful products, like gasoline or jet fuel, to special refineries, most of which are in
the United States; heavy oil costs more to refine than light.

15. "A High Stakes Conflict," *New York Times,* April 10, 2007.

16. "Short-Term Energy Outlook," Energy Information Administration, August 12, 2008:
Table 3c, http://tonto.eia.doe.gov/cfapps/STEO_Query/steotables.cfm?periodType=
Annual&startYear=2005&startQuarter=1&startMonth=1&endYear=2009&endQuar
ter=4&endMonth=12&tableNumber=7&noScroll=false.

17. U.S. government Energy Information Administration's "Venezuela Energy Profile,"
www.eia.doe.gov. Also: www.venezuelatoday.org/05-05-18_es.htm. Also: www.guia
.com.ve/noticias/?id=2470.

18. www.eia.doe.gov.world/oil/production/data.

19. Venezuela subsidizes gasoline to the tune of $9 billion in 2007 so that it sells for U.S. 20
cents a gallon. See: www.venezuelatuya.com/historia/27_febrero.htm.

20. Michael Rowan and Douglas Schoen, "The Terrorist in the $10 Gallon Hat," *Huffington
Post,* July 4, 2008, www.huffingtonpost.com/michael-rowan-and-douglas-schoen/the-
terrorist-in-the-10-g_b_110858.html?page=4. Also: www.analitica.com/va/economia/
opinion/5056492.asp; Also: www.soberania.org/Articulos/articulo_2144.htm; and www
.soberania.org/Articulos/articulo_073.htm.

21. On Transparency International's global corruption scale, Venezuela under Chávez fell
to an all-time low, 162 out of 179 countries rated in 2007, www.transparency.org/
policy_research/surveys_indices/cpi/2007.

22. Reid, *Forgotten Continent,* 164–170 (see full citation, page 193, note 16).

23. "Global Conflict," in *The World Today, Essential Atlas of the World* (London: Dorling
Kindersley, 2003).

24. Economics Focus, *The Economist,* November 17, 2007, 92.

25. Ibid.

26. Andrés Oppenheimer, *Saving the Americas,* from the afterword (New York: Random
House, 2007).

27. "Short-Term Energy Outlook," Energy Information Administration, August 12, 2008:
Figure 5, www.eia.doe.gov/emeu/steo/pub/gifs/Fig5.gif; "International Energy Annual," Energy Information Administration, 2005: Table 1.2, www.eia.doe.gov/pub/
oil_gas/petroleum/analysis_publications/oil_market_basics/dem_image_consump
tion.htm

28. Wilfred L. Kohl, "The Perfect Storm: OPEC and the World Oil Market," *Harvard International Review*, Vol. 26 (2005).

29. Mohammad bin Ahaen al-Hamli, oil minister for the United Arab Emerites and president of OPEC, in "Why Oil May Not Stop at $100," Neil King, *Wall Street Journal*, October 31, 2007.

30. Chávez on Venezuelan TV, March 20, 2008.

31. Javier Blas, "OPEC Income Hits Record as Oil Prices Soar," *Financial Times*, August 10, 2008; and "The Biggest Transfer of Wealth in History," Jutia Group, July 12, 2008. Also: Steven Mufson, "Oil Prices Cause Global Shift in Wealth," *Washington Post*, November 10, 2007, http://bartblog.bartcop.com/2007/11/11/rising-oil-prices-cause-global-shift-in-wealth/.

32. "Shock Treatment," *The Economist*, November 15, 2007, www.economist.com/finance/displaystory.cfm?story_id=10130655. Twenty years ago, private oil companies controlled more than half the earth's oil reserves; today it is less than 5 percent. See: "Role of National Oil Companies in the International Oil Market," Robert Pirog, Congressional Research Service, August 21, 2007, 3–4, www.fas.org/sgp/crs/misc/RL34137.pdf.

33. Jad Mouawad, "The Big Thirst," *New York Times*, April 20, 2008, www.nytimes.com/2008/04/20/weekinreview/20mouawad.html. Also: www.nacion.com/ln_ee/2007/abril/30/mundo1079439.html. Also: http://news.bbc.co.uk/hi/spanish/latin_america/newsid_4963000/4963342.stm. Also: http://ipsnoticias.net/nota.asp?idnews=40815.

34. Ibsen Martinez, "On Price Controls and Populist 'Double Think,'" *Reflections from Latin America*, The Library of Economics and Liberty, March 3, 2008. www.econlib.org/LIBRARY/Columns/y2008/Martinezdoublethink.html. Also, *El Universal:* "Carnicerías pequeñas afectadas por actuales precios regulados," March 2, 2007; *El Universal:* "Se requiere cambiar el control de precios para reducir escasez," May 28, 2007; *El Universal:* "Gobierno descarta medidas adicionales para frenar precios," August 3, 2007; *El Universal:* "Persiste explosión de consumo pero con alto desabastecimiento," August 4, 2007. Also: http://broward.el-venezolano.net/articulo.asp?id=4649&edition=173. Also: www.tendenciaeconomica.com/inflacion/la-economia-venezolana-el-talon-de-aquiles-de-chavez.html.

35. Mark Lander, "High Priced Oil Adds Volatility to Global Scramble for Power," *New York Times*, November 7, 2007.

36. Energy Information Administration, http://tonto.eia.doe.gov/dnav/pet/pet_move_neti_a_ep00_IMN_mbblpd_a.htm.

37. UCLA political scientist Michael L. Ross using a statistical analysis of 113 states between 1971 and 1997, concluded that a state's "reliance on either oil or mineral exports tends to make it less democratic."

38. Thomas Friedman, *The First Law of Petropolitics, Foreign Policy* (May/June 2006).

39. *Aló Presidente*, Venezuelan TV program, June 2, 2007.

40. "The Not So Odd Couple: Venezuela's Hugo Chávez and Cuba's Fidel Castro," Council on Hemispheric Affairs paper, June 21, 2005. Also: Jorge Castañeda, "Chavez Lives Castro's Dream," *Newsweek*, February 19, 2007, www.newsweek.com/id/68391?tid=relatedcl

41. While retaining sovereignty, Cuba and Venezuela share a condominium relationship of mutual help—investment and defense agreed by Fidel Castro and Hugo Chávez

on December 14, 2004. Whether Fidel's brother Raúl Castro, the new president of Cuba, will maintain the same closeness to Chávez as Fidel did, is speculative. Also: "Impulsan Cuba y Venezuela su relación," April 28, 2005, www.esmas.com/noticierostele visa/internacionales/442287.html.

42. "The Not So Odd Couple: Venezuela's Hugo Chávez and Cuba's Fidel Castro," Council on Hemispheric Affairs, June 21, 2005, www.coha.org/NEW_PRESS_RELEASES/ New_Press_Releases_2005/05.62_The_Not_So_Odd_Couple_Venezuelas_Hugo_Cha vez_and_Cubas_Fidel_Castro.htm. Also: "Factura petrolera de Cuba con Venezuela sumará $4 millardos?," *El Universal*, August 4, 2007, 1–10.

43. Otto J. Reich, "Latin America's Terrible Two," *National Review*, April 11, 2005 http://ar ticle.nationalreview.com/?q=YTM0NTcxM2ZiZWJjZWM5Y2ZiYmQyYzQ4M2M4O Tc0MDE=.

44. For comparison, the U.S. has provided $6 billion to Colombia to fight the drug war during the same 1999-to-present period, while Venezuela has provided $24 billion to Cuba. See www.ciponline.org/facts/0512eras.pdf.

45. The numbers for just about anything in Chávez's government vary and are generally state secrets, especially the oil, money, and security personnel numbers. Castro and Chávez applied the same program to Bolivia, Ecuador, and Nicaragua from 2006 to 2008, which is stretching Cuba's vaunted health program very thin. See: Argiris Malapanis and Roger Calero, "Clínicas con médicos cubanos ganan popularidad por toda Venezuela," December 22, 2006, www.granma.cu/espanol/2006/diciembre/ vier22/militante.html.

46. Castro claims that the U.S. has attempted to assassinate him some 300 times since 1960 and plenty of evidence exists that the U.S. tried to do so during the administrations of presidents Kennedy, Johnson, Nixon, and Reagan; Chávez claims that the U.S. has attempted to assassinate him every year since 1999, but no evidence exists that the U.S. has tried to do so. Chávez's speeches are filled with references to U.S. assassination attempts against Castro, Chile's Sálvador Allende in 1973, and himself as a kind of proof by association. See: "Chávez aseguró que ahora sí Bush ordenó matarlo," *El Universal*, September 2006.

47. When Castro took over Cuba it was the wealthiest country in Latin America, while today it is tied with Haiti for being the poorest. However, Castro's lack of performance has not prevented him from claiming 99 percent approval in sham elections that Cuba has run throughout the period of Castro's dictatorship, as if he is the will of the people. Chávez is obviously headed down the same track as following chapters of this book document.

48. Testimony to the U.S. Congress by Gal Luft, quoted in Henry Blodget, "OPEC Oil Reserves Worth 3X as Much as All Companies on All World Stock Exchanges Combined," ClusterStock, July 23, 2008. www.clusterstock.com/2008/7/opec-oil-reserves-worth -3x-as-much-as-all-companies-on-all-world-stock-exchanges-combined.

49. Elizalde and Báez, *Our Chávez*, 339 (see note 4, ch. 1). Also: Daniel Williams and Maher Chmaytelli, "Chavez Tells OPEC to Use Politics, Curb 'Imperialism,'" Bloomberg Press, November 19, 2007, www.bloomberg.com/apps/news?pid=20601087&sid=aN mE.oybx0H0&refer=worldwide. This mentions the 1973 embargo, and discusses Chávez's call for OPEC to return to its anticolonial roots, but it does not mention Chávez's stance on embargo as a cadet.

50. Natalie Chen et al., "Oil Prices, Profits and Recessions: An Inquiry Using Terrorism as an Instrumental Variable," University of Warwick, 2007. Also: Scott D. Sagan, "How to

Keep the Bomb from Iran," *Foreign Affairs*, September/October 2006, 1, 3. Also: www
.nytimes.com/cfr/world/20060901faessay_v85n5_sagan.html?pagewanted=1&sq=iraq-
iran war nuclearweapons&st=cse&scp=65

51. Gregory Wilpert, "The Economics, Culture, and Politics of Oil in Venezuela," (see full
citation, page 197, note 5). Also: "Venezuela preside la OPEP. El Ministro de Energía y
Minas, Alí Rodríguez Araque fue elegido para encabezar cartel con motivo de la Con-
ferencia de Jefes de Estados y Ministerial que se celebrará en Caracas," *El Universal*,
March 22, 2000, 2–13.

52. "Chavez Goes His Own Way—To Iraq," BBC News, August 10, 2000, http://www
.cbsnews.com/stories/2000/08/09/world/main223125.shtml. Also: *El Universal*:
"Washington critica viaje de Chávez a Irak," August 8, 2000; *El Universal*: "Hugo Chávez
entrará a Irak a pie," August 9, 2000, first page; *El Universal*: "Rancel fustiga oposición de
Washington a visita Irak," August 9, 2000; *El Universal*: "Casa Blanca suaviza criticas de
encuentro Chávez–Hussein," August 10, 2000.

53. *El Universal*: "OPEP consulta para paliar caída de precios," January 10, 2007; *El Universal*:
"OPEP mantendrá producción sin cambios al menos hasta febrero," December 6,
YEAR? Also: www.aporrea.org/actualidad/a7859.html. Also: http://209.85.215.104/
search?q=cache:D8c8G55ccTwJ:www.analitica.com/va/economia/opinion/1456174
.asp+venezuela+e+iran+presiona+baja+suministro+y+aumentar+precios+opep+
1999&hl=es&ct=clnk&cd=2&gl=ve.

54. Rania el Gamal, "Could OPEC Drop Dollar for Euro?" *Kuwait Times*, December 19,
2007; and "The USD Agony," *China Daily*, June 4, 2008. Also: Jad Mouawad, "Critics As-
sail Weak Dollar at OPEC Event," *New York Times*, November 19, 2007, www.nytimes
.com/2007/11/19/business/19opec.html?scp=1&sq=opec_chavez_ahmadinejad_saudi
&st=cse

55. "OPEC Urged to End Use of Dollar," Al Jazeera news, November 19, 2007.

56. Venezuela produces only 2.4 mbd in 2008, one third of which is used internally, so it
is now fourth among exporters to the U.S. "Crude Oil and Total Petroleum Imports
Top 15 Countries," August 26, 2008, Energy Information Agency, www.eia.gov.doe
.gov/pub/oil_gas/petroleum/data_publications/company_level_imports/current/im
port.html.

57. Reid, *Forgotten Continent*, 161–63.

58. "A High-Stakes Conflict: Venezuela's Reserves And U.S. Energy Needs," *New York Times*,
April 10, 2007.

59. Oil is "the devil's excrement" according to Juan Pablo Pérez Alfonso, a Venezuelan and
one of the founders of OPEC. See Jerry Useem, "The Devil's Excrement," *Fortune* magazine, February 3, 2003. See also: www.eluniversal.com/2008/08/17/til_art_omar
-lares_998056.shtml; www.soberania.org/Articulos/articulo_2061.htm; www.derevis
tas.com/contenido/articulo.php?art=64

60. Terry Lynn Karl, *The Paradox of Plenty: Oil Booms and Petro-States* (Berkeley: University
of California Press, 1997).

61. Robert Klitgaard, *Corrupt Cities: A Practical Guide to Cure and Prevention* (Oakland, CA:
ICS Press, 2000), 26.

Chapter 5: Bad Neighbor

1. www.newyorker.com/reporting/2008/06/23/080623fa_fact_anderson.

2. *El Universal*: "Venezuela facilita adquisición de crudo a países del Caribe"; *El Universal*:

"Petrocaribe nació bajo la duda," Tema del Día, June 30, 2005; El Universal: "Fondos del Banco del Sur se usarán para atender crisis fiscales," April 12, 2007.

3. El Universal: "La demanda por el bono del sur supera la oferta de finanzas," March 2, 2007; El Universal: "330 mil inversionistas demandaron por bono del sur," March 3, 2007.

4. "Acabar con petrodiplomacia," El Nacional, December 23, 2007, 2.

5. Natalie Obiko Pearson and Ian James, "Chavez offers billions in Latin America," USA Today, August 26, 2007, www.usatoday.com/news/topstories/2007-08-26-1322251005_x.htm.

6. The votes that side with the U.S. at the thirty-five-nation OAS are Canada, Chile, Colombia, El Salvador, and Mexico; on matters of controversy, several of those countries abandon the U.S. position.

7. In the opinion of Diego Arria, former ambassador to the United Nations from Venezuela in the 1990s.

8. Natalie Obiko Pearson and Ian James, "Venezuela Offers Billions to Countries in Latin America," Associated Press, August 28, 2007, www.venezuelanalysis.com/news/2571.

9. "Chávez bate récords en diez años de gobierno," El Nuevo Herald, July 28, 2008, http://realidadalternativa.wordpress.com/2008/07/30/el-nuevo-herald-chavez-bate-records-en-10-anos-de-gobierno.

10. "Iranian Regime Emerges as Central Player in Probe of Money-Laundering by UBS," October 15, 2005, www.freedomzone.com/archives/2005/10/iranian_regime_emerges_as_cent.php. Also: Kenneth Rijock, "US Slams Venezuela on Money-Laundering," World-Check, www.world-check.com/articles/2008/03/01/us-slams-venezuela-money-laundering/ 1 March 08.

11. Parag Khanna, "Conclusion: Beyond Monroe," The Second World: Empires and Influence in the New Global Order (New York: Random House, 2008), 166.

12. Tim Rogers, "Chávez plays oil card in Nicaragua," Christian Science Monitor, May 5, 2006, www.csmonitor.com/2006/0505/p01s04-woam.html. Also: "Chávez condonó deuda de Nicaragua por $32.8 millardos," El Universal, January 12, 2007, 1–5. Also: www.heritage.org/Press/Commentary/ed011508c.cfm. Also: www.europapress.es/internacional/noticia=Venezuela-Acusan-Hugo-Chavez-influir-ultimas-elecciones-de-Argentina-juicio-caso-maletin20080910081738.html. Also: www.laregion.es/noticia/68375/Venezuela/acusaci%C3%B3n/Ch%C3%A1vez/Hugo/caso/malet%C3%ADn/elecciones/Argentina/. Also: http://noticiasyciencias.blogspot.com/2006/05/alan-garca-hugo-chvez-no-influir-en.html.

13. One of the authors was a consultant for a competing presidential campaign in Bolivia.

14. Kiraz Janicke, "Chávez Warns that Bolivia is Being Destabilized by U.S. Just as Venezuela," September 10, 2007, www.venezuelanalysis.com/news/2593. Also: "Bachelet cree 'normal' acuerdo militar entre Venezuela–Bolivia," El Universal, October 11, 2006, 1–4.

15. "Ortega anuncia incorporación de Nicaragua al ALBA," El Universal, January 11, 2007, 1–5. www.noticiasdegipuzkoa.com/ediciones/2006/04/30/politica/espana-mundo/d30esp22.177687.php. Also: www.usatoday.com/news/world/2006-04-29-alba_x.htm.

16. Statement by Senate president Oscar Ortiz Antelo in Ambito Financiero newspaper, Bolivia, April 4, 2008.

17. Of the thirty-five nations in the OAS, most are run by socialists, populists, leftists, or communists by our count.

18. *El Universal:* "Empresas de Brasil solicitan que Venezuela no ingrese al MERCOSUR," November 30, 2007, 1–20. *El Universal:"* Chávez emprenderá gira con la mirada hacia el MERCOSUR," August 5, 2007, 1–4. Also: http://english.eluniversal.com/2008/03/28/en_ing_art_chavez-signs-energy_28A1468519.shtml.

19. *New York Times,* April 3, 2008, A10.

20. "Chavez Backs Ecuador in Bid to Rejoin Cartel," *The Toronto Star,* business section, October 9, 2007, B02. Also: www.lukor.com/not-mun/america/0711/15012158.htm. Also: http://news.bbc.co.uk/hi/spanish/business/newsid_5035000/5035834.stm. Also: www.adnmundo.com/contenidos/energia/opep_ecuador_chavez_en_06_06_01.html

21. www.nytimes.com/2007/11/04/magazine/04oil-t.html?pagewanted=7&n=Top/News/World/Countries%20and%20Territories/Bolivia.

22. www.stwr.org/latin-america-caribbean/oil-politics-in-nicaragua-a-chavez-wave.html. Also: www.hemisferio.org/al-eeuu/boletines/02/84/reg_03.pdf. Also: www.reuters.com/article/worldNews/idUSN0139469120070802. Also: www.radiolaprimerisima.com/noticias/5685.

23. In 2008, Mayor Ken Livingstone (Labour) was defeated by the conservatives—the Chávez oil-for-traffic-advice deal was prominent in the campaign. In the summer of 2008, Livingstone announced that he was becoming a traffic consultant for Chávez in Caracas (see: Fiona Hamilton, "Former Mayor Ken Livingstone is Hugo Chávez's New Adviser," *The Australian,* August 29, 2008). Also: www.guardian.co.uk/world/2006/may/14/oil.venezuela.

24. Andrés Oppenheimer, *Saving the Americas,* 300, (see note 26, chapter 4).

25. One of the authors advised Dr. Oscar Arias in the campaign.

26. Authors' notes from the campaign.

27. Authors' notes from the campaign

28. *Christian Science Monitor,* April 3, 2008.

29. www.elpais.com.co/paisonline/notas/marzo052008/llamadachavez.html.

30. Jackson Diehl, "The FARC's Guardian Angel," March 10, 2008, A15, www.washingtonpost.com/wp-dyn/content/article/2008/03/09/AR2008030901429.html.

31. Ibid.

32. Thor Halvorssen, "Venezuela's Charades" (editorial), February 7, 2008. Courtesy of the *Washington Times.* www.washingtontimes.com/news/2008/feb/07/venezuelas-charades/.

33. www.state.gov/s/ct/c14151.htm.

34. http://uk.reuters.com/article/email/idukn0328060920080403.

35. Reid, *Forgotten Continent,* 257.

36. Ibid, 258.

37. Ibid.

38. Ibid.

39. www.washingtonpost.com/wp-dyn/content/article/2007/07/25/AR2007072501093.html?nav=rss_world/southamerica. Also: http://hrw.org/english/docs/2005/04/15/colomb10496.htm. Also: http://hrw.org/english/docs/2005/02/22/colomb10202.htm. Also:www.hchr.org.co/documentoseinformes/informes/altocomisionado/Informe2004_eng.pdf.

40. Halvorssen, "Venezuela's Charades."

41. Agence France Press, March 18, 2008.

42. Kim Cragin, et al., "Sharing the Dragon's Teeth: Terrorist Groups and the Exchange of New Technologies," RAND Corporation, 2007, 72, www.rand.org/pubs/monographs/2007/RAND_MG485.pdf.

43. www.state.gov/s/ct/rls/fs/2001/6531.htm. Also: http://eur-lex.europa.eu/LexUriServ/site/es/oj/2005/l_272/l_27220051018es00150017.pdf.

44. Reid, *Forgotten Continent*, 259.

45. "Colombian army moves against rebels," BBC news, February 21, 2002, http://news.bbc.co.uk/2/hi/americas/1832060.stm.

46. A comparison between what the Iraqi and Colombian governments have achieved militarily, politically, and economically against their respective insurgencies since 2004 would be instructive to U.S. taxpayers, whose $6 billion investment in Colombia would be eaten up in two weeks in Iraq.

47. "Colombia's rebels: a fading force?" BBC news, February 1, 2008, http://news.bbc.co.uk/2/hi/americas/7217817.stm.

48. Reid, *Forgotten Continent*, 257–261.

49. www.eluniversal.com/2008/03/03/en_pol_art_chavez-sends-troops,_03A1402645.shtml.

50. http://english.eluniversal.com/2008/02/01/en_ing_art_dangerous-alliances_01A134 4453.shtml. Also: www.infolatam.com/entrada/venezuela_hugo_chavez_entre_el_ nacionali-7301.html. http://archivo.eluniversal.com/2008/01/27/pol_art_alianzas-peligrosas_685043.shtml.

51. Mary Anastasia O'Grady, *Wall Street Journal*, opinion page, March 10, 2008.

52. http://gatewaypundit.blogspot.com/2008/05/interpol-confirms-authenticity-of-raul .html. The Southern Command of the U.S. apparently has intelligence on Chávez's connections to the FARC, terrorists, and drug trafficking; Homeland Security and the Department of Justice apparently possess intelligence on Chávez's connections to money laundering; the DEA and Congress have conducted investigations on these matters, many of which are ongoing. Whether the U.S. fully discloses all that it knows about Chávez remains an open question.

53. Mary Anastasia O'Grady, "The FARC Files," *Wall Street Journal*, March 10, 2008.

54. Ibid.

55. Romero, "Venezuela threatens war with Colombia," March 4, 2008 (see note 103, ch 5).

56. Peter DeShazo, "The OAS," paper by the former deputy permanent representative to the OAS, World Affairs Council of San Antonio, Texas, November 8, 2002. Also: www .un.org/News/Press/docs/2001/sc7158.doc.htm.

57. Ken Rijock, www.world-check.com.

58. Ibid.

59. According to Rijock, the most valuable file of all the 37,000 is definitely the unreleased (so far) FARC membership list, which may break open the financial dealings of al-Qaeda, Iran, Hezbollah, Hamas, and ETA, not just the FARC and ELN of Colombia, the Shining Path of Peru, and whatever Chávez has been up to.

60. Rijock, world-check.com.

61. World-Check is a prime example of this. It is a consultancy advising securities rating agencies, global banks, and investors of political risk in developing nations. For several years, Ken Rijock of World-Check has been advising clients of the enormous risk Chávez presents. While not disclosing his sources, Rijock has been "on the money" in his assessments and early re: Chávez's connections to terrorism, drugs, and money-laundering.

62. Rijock, world-check.com.

63. Ibid.

64. John Carlin, "Revealed: Chávez role in cocaine trail to Europe," *Guardian*, February 3, 2008.
65. Ibid.
66. Ibid.
67. Latin American Drugs I: Losing the Fight, Crisis Group Latin America Report No. 25, March 14, 2008, 11.
68. Reported in a meeting of one of the authors with Ambassador William Brownfield and DEA administrators in Caracas in 2004. The following year the DEA was expelled from Venezuela.
69. Latin American Drugs II: Improving Policy and Reducing Harm, Crisis Group Latin America Report No. 26, March 14, 2008.
70. www.state.gov/p/inl/rls/nrcrpt/2008/vol1/html/100776.htm.
71. Latin American Drugs II, Report No. 26, 23 (see note 69, above).
72. Ibid, 25.
73. Latin American Drugs I, Report No. 25, 11 (see note 67, above).
74. Carlin, *Guardian*, February 3, 2008 (see note 64, above).
75. Rafael was the name the *Guardian*'s journalist gave to his former FARC guerrilla sources to protect them from reprisals.
76. The ETA (Basque Homeland and Freedom), a separatist group that is responsible for more than eight hundred murders and kidnappings, is designated as a terrorist group under the laws of Spain, France, and the European Union.
77. Carlin, *Guardian*, Feb 3, 2008.
78. "Chávez embraces Colombian narco-terrorists," *VenEconomy Weekly*, January 16, 2008.
79. http://news.bbc.co.uk/nolpda/ifs_news/hi/newsid_6972000/6972901.stm. Also: www.iht.com/articles/ap/2007/09/01/america/LA-GEN-Venezuela-Colombia-Pris oners.php. Also: www.washingtonpost.com/wp-dyn/content/article/2007/09/08/AR2007090802126_pf.htm. Also: http://actualidadhispana.blogspot.com/2008/01/presidente-chvez-hace-un-llamado-uribe.html. (Note: chvez [*sic*].)
80. Kevork Djansezian, "Is Bono among record number of Nobel Peace Prize nominees?" February 24, 2005. www.usatoday.com/news/world/2005-02-24-nobel-list_x.htm.
81. *El Universal:* "Chávez pide trasladar a Ingrid a un lugar seguro," March 1, 2008, 1–18; *El Universal:* "Pulecio está consternada por situación de Ingrid," March 1, 2008, 1–18.
82. www.publico.es/124270/chavez/pide/lider/farc/liberacion/unilateral/rehenes.
83. Jenny Barchfield, "Chavez Visits Paris for Hostage Talks," Associated Press, November 20, 2007, www.washingtonpost.com/wp-dyn/content/article/2007/11/20/AR200711 2001859_pf.html. Also: www.minci.gob.ve/noticias_-_prensa/28/15537/presidente_chez_aspira.html.
84. www.csmonitor.com/2007/0906/p01s01-woam.html?page=1. Also: Humberto Márquez, "Colombia: Chavez Asks Bush, FARC Head To Support Hostage Swap," Inter Press Service (IPS), September 26, 2007. Also: www.elpais.com.co/paisonline/notas/Agosto202007/chavezvene.html.
85. www.csmonitor.com/2007/0906/p01s01-woam.html?page=1. Also: www.sptimes.com/2007/09/25/Worldandnation/Florida_parents_enlis.shtml. Also: Humberto Márquez, "Colombia: Chavez Asks Bush, FARC Head To Support Hostage Swap," IPS, September 26, 2007. Also: www.iht.com/articles/ap/2007/08/20/america/LA-GEN-Venezuela-Colombia-Hostages.php. Also: www.lukor.com/not-mun/america/portada/07082113 .htm.
86. www.guardian.co.uk/world/2008/jan/06/film.usa. Also: http://vulcano.wordpress

.com/2008/01/07/oliver-stone-defiende-a-chavez-y-critica-trato-que-da-eeuu-a-patio
-trasero/.

87. www.csmonitor.com/2007/0906/p01s01-woam.html?page=1. Also: www.washington
post.com/wp-dyn/content/article/2007/09/27/AR2007092701137.html. Also: Ana
Carrigan, "Colombia: Venezuela, Europe Attempt To Ease Hostage Crisis." IPS, November 2, 2007. Also: www.bloomberg.com/apps/news?pid=20601086&sid=aVhQaT
Q9GbNs&refer=latin_america.

88. www.washingtonpost.com/wp-dyn/content/article/2007/09/26/AR2007092602021_
pf.html.

89. http://nl.newsbank.com/nl-search/we/Archives?p_product=MH&s_site=miami&p_
multi=MH&p_theme=realcities&p_action=search&p_maxdocs=200&p_topdoc=1&
p_text_direct-0=11C1F47FCE7003B0&p_field_direct-0=document_id&p_perpage=10
&p_sort=YMD_date:D&s_trackval=GooglePM.

90. "Death or Freedom," *The Economist,* April 5, 2008, 42.

91. Ibid.

92. Jackson Diehl, *Washington Post,* March 10, 2008, A15.

93. As a legitimate belligerent under the Geneva conventions, the FARC could distance itself somewhat from its past criminal behavior and protect itself (and Chávez) from
charges of crimes against humanity stemming from kidnapping, murder, extortion, and
drug trafficking, which both the FARC and Chávez know happened and fear greatly.

94. "Familiares esperan resultados de ADN," *El Universal,* January 2, 2008. Also: www.elco
mercio.com.pe/ediciononline/HTML/2007-12-31/Hugo-Chavez-duda-respecto-hipote
sis-sobre-emmanuel-dada-alvaro-uribe.html. Also: www.usaid.gov/our_work/cross-
cutting_programs/transition_initiatives/country/venezuela/rpt1207.html. Also: www
.sptimes.com/2008/01/12/Worldandnation/FARC_hostage_release_.shtml. Also: *El
Universal,* "Familiares esperan resultados de AND," January 2, 2008, 1–14.

95. www.humanevents.com/article.php?id=24455. Also: *El Universal:* "Cuatro rehenes re-
gresan a la vida," February 28, 2008, 1–16.

96. *Washington Post* editorial, January 15, 2008.

97. Ibid.

98. "Sad pawn sent to freezer; Colombia and Venezuela," *The Economist,* Americas section,
December 1, 2007. Also: *El Universal,* "En vilo negocios con socio estratégico," November 27, 2007, 1–12; *El Universal:* "En Colombia hacen llamado a la calma," November 27,
2007, 1–23; *El Universal:* "Lo que he hecho es poner en su sitio al presidente de Colombia," November 27, 2007, 1–24; *El Universal:* "Uribe analizará impasse con asesores,"
November 30, 2007, 1–22.

99. www.nytimes.com/2008/01/02/world/americas/02colombia.html.

100. Rory Carroll, "The Long Slide," *Guardian,* May 17, 2008, www.guardian.co.uk/
world/2008/may/17/venezuela.hugo.chavez. Also: www.perfil.com/contenidos/
2008/01/05/noticia_0021.html. Also: www.elespectador.com/noticias/politica/arti
culo-chavez-critica-farc-tengan-personas-secuestradas. Also: www.fac.mil.co/?idcate
goria=24960&facmil_2007=fe2958d2bfc1a59.

101. Catalina Holguín, "Colombia: networks of dissent and power,"Open Democracy, www
.opendemocracy.net/article/democracy_power/politics_protest/facebook_farc.

102. Simon Romero, "Troops Mass at Colombian Borders in Crisis Over Killing of Rebel,"
New York Times, section A, March 3, 2008, 9.

103. "Flying With Hugo Chavez: One Writer's Experience," an NPR interview with Jon Lee
Anderson of the *New Yorker* magazine, June 25, 2008. Also: Simon Romero, "Venezuela

threatens war with Colombia: Cross-border raid in Ecuador territory," *International Herald Tribune,* New York Times Media Group, March 4, 2008, 6.

104. *El Universal:* "Chávez envía tanques y tropas a la frontera con Colombia," March 3, 2008, 1–14; *El Universal:* "Se declaró ruptura de relaciones 'de hecho,' " March 3, 2008, 1–17; *El Universal:* "Militares se dirigen hacia la frontera con Colombia," March 5, 2008, 1–19.

105. A Reyes e-mail to the FARC secretariat notes that Correa, Morales, and Ortega are "with Chávez to the death." Also see O'Grady, *Wall Street Journal,* March 10, 2008.

106. *Tal Cual* editorial; Also: *New York Times,* March 4, 2008, A3.

107. *Miami Herald,* March 23, 2008.

108. Interview in *La Nacion* newspaper of Argentina, March 31, 2008.

109. Manny Fernandez and Annie Correal, *New York Times,* March 9, 2008, Angelica Medaglia contributed reporting. www.latinamericanpost.com/index.php?mod=seccion& secc=3&conn=5271. Note: Since Chávez took power in 1999 there have been 114,000 homicides with only one remembered by a moment of silence—Raúl Reyes. Also: www.terra.com.ve/actualidad/articulo/html/act1270239.htm. Also: http://informativo-venezuela.com/index.php?option=com_content&task=view&id=128&Itemid=31.

110. "Uribe irá a Corte Penal Internacional," *El Universal,* March 5, 2008, 1–15.

111. News Agency Anncol, which is closely linked to the FARC, reported in *El Universal,* April 3, 2008.

112. "Sarkozy asks Chavez to help free hostage," *Oakland Tribune,* April 6, 2008.

113. Diehl, "The FARC's Guardian Angel," *Washington Post,* March 10, 2008; and *Washington Post* editorial on March 15, 2008.

114. "Sarkozy asks . . . ," *Oakland Tribune,* April 6, 2008.

115. Chris Kraul and Patrick J. Mcdonnell, "Freed hostage Ingrid Betancourt reunited with children in Colombia," *Los Angeles Times,* July 4, 2008, http://articles.latimes.com/2008/jul/04/world/fg-hostages4.

Chapter 6: The Real Axis of Evil

1. Parisa Hafezi, "Iran, Venezuela in 'Axis of Unity' Against U.S.," Reuters, Tehran, July 2, 2007.

2. "U.S.: Will Oil Worries Send the Economy Skidding?" *Business Week,* January 20, 2003. www.businessweek.com/magazine/content/03_03/b3816047.htm.

3. www.opecfund.org. Also: "OPEC Should Become a Political Actor against Imperialism, Venezuela Argues." Also: Kiraz Janicke, venezuenanalysis.com, November 19, 2007, *Marxist-Leninist Daily,* www.cpcml.ca/Tmld2007/D37188.htm.

4. Chávez made the comment on August 12, 2000, during a press conference in Indonesia, which he visited after Iraq and Iran.

5. *Aló Presidente* TV program, No. 263, January 21, 2007.

6. Fred Pais, "Chavez Pushes for OPEC unity," Associated Press, August 5, 2000.

7. Bolivar's birthplace museum guestbook, old city of Caracas, Venezuela.

8. Venezuela's RCTV news, September 29, 2000.

9. "Chávez Visits 'Brother' Ahmadinejad," Al Jazeera News, July 2, 2007. Also: "Iran, Venezuela ink several agreements," IranMania.com, March 12, 2005; www.bilaterals.org. Also: www.agenciaperu.com/columnas/2005/mar/internacional2.htm. Also: www.socialismo-o-barbarie.org/venezuela/050320_c_pactosconiran.htm.

10. *El Universal:* "Hugo Chávez de visita en Irán hasta el Lunes," May 18, 2001. Also: *El Universal,* "Chávez estrecha lazos con Khatami," 2–4.

11. "Iran, Venezuela welcome expansion of investment, trade ties," Iran news agency, August 29, 2004.

12. This intelligence honor belongs to World-Check, in the opinion of the authors.

13. "Profile: Mahmoud Ahmadinejad," BBC News, April 28, 2006.

14. Michael Rowan, "Brothers," El Universal, September 26, 2006.

15. El Universal, June 28, 2005, 1.

16. Ibid., 1654.

17. Ibid.

18. "Venezuela's Chavez, Iran's Ahmadinejad Pledge Mutual Support," Associated Press, via Fox News, July 29, 2006.

19. Ibid., Associated Press.

20. Nasser Karimi, "Hugo Chavez receives Iran's highest honor," Associated Press, July 30, 2006.

21. Ibid.

22. Ibid.

23. Ibid.

24. El Universal, in Caracas, September 17, 2006. Also: http://74.125.45.104/search?q=cache: Xl9nzwEqMvsJ:peakoil-illustrated.blogspot.com/2006_09_01_archive.html+ahmadine jad+orden+libertador&hl=es&ct=clnk&cd=1&gl=ve. http://74.125.45.104/search? q=cache:ukkSNcYi1MMJ:news.bbc.co.uk/hi/spanish/latin_america/newsid_5355000/ 5355024.stm+ahmadinejad+orden+libertador&hl=es&ct=clnk&cd=2&gl=ve.

25. El Universal, Caracas, September 18, 2006.

26. Aló Presidente, TV program no. 281, April 12, 2007.

27. David Stout, "Chávez Calls Bush 'the Devil' in U.N. Speech," New York Times, September 20, 2006, www.nytimes.com/2006/09/20/world/americas/20cnd-chavez.html?ex =1158984000&en=aa643a6bdfaf2377&ei=5087%0A.

28. Warren Hoge, "Venezuela Slips in Voting for U.N. Seat," New York Times, October 16, 2006.

29. Simon Romero, "Iranian President Visits Venezuela to Strengthen Ties," New York Times, January 14, 2007. Also: www.radiolaprimerisima.com/noticias/8507. Also: http:// alexisrojas.blog.com.es/2007/01/16/fondo_de_inversiasn_venezuela_irain_abre~1563201.

30. Aló Presidente, January 27, 2007. Also: "Hugo Chavez Urges Allies to Form Military Alliance Against U.S.," News Agency Trend, January 28, 2008, www.newstrendaz.com.

31. www.radiosantafe.com/2008/01/28/chavez-propone-crear-fuerza-armada-conjunta-con -nicaragua-bolivia-cuba-r-dominicana-para-enfrentar-a-eu-y-colombia/. Also: www.abn .info.ve/go_news5.php?articulo=118202&lee=16.

32. Parisa Hafezi, "Iran, Venezuela in 'axis of unity,' " Reuters, July 2, 2007.

33. Ibid.

34. Aló Presidente, TV program no. 295, September 23, 2007.

35. "Iran leader visits Venezuela, Bolivia," Associated Press, La Paz, Bolivia, September 27, 2007. Also: Ian James, "Iran Leader Visits Venezuela, Bolivia," FoxNews.com, September 27, 2007. Note: Alan Clendenning contributed to article from La Paz, Bolivia.

36. http://english.aljazeera.net, November 20, 2007. Also: "U.S. Agrees to New Talks with Iran on Iraq," CBSNews.com, November 20, 2007.

37. "Chavez, Ahmadinejad Meet in Iran, Promise to Work Against U.S.," Associated Press, November 19, 2007, as reported in Canadian Press, cbcnews.ca.

38. "Iran and Venezuela in air link up," Al Jazeera News, March 4, 2007.

39. "Iran Air Launches Weekly Flights to Venezuela Through Syria, Damascus Official

Says," *International Herald Tribune,* March 2, 2007. Also: *El Universal,* "Inaugurada ruta aérea entre Caracas, Damasco y Teherán," March 3, 2007, 1–14.

40. "Iran Air launches weekly flights to Venezuela through Syria, Damascus official says," Associated Press, March 2, 2007, www.iht.com/articles/ap/2007/03/02/africa/ME-GEN-Syria-Iran-Venezuela.php.

41. "Alert for Iranian checks coming into US," World-Check, February 10, 2007.

42. www.primera-clase.com/2008/09/09/tsa-no-reconoce-seguridad-en-aeropuertos-de -venezuela/.

43. "Ahmadinejad bolsters Iranian ties with Bolivia and Nicaragua," Associated Press, September 28, 2007, www.iht.com/articles/2007/09/28/america/iran.php.

44. Ian James, "Iran leader visits Venezuela, Bolivia," Associated Press, September 27, 2007.

45. In mid-2003, Goni's government was barraged by indigenous protests over a rise in taxes and prices imposed by the IMF rules. It was organized by the supporters of Evo Morales. Goni had visited President George W. Bush in the Oval Office and asked for $50 million to tide him over the IMF-demanded tax he was imposing, but Bush apparently declined.

46. Ron Nathan, "Greenspan Predicting Recession," *Philippine Daily Inquiry,* May 13, 2008; Shepherd Bliss, "US Economy Declines," *Atlantic Free Press,* November 22, 2007.

47. Jad Mouawad, "OPEC event is clouded by criticism of the dollar," *New York Times,* November 19, 2007.

48. "Chávez aims to topple the US dollar," *VenEconomy Weekly,* November 21, 2007.

49. "Losing Faith in the Greenback," *The Economist,* December 1, 2007, 85.

50. Gary Dorsch, "Can the 'Axis of Oil' Topple the U.S. dollar?" *Global Money Trends,* May 1, 2007.

51. Thom Shanker, "Iran Encounter Echoes Troubling '02 War Game," *New York Times,* January 12, 2008. Also: Mike Nizza, "U.S. Military Reports Skirmish with Iran," *New York Times,* January 7, 2008.

52. Shanker, "Iran Encounter Echoes."

53. Kenneth Rijock, "Iranian missiles are pointed at Colombia, increasing country risk," World-Check, Februrary 13, 2008, www.world-check.com/articles/2008/02/13/ira nian-missiles-are-pointed-colombia-increasing-c/. Also: Kenneth Rijock, "Did US sanc-tion Russian arms companies because of Venezuela?" World-Check, January 11, 2007, www.world-check.com/articles/2007/01/11/did-us-sanction-russian-arms-companies -because-ven/.

54. "At the end of the first Bush Administration, I posed this question during an interview in a Washington restaurant with a top Pentagon official who closely followed Colombia and the situation in Venezuela. He had just recited to me a long series of examples of alleged Venezuelan aid to the Colombian guerrillas. But when I took my pen out of my pocket to write down what he was saying, he cut me off, saying that everything he was telling me was off the record and couldn't be published. Why? I asked, perplexed . . . The official gave me a three-letter answer: WMD—weapons of mass destruction. I didn't understand. What did weapons of mass destruction, like those the government had never found in Iraq, have to do with Chávez's aid to Latin American rebels? 'A lot,' he answered, and explained that, after the international ridicule heaped on the U.S. for claiming that Saddam Hussein's regime had weapons of mass destruction, the CIA and other U.S. intelligence agencies were under strict orders to leak nothing that wasn't '100 percent' backed by documents, recordings, or other irrefutable evidence. 'In Chávez's

case, we've got intelligence corroborating about 95 percent of the information about his support for violent groups in other countries, but after Iraq we're not going public until we've got 150 percent corroboration.'—Andrés Oppenheimer, *Saving the Americas,* 79–80. Note: With the Reyes computer, the Pentagon now has 1,000 percent corroboration.

55. Douglas Farah, "Chavez's Favorite Pariahs," *Washington Post,* January 26, 2008.
56. Russ Buettner, "Hugo Chávez Is Tied to Guiliani Firm," *New York Times,* March 15, 2007. Also: www.voanews.com/spanish/archive/2006-05/2006-05-17-voa22.cfm; and http://impreso.elnuevodiario.com.ni/2006/05/16/internacionales/19506.
57. Chris Kraul, "U.S. is monitoring commercial presence of Iran in Venezuela," *LA Times,* June 25, 2006.
58. Simon Romero, "Venezuela Strengthens Its Relationships in the Middle East," *New York Times,* August 21, 2006.
59. Larry Rohter, "Venezuela's leader covets a nuclear energy program," *New York Times,* November 27, 2005.
60. Ewen McAskill and Simon Tisdell, "Iran seeks links with Venezuela," *Guardian,* June 23, 2006.
61. Natalie Obiko Pearson, "Iran and Venezuela Plan Anti-US Fund," Associated Press, January 14, 2007.
62. Kenneth Rijock, "Why is the United States ignoring terrorist activity in Venezuela?" World-Check, September 19, 2007, www.world-check.com/articles/2007/09/19/why-united-states-ignoring-terrorist-financing-wes/.
63. Natalie Pearson, "Iran and Venezuela Plan Anti-U.S. Fund," www.venezuelanalysis.com/news/2178, August 15, 2008.
64. "Venezuela is Selling Oil to China Instead of the US," Transpacifica.com, July 2, 2008. Also: www.pdvsa.com/index.php?tpl=interface.sp/design/salaprensa/readesp.tpl.html&newsid_obj_id=4674&newsid_temas=54.
65. Kenneth Rijock, "Why is the United States ignoring terrorist activity in Venezuela?" www.world-check.com/articles/2007/09/19/why-united-states-ignoring-terrorist-financing-wes/.
66. "Is Venezuela Mining Uranium for Iran?" gatewaypundit.blogspot.com, originally posted by VCrisis.com on September 8, 2006.
67. "Iranian missiles are pointed at Colombia, increasing country risk," World-Check, February 13, 2008; "Alert for Iranian checks coming into the US," World-Check, February 10, 2007; "Warning on deceptively-named bank in Venezuela," World-Check, March 22, 2008; "US sanctions against Iran make Venezuelan banks and bankers targets," World-Check, October 26, 2007.
68. Kenneth Rijock, "Colombia confirms that FARC cache is Uranium, could be the 30 Kilos mentioned on Reyes' computer," March 27, 2008, www.world-check.com/articles/2008/03/27/colombia-confirms-farc-cache-uranium-could-be-30-k/.
69. Ibid.
70. On December 24, 2005, in his TV Christmas address to Venezuela, Chávez said, "The descendents of those who crucified Christ . . . have taken over the wealth of the world." In his January 21, 2006, address at the UN General Assembly, he said, "Imperialist fire, fascist fire, assassin fire, genocidal fire!—The empire's and Israel's, against the innocent people of Palestine and the people of Lebanon. That is the truth!" During a visit to Iran on July 29, 2006, he said, "It's also fascism what Israel is doing to the Palestinian people . . . terrorism and fascism . . . Israel is doing the same that Hitler did against the

Jews. They are killing innocent children and whole families." On August 8, 2006, he said, "I have no interest whatsoever in keeping diplomatic relations, or office, or trade, or anything with a state like Israel." On August 6, 2006, he said: "Israel has gone mad, attacking the people of Palestine and Lebanon . . . This is a new holocaust." In Beijing on August 26, 2006, he said: "Israel should be presented before the international tribunals for that genocide in Lebanon."

71. Chávez's December 24, 2005, TV address in Venezuela.
72. Ibid.
73. Carlos Alberto Montaner, "Hugo Chávez's Anti-Semitism and Anti-Israelism," http://canadiancoalition.com/forum/messages/29904.shtml.

Chapter 7: Chávez and the Jihad

1. www.cbsnews.com/stories/2003/04/18/60minutes/main550000.shtml.
2. U.S. Department of State, Country Reports on Terrorism, www.state.gov/s/ct/rls/crt/2006/82736.html, April 30, 2007.
3. From Country Reports on Terrorism 2006, U.S. State Dept., released by the Office of the Coordinator for Counterterrorism, April 30, 2007, www.state.gov/s/ct/rls/crt/2006/; and Country Reports on Terrorism 2007, U.S. State Dept., released by the Office of the Coordinator for Counterterrorism. April 30, 2008, www.state.gov/s/ct/rls/crt/2007/.
4. Elise Labott, CNN State Department producer, "U.S. terror report cites Venezuela, Iran," April 30, 2008.
5. "Venezuela: Terrorism Hub of South America?" Hearing before the subcommittee on International Terrorism and Nonproliferation, Committee on International Relations, House of Representatives, 109th Congress, second session, serial No. 109–189, Washington, D.C., July 13, 2006, http://commdocs.house.gov/committees/intlrel/hfa28638.000/hfa28638_0.htm.
6. "Man charged over Gatwick grenade," BBC, London, February 17, 2003, 13:28 gmt.
7. Linda Robinson, "Terror Close to Home in Venezuela, a Volatile Leader Befriends Mideast, Colombia, and Cuba," *U.S. News and World Report*, October 6, 2003, www.freerepublic.com/focus/f-news/993592/posts or www.usnews.com/usnews/news/articles/0310066venezuela.htm.
8. Deann Alford, "Why Is Venezuela's Chavez Singling Out New Tribes Mission? Charges sound eerily familiar to Latin American missionaries," October 27, 2005, 12:00 a.m., www.christianitytoday.com/ct/2005/octoberweb-only/43.0c.html.
9. "Peruvian Paper Claims Venezuela Supporting Hezbollah Groups In Amazon," BBC Monitoring International Reports, October 31, 2007 (Text of report by Peruvian newspaper *La Razon* website on October 29, 2007).
10. Gustavo Coronel, "Chavez joins the terrorists: his path to martyrdom," September 2, 2006, http:wincoast.com/forum/archive/index.php.
11. "Venezuela: Terrorism Hub of South America?" Hearing before the subcommittee on International Terrorism and Nonproliferation, Committee on International Relations, House of Representatives, 109th Congress, second session, serial No. 109–189, Washington, D.C., July 13, 2006, http://commdocs.house.gov/committees/intlrel/hfa28638.000/hfa28638_0.htm.
12. Originally from Noticias 24, Patricia Poleo, translated and posted on Fausta's Blog, delivered by Newstex, June 11, 2008, 8:45 a.m. EST. "Venezuelans recruited by the Interior Ministry trained by Hezbollah."

13. "Venezuela's Youth and Hezbollah," June 11, 2008, http://jewishinfonews.wordpress .com/2008/06/11/venezuelas-youth-and-hezbollah/.

14. Chris Kraul and Sebastian Rotella, "Hezbollah Presence in Venezuela Feared," *Los Angeles Times,* August 27, 2008.

15. Ibid.

16. "Chávez in Damascus today and will meet Mish'al; Al-Asad to Cuba next month to attend non-aligned summit," text of report by Ibrahim Humaydi in Damascus, published by London-based newspaper *Al-Hayat* on August 30, 2006.

17. "Venezuela's president to meet Hamas leader during Damascus visit," BBC Worldwide Monitoring, Middle East–Political, August 30, 2006. Source: *Al-Hayat,* London, in Arabic, August 30, 2006.

18. "Venezuela would receive Hamas leaders 'with pleasure,' vice president says," Associated Press, February 14, 2006, 12:59 a.m.

19. Art Moore, "Defector: Chavez gave $1 million to al-Qaida; Venezuelan leader endangering region with increasing ties to terrorism," WorldNetDaily.com, January 7, 2003.

20. "Mission Manager for Cuba and Venezuela Announced," Office of the Director of National Intelligence, Public Affairs Office, Washington, D.C., 20511, press release, Odni News Release No. 16-06, August 18, 2006, hwww.dni.gov/press_releases/News_ Release_16_08_18_06.pdf.

21. "Treasury Targets Hizballah in Venezuela," press release hp-1036, Washington, D.C. www .treas.gov/press/releases/hp1036.htm, June 18, 2008.

22. James Suggett, "U.S. Accusations of Venezuelan Support for Hezbollah 'Mud Slinging' Says Venezuelan Official," Venezuelanalysis.com, June 19, 2008, www.venezuelanalysis .com/news/3575.

23. Martin Arostegui, "U.S. ties Caracas to Hezbollah aid," *Washington Times,* July 7, 2008.

24. James Suggett, "U.S. Accusations of Venezuelan Support for Hezbollah," Venezuel analysis.com, June 19, 2008.

Chapter 8: Useful Idiots

1. http://informativovenezuela.com/index.php?option=com_content&task=view&id= 128&Itemid=31.

2. "What Candidates Have Raised and Spent," *New York Times,* February 22, 2008, www .nytimes.com/imagepages/2008/02/22/us/20080222_CLINTON_GRAPHIC.html.

3. Emilce Chacón, "En Venezuela disminuye la pobreza progresivamente," October 17, 2006, www.minci.gob.ve/reportajes/2/5828/en_venezuela_disminuye.html.

4. "Hunger strike spreads to a third of Venezuela's 21,000 inmates," EFE News service, April 20, 2008.

5. In *Guide to the Perfect Latin American Idiot* (Lanham, MD: Madison Books, 2000), Plinio Apuleyo Mendoza, Carlos Alberto Montaner, and Álvaro Vargas Llosa describe the original misguided populists of Latin America. Vargas Llosa is also the author of *Liberty for Latin America: How to Undo Five Hundred Years of State Oppression* (New York: Farrar, Straus and Giroux, 2005).

6. Álvaro Vargas Llosa, "The Return of the Idiot," *Foreign Policy* (May/June, 2007) www .foreignpolicy.com/story/cms.php?story_id=3805.

7. Ibid.

8. Ibid.

9. "Chávez concedes he failed to solve Venezuelans' most serious problems," *El Universal,* January 29, 2008.

10. Ana Maria Ortiz and Matthew Vadum, "The American Friends of Hugo Chávez," *Organization Trends* magazine, March 2008.

11. "Chomsky on Chavez," August 29, 2008, www.democraticunderground.com.

12. Reported to one of the authors by a Venezuelan source who prefers to remain anonymous.

13. "Joseph Stiglitz Praises Venezuela's Economic Policies," www.venezuelanalysis.com/news/2719, October 11, 2007. Also: *The Cato Journal Book Review*, vol. 16, no. 2, www.cato.org/pubs/journal/cj16n2-10.html.

14. Op-Ed page, *New York Times*, Earth Day, 2006. Also: Joseph Stiglitz, "Will the dam break in 2007?" *Guardian* (comment in Free Blog), December 27, 2006.

15. Marcel Granier, "Remote Control," *El Universal*, January 24, 2007. Also: www.pagina12.com.ar/diario/elmundo/4-85488-2007-05-25.html; www.postwritersgroup.com/spanish/varg070530.html; http://impreso.elnuevodiario.com.ni/2007/05/28/nacionales/49854.

16. Victor Navasky, "Mission to Caracas," *The Nation*, released February 9, 2007.

17. Sol Stern, "The Bomber as School Reformer," *City Journal*, Manhattan Institute, Autumn 2008.

18. Ortiz and Vadum, "American Friends of Chávez."

19. Ibid.

20. "Chávez has a photo obsession for photo-op sessions with anti-American Americans," a Venezuelan journalist who prefers to be anonymous noted about the media-savvy Chávez, in conversation with the authors in September, 2006.

21. Ortiz and Vadum, "American Friends of Chávez."

22. "Hugo Chávez and the Politics of Race," October 15, 2005, www.venezuelanalysis.com/analysis/1414. Also: Hugh O'Shaughnessy, "Chavez offers fuel at 40% discount to poor US citizens," *Irish Times*, August 30, 2005.

23. "Chávez, Venezuela, United States and You," unpublished manuscript by Kyle D. Guerrero, a pseudonym for an American author living in Caracas.

24. "Belafonte Calls Bush 'Greatest Terrorist'–Americas," www.MSNBC.com, January 8, 2006, www.msnbc.msn.com/id/10767465/. Also: http://alberdianos.blogspot.com/2008/04/estrellas-de-hollywood-demuestran.html. Also: http://rayma.eluniversal.com/2006/01/07/pol_art_07105F.shtml.

25. "Chávez calls Bush a 'genocidal terrorist,'" Agence France-Presse, in *Deccan Herald*, March 17, 2008.

26. African American Environmental Association, January 2006, www.aaenvironment.blogspot.com/2006_01_01_archive.html.

27. Gregory Wilpert, "Delegation of Prominent U.S. Progressive Leaders Visits Venezuela," Venezuelanalysis.com, January 8, 2006.

28. "Entrevista//Diego Rísquez, cineaste: Es un error del ministro meterse con los cineastas: Considero que darle 18 millones de dólares a una sola persona (Glover) es poner todos los huevos en una sola cesta," June 4, 2007. Also: "Venezuela pagará 60% de la producción de Danny Glover," *El Universal*, April 11, 2008, 3–8.

29. "Hugo Chavez to Finance Danny Glover Movies," Fox News, May 22, 2007. Also: "Entrevista//Diego Rísquez, cineaste."

30. "Interview with Aram Aharonian, director general of Telesur," *New Internationalist*, issue 386 (January 2006). Also: http://blogs.elcomerciodigital.com/guarandol/2007/1/21/telesur-abrira-oficina-madrid-antes-del-mes-mayo-.

31. James Painter, "The Boom in Counter-Hegemonic News Channels: A case study of Telesur," Reuters Fellowship Paper, Oxford University, Reuters Institute for the Study

of Journalism, Michaelmas, September 29, 2006. http://reutersinstitute.politics.ox.ac.uk/fileadmin/documents/Publications/fellows__papers/James_Painter.pdf. Also: www.eluniversal.com/2005/05/25/til_art_25314A.shtml; and www.webislam.com/?idn=1707; and www.venezuelanalysis.com/analysis/976; and www.eluniversal.com/2008/07/03/pol_art_ponen-telesur-a-la-o_930279.shtml.

32. Ortiz and Vadum, "American Friends of Chávez."

33. "Actor Kevin Spacey Meets Hugo Chavez in Venezuela," *Herald Sun*, September 26, 2007.

34. "Sean Penn Meets Chavez in Venezuela," August 3, 2007, www.washingtonpost.com/wp=dyn/content/article/2007/08/03/AR200708300657.html. Also: Ian James, "On the road with Sean Penn and Chávez," Associated Press, in *USA Today*, August 4, 2007. Also: "Sean Penn considerará producción con la Villa," *El Universal*, August 3, 2007, 3–8.

35. Ortiz and Vadum, "American Friends of Chávez."

36. "Sean Penn Meets Chavez," *Washington Post;* and "On the road with Sean Penn and Chávez," Associated Press; and "Sean Penn considerada producción," *El Universal*.

37. Michael Rowan, "Sean's Questions," *El Universal*, August 14, 2007.

38. Dan Glaister, "Campbell Meets Chávez," *Guardian*, November 1, 2007, www.guardian.co.uk/world/2007/nov/01/venezuela.international; Francisco Rodríguez, "Venezuela's Empty Revolution," *Foreign Affairs* (March/April 2008).

39. Glaister, "Campbell meets Chávez."

40. Christopher Toothaker, "Filmmaker Oliver Stone shadows Hugo Chavez on hostage recovery mission," Associated Press, December 29, 2007, www.iht.com/articles/ap/2007/12/29/news/People-Stone.php.

41. "Así manejan sus finanzas las Farc," Caracol Radio, January 31, 2005, www.caracol.com.co/nota.aspx?id=142347.

42. "Director Oliver Stone Joins Hostage Rescue Team," December 30, 2007, www.cnn.com/2007/WORLD/americas/12/30/stone.colombia/index.html. Also: Toby Muse, "Stone joins hostage-release mission," *USA Today*, December 12, 2007, www.usatoday.com/life/movies/2007-12-30-stone-N.htm.

43. "Director Oliver Stone," (CNN.com, December 30, 2007). Also: "Filmmaker Oliver Stone shadows Hugo Chávez on hostage recovery mission," Associated Press, *International Herald Tribune,* December 29, 2007, www.iht.com/articles/ap/2007/12/29/news/People-Stone.php.

44. Ortiz and Vadum, "American Friends of Chávez" (see note 10, ch. 8).

45. Ibid.

46. Charlie Devereux, "Anger as Chávez gives Hollywood star pounds 9m," *Sunday Telegraph*, London, April 20, 2008.

47. "Letter to President Bush about Venezuela from Congress and You," Portland Independent Media Center, December 13, 2002, http://portland.indymedia.org/en/2002/12/37845.shtml.

48. ABC News, Democratic Presidential Primary Debate in Iowa, August 19, 2007. Also: "Beyond Iraq and into an Era of Bold Engagement," speech by Christopher Dodd, published by Council on Foreign Relations—Essential Documents, April 12, 2007.

49. Ortiz and Vadum, "American Friends of Chávez."

50. Fund-raising letter from Jimmy Carter to one of the authors, November 19, 2007.

51. Emphasis is in the Carter fund-raising letter.

52. Ibid.

53. "Carter meets with embattled Chávez on political bridge-building mission," Agence France-Presse, July 9, 2002. Also: www.venezuelatoday.org/02-07-15_es.htm.

54. "President Carter's Statement at Conclusion of Venezuela Trip," www.embavenez-us.org/news.english/president_carter.htm.

55. "Castro Opens Doors Wide for Carter," http://archives.cnn.com/2002/WORLD/americas/05/12/carter.visit/index.html, May 13, 2002. Also: Scott Wilson, "Another Political Confrontation Looming in Venezuela; Opposition to Chavez Seen Hardening Despite President's Moves Since Coup," Washington Post, July 6, 2002.

56. Mary Anastasia O'Grady, "Observers Rush to Judgment: Jimmy Carter gets rolled—first by Fidel Castro, now by Hugo Chávez," Wall Street Journal, August 21, 2004, www.opinionjournal.com/wsj/?id=110005509. Also: Jake Keaveny, "Crisis! The often overlooked backdrop to Venezuela's political upheaval is an economic disaster," Capital Markets, Institutional Investor, international edition, July 1, 2002.

57. "Venezuelan Opposition Rejects Jimmy Carter's Invitation," Times-News, 2002. Also: Scott Wilson, "Another Political Confrontation Looming in Venezuela; Opposition to Chavez Seen Hardening Despite President's Moves Since Coup," Washington Post, July 6, 2002.

58. Stentor Danielson, "Jimmy Carter Calls for Better Approach to Foreign Aid in Speech at Geographic," National Geographic News, July 11, 2002, http://news.nationalgeographic.com/news/2002/07/0711_020711_jimmycarter_2.html.

59. "Chávez Calls Carter Talks 'Historic,' " Wall Street Journal Abstracts, July 10, 2002, World Watch—The Americas.

60. www.aporrea.org/actualidad/a420.html.

61. Alan Riding, "The Nobel Award: Reaction; Praise and Blame for Prize to Carter, and Message to Bush," New York Times, October 12, 2002.

62. "Venezuela Violence Warning," BBC News, February 26, 2003, http://news.bbc.co.uk/1/hi/world/americas/2801257.stm.

63. Mark Weisbrot, "The other side of the story; Venezuela's recall," International Herald Tribune, August 29, 2003.

64. Phil Gunson, "Chavez's grip on media getting stronger," Miami Herald, March 26, 2008.

65. www.analitica.com/va/politica/opinion/1345036.asp. Also: www.elpais.com/articulo/internacional/oposicion/acusa/Chavez/intentar/retrasar/referendum/elpepiint/2003 0918elpepiint_13/Tes.

66. "Venezuela: Highlights of Radio Nacional de Venezuela news 2200 gmt 27," BBC Worldwide Monitoring, Latin America–Political, January 28, 2004.

67. Rodríguez, "Venezuela's Empty Revolution" (see page 190, note 21).

68. "Visitors Seek a Taste of Revolution in Venezuela," New York Times online, www.nytimes.com/2006/03/21/international/americas/21venezuela.html.

69. Mike Ceaser, "Anti-Chavez Leader Under Fire," Christian Science Monitor, July 5, 2005, www.csmonitor.com/2005/0705/p06s01-woam.html. Also: www.aporrea.org/actualidad/n13943.html.

70. Jimmy Carter, Beyond the White House: Waging Peace, Fighting Disease, Building Hope (New York: Simon & Schuster, 2007).

71. Jason Barnes, "Congressman Dan Burton: Don't Threaten Chavez," Newsmax, October 26, 2005, http://vcrisis.com/index.php?content=letters/200510261458.

72. Estimates made by two former presidents of PDVSA who wish to remain anonymous. Also: Gustavo Coronel, "Hugo Chavez's Big Splurge: Buying Few Real Friends," Human Events.com, August 22, 2007, www.humanevents.com/article.php?id=22011.

73. Ibid.

74. Ibid.

75. Ibid.

76. The $250 million appropriated in 2007 for "North American" activities plus the $250 million the oil program costs.

77. "Is CITGO Program for Poor or for Chavez?" February 23, 2007, www.washingtonpost .com.

78. Ibid.

79. Erik Ekholm, "Barely getting by, too proud to seek help and facing a cold Maine winter," *New York Times,* November 24, 2007.

80. Ralph Nader, "Big Oil's Profits and Plunder," Corporate Accountability and Workplace website, January 8, 2008. Also: Dan Brown, "Bush's Poor Kids First Kept Sick and Freezing," *Huffington Post,* October 22, 2007, www.huffingtonpost.com/dan-brown/bushs -poor-kids-first-_b_69333.html.

81. "Jack Kemp's Shady Business Deal," www.michellemalkin.com/2005/03/16/jack- kemps-other-shady-business-deal/. Also: Thor Halvorssen, "Hugo Chávez vs. the Media: The Venezuelan strongman tries to crack down on his country's journalists while Jack Kemp shills for him in America," *The Weekly Standard,* June 09, 2003, www .weeklystandard.com/Content/Public/Articles/000/000/002/785ruylo.asp?pg=1.

82. Quote to the authors from a person who attended a 2004 luncheon of former members of Congress in Washington, D.C., and who wishes to remain anonymous.

83. Mary Anastasia O'Grady, "Perspectives," *Wall Street Journal,* May 25, 2003.

84. U.S. Rep. Duncan Hunter in Republican presidential primary race in "Romney, Bain and Chavez," www.astrodatabank.com/romney 2007.

85. Russ Buettner, "Company Chávez Controls Is Client of Giuliani Firm," *New York Times,* March 15, 2007.

86. "Rudy Giuliani Says Law Firm Protects American Jobs by Representing Venezuela- Owned Citgo," Associated Press, via FoxNews.com, March 18, 2007, www.foxnews .com/story/0,2933,259502,00.html.

87. Ortiz and Vadum, "American Friends of Chávez," (see note 10, ch. 8).

88. "'The meaning of Hong Kong WTO," *Common Dreams,* January 14, 2006, www.com mondreams.org/views06/0114-29.htm

89. Observation by a European ambassador to Venezuela who requests anonymity, in conversation with the authors in 2006.

90. "Political tourism to Venezuela a hot item," *VenEconomy Monthly,* December 2006.

91. Ortiz and Vadum, "American Friends of Chávez."

92. The precise number of visitors has not been disclosed.

93. Ortiz and Vadum, "American Friends of Chávez."

94. Ibid.

95. John J. Miller, *The National Review,* December 15, 2004.

96. According to Alex Boyd of http://vcrisis.com/index.php?content=letters/200406211040, the VIO suppliers under U.S. law reported $5.7 million in lobbying from 1999 to 2003, plus $1.2 million in 2001 alone to Patton Boggs for lobbying and legal, plus $4.4 million to Arnold Porter from 1998 to 2001 for legal and lobbying work for PDVSA and CITGO. Reporting since 2004 has become very difficult to track but is assumed to have increased vastly.

97. Casto Ocando, "Chavez budgets $250 million for 'alternative' groups," *Miami Herald,* November 24, 2007.

98. Ibid.

99. "A helping hand here and a leg-up there," *VenEconomy*, August 2, 2007, http://mega resistencia.com/foro/viewtopic.php?t=1013. Also: *El Universal*, "Permiten a Fonden re-comprar deuda," June 29, 2005, 2–4. *El Universal:* "Para 2008 Fonden trendrá 28 bil-lones," September 6, 2007, 1–16. *El Universal:* "BCV obtuvo 46% de divisas petroleras del primer trimestre," May 28, 2007, 1–16; *El Universal:* "Con Fonden se capitalizó Fondafa y el Banco agrícola," May 12, 2007, 1–12; *El Universal:* "Aportes al Fonden total-izarán $ 31,4 millardos," November 23, 2007, 1–17; http://blogs.noticierodigital.com/penzini/?p=1.

100. http://eriksez.wordpress.com/2008/04/14/hinterlaces-respaldo-electoral-chavez-35-op osicion-15-17-50-ninguno-de-los-anteriores/.

101. "Has Citgo Become a Political Tool for Hugo Chavez?" *USA Today*, January 11, 2006.

102. Chuck Angier, "$8 Billion in US Foreign Aid to Russia," August 15, 2008, www.no lanchart.com/article4509.html.

103. "The 'New' PDVSA: Lies, Deceptive Statistics and Bad Management," vcrisis.com, Au-gust 19, 2006 (reports 18 percent drop in Venezuelan oil exports to U.S. from 1998 to 2006), http://vcrisis.com/index.php?content=letters/200608190636.

104. ABC's *Nightline*, March 16, 2007.

Chapter 9: Chávez as Spin Doctor

1. Chávez's *Aló Presidente* TV program airs every Sunday at 11:00 a.m. and has been known to exceed eight hours; see www.alopresidente.gob.ve for archives and streaming videos.

2. *The Economist*, June 14, 2008, 47.

3. "Russia and Venezuela Will Coordinate Energy Policies," *New York Times*, July 23, 2008.

4. "Russia Sets War Games in the Caribbean," *New York Sun*, September 8, 2008.

5. "Russian Bombers Land in Venezuela," BBC News, September 11, 2008, http://news .bbc.co.uk/2/hi/americas/7609577.stm.

6. "Venezuela Plays The Russia Card," *Investor's Business Daily*, September 8, 2008.

7. *The Economist*, June 14, 2008, 47.

8. "Chávez Decree Tightens Hold on Intelligence," *New York Times*, June 3, 2008.

9. Jon Lee Anderson, "Fidel's Heir," *The New Yorker*, June 23, 2008, www.newyorker.com/reporting/2008/06/23/080623fa_fact_anderson.

10. William Falk, "The Two Weeks You Missed," *New York Times*, September 6, 2008, A17.

11. "Treasury Targets Hizballah in Venezuela," U.S. Department of the Treasury, June 18, 2008, www.ustreas.gov/press/releases/hp1036.htm.

12. Richard Lapper, "Uribe ascendant: Defeats for the FARC mark a shift of power in Latin America," *Financial Times*, July 6, 2008, www.consuladodecolombiany.com/new_page/prensa/2008/JUNIO/070820082.htm.

13. Simon Romero, "A Little Insult Is All the Rage in Venezuela: 'Pitiyanqui,' " *New York Times*, September 6, 2008, A9.

14. www.cia.gov/library/publications/the-world-factbook/geos/ve.html.

Chapter 10: The Alliance of the Americas

1. For more on this subject see Parag Khanna, *The Second World: Empires and Influence in the New Global Order* (New York: Random House, 2008).

2. Council on Foreign Relations, *The Chronicle*, 1.
3. "A Decade Under Chávez: Political Intolerance and Lost Opportunities for Advancing Human Rights in Venezuela," www.hrw.org/reports/2008/venezuela0908/6.htm#_ftn684. Also: *El Universal*, "Problemas del Venezolano sin respuesta en la reforma," November 6, 2007.
4. "Deadly Massage," *The Economist*, July 19, 2008, 47.
5. "Fidel's Heir," *The New Yorker*, June 23, 2008, 53.
6. J. M. Briceño Guerrero, *El Laberinto de los Tres Minotauros* or *The Labyrinth of the Three Minotaurs* (Caracas: Monte Avila, 1994).
7. Latin America includes Mexico, which is considered part of North America.
8. "Latin America and the Caribbean Poverty Analysis Brief," World Bank, March 2007, http://go.worldbank.org/UWBB738R80.
9. Ibid.
10. The GDP per capita is calculated by dividing the national income by the national population to produce an international comparative measure and is not an indication of individual annual disposable income.
11. Angus Maddison, *Monitoring the World Economy 1820–1920*, Organization for Economic Co-operation and Development, 1995.
12. Thomas Malthus had predicted the opposite to occur in *An Essay on the Principal of Population* in 1798. Malthus asserted that humanity was doomed to fail since food production would never grow as rapidly as population.
13. Maddison, *Monitoring the World Economy*.
14. Andrés Oppenheimer, "Chavez Destabilizes, and U.S. Pays Bill," *Miami Herald*, October 18, 2007, www.cubanet.org/CNews/y07/oct07/18e6.htm.
15. Thomas Friedman, "Dumb as We Wanna Be," *New York Times*, April 30, 2008, A19.
16. "Resolution 1737 (2006)," United Nations Security Council, December 23, 2006, www.un.org/News/Press/docs/2006/sc8928.doc.htm.
17. "What You Need To Know About U.S. Sanctions Against Drug Traffickers," U.S. Department of the Treasury Office of Foreign Assets Control, August 28, 2008, www.treas.gov/offices/enforcement/ofac/programs/narco/drugs.pdf.
18. Jad Mouawad, "Oil and Gasoline Prices Climb Higher," *New York Times*, April 21, 2008, www.nytimes.com/2008/04/21/business/21cnd-oil.html?scp=68&sq=oil u.s. april 2008&st=cse.
19. OPEC and International Energy Administration estimate 2.4 mbd; Chávez says 3.3 mbd—but won't open PDVSA's books to prove it—since 2003.
20. Karen A. Harbert, "Western Hemisphere Energy Security," U.S. Department of Energy, March 2, 2006, 6, http://64.233.169.104/search?q=cache:pCOu7cX1q5IJ:www.pi.energy.gov/documents/HarbertTestimony.pdf+venezuelan+oil+u.s.+consumption+site:energy.gov&hl=en&ct=clnk&cd=8&gl=us&client=safari.
21. Cesar J. Alvarez and Stephanie Hanson, "Venezuela's Oil-Based Economy," Council on Foreign Relations, June 27, 2008, www.cfr.org/publication/12089/.
22. Chávez and PDVSA claim 2007 and 2008.
23. Cesar J. Alvarez and Stephanie Hanson, "Venezuela's Oil-Based Economy."
24. "Subsidized Gasoline Prices Eat Into Venezuelan Oil," www.futurepundit.com/archives/004735.html. October 29, 2007. Also: Brian McBeth and Christina Stansell, "Petroleos de Venezuela S.A.," *International Directory of Company Histories*, vol. 74 (2003).
25. "Polls: Support for Chavez Government Falling," *USA Today*, March 18, 2008. www.usatoday.com/news/world/2008-03-18-chavez-venezuela_n.htm?loc=interstitialskip. Also:

http://realidadalternativa.wordpress.com/2008/04/15/encuesta-hinterlace-cree-que
-convocatoria-la-tendria-candidato-independiente/.

26. "Global Unease With Major World Powers," Pew Global Attitudes Project, June 27, 2007, 3–4, http://pewglobal.org/reports/pdf/256.pdf.

27. Oil is fungible, so Venezuelan oil not sold to the U.S. can be sold elsewhere and does not disappear from the world market. The 700,000 barrels of heavy oil would temporarily disappear because they cannot be refined anywhere but in the U.S.

28. The assumption here is that all of Venezuela's oil would go elsewhere in the market except the 700,000 barrels per day of heavy oil that can be refined only in the U.S.

29. "Mack to Bush: Name Venezuela as State Sponsor of Terror," March 6, 2008, http://mack.house.gov/index.cfm?FuseAction=PressReleases.View&ContentRecord_id=549.

30. Pew Global Attitudes Project, pewglobal.org/.

31. Graham Bowley, "How to show a dictator the door," New York Times, Week in Review, April 27, 2008, 5.

32. Economist magazine's World in Figures, 2007 edition.

33. Ibid.

34. 2007 World Development Indicators, World Bank, 2008, 186, http://siteresources.worldbank.org/DATASTATISTICS/Resources/WDI07section4-intro.pdf.

35. Ibid.

36. Former president and the socialist disaster Alan García, who now embraces market economy, narrowly defeated Ollanta Humala, an indigenous leader who supports Chávez's Bolivarian Revolution. www.electoralgeography.com/new/en/countries/p/peru/peru-presidential-election-2006.html.

37. This table is drawn from Economist online, "Forecasts for 66 Countries," World in Figures, World in 2007, and refers to data from 2006; www.economist.com/theWorldIn/index.cfm?d=2007&Go=GO. Accessed March 2008.

38. "Heinsohn's Theory: Countries With Young Populations Are More Violent," www.dailyreckoning.co.uk. Also: Celia W. Dugger, "Very Young Populations Contribute to Strife, Study Concludes," New York Times, April 4, 2007, www.nytimes.com/2007/04/04/world/04youth.html.

39. Benjamin Friedman, "Industrial Evolution," reviewing A Farewell to Alms by Gregory Clark in The New York Times Book Review, December 9, 2007, 21. Also: Paul Collier, The Bottom Billion: Why the Poorest Countries are Failing and What Can Be Done About It (New York: Oxford University Press, April 2007).

40. Jared Diamond makes the same connection between poverty and terrorism. In "What's Your Consumption Factor?" New York Times, January 2, 2008, he argues that disparity in oil consumption rates reflect the larger wealth inequality that gives root to terrorism. www.nytimes.com/2008/01/02/opinion/02diamond.html.

41. www.businessroundtable.org//taskforces/taskforce/document.aspx?qs=6956BF807822B0F1AD6428122FB51711FCF539CFC3D33B8.

42. These figures are drawn from Puerto Rican elections from 1968 to the present for the statehood party (PNP), the commonwealth party (PDP), and the independence party, www.electionspuertorico.org.

43. Emmanuel Jiminez, 2007 World Bank Report: The Next Four Billion.

44. Douglass C. North, The Economic Growth of the United States, 1790–1860 (New York: Norton, 1966).

45. Douglass C. North, Understanding the Process of Economic Change (New Jersey: Princeton University Press, 2005).

46. Ibid.

47. Rowan, *Getting Over Chávez and Poverty* (Caracas: El Nacional Books, 2006). Also: www .latinbusinesschronicle.com/app/article.aspx?id=105.

48. Rowan, ibid.

49. "Brazilian Retailer Courts the Poor," Harvard case study, www.allbusiness.com/ retail-trade/4554306-1/.html, August 26, 2007, and http.//money.cnn.com/fortune_ archive/2004/11/15/8191101/index.htm.

50. Nicholas Sullivan, *You Can Hear Me Now: How Micro-loans and Cell Phones Are Connecting the World's Poor to the Global Economy* (New York: John Wiley & Sons, 2007). Also: Sara Corbett, "Can the Cellphone Help End Global Poverty?" *The New York Times Magazine,* April 13, 2008, 4, www.nytimes.com/2008/04/13/magazine/13anthropology-t.html? pagewanted=4&sq=grameen bank bangladesh &st=nyt&scp=5.

51. Nicolaus Mills, "A Globalism for Our Time," *The American Prospect,* July/August 2007.

52. "Marshall Plan Speech," June 5, 1947, remarks delivered at Harvard University, Cambridge, Mass., U.S. Department of State, www.america.gov.

53. See table on page 186.

54. From Secretary of State George C. Marshall's commencement address at Harvard University, June 5, 1947, accessed at www.usaid.gov/multimedia/video/marshall/marshall speech.html.

55. This table is also drawn from *The Economist* online, "Forecasts for 66 Countries," World in Figures, World in 2007, and refers to data from 2006; www.economist.com/the WorldIn/index.cfm?d=2007&Go=GO. Accessed in March 2008.

56. www.Presidency.ucsb.edu.

About the Authors

DOUGLAS SCHOEN has been a consultant for the Democratic Party for the past thirty years. A founding partner of Penn, Schoen, and Berland Associates, Inc., he was former President Bill Clinton's research and strategic consultant during the 1996 reelection campaign and has worked for major corporations and nineteen heads of state around the world, including Silvio Berlusconi, Shimon Peres, Yitzhak Rabin, and Ehud Barak. He is the author of five books.

MICHAEL ROWAN has a long history as a successful political consultant both here and in Venezuela, and also as a newspaper columnist in Latin America. In the United States, he has advised winning candidates in twenty-six states; he has also advised presidential and other candidates in thirteen foreign countries, including Governor Manuel Rosales of Venezuela, former President Jaime Paz Zamora of Bolivia, and President Oscar Arias of Costa Rica.